THE STORY OF
THE CHURCH

peyton

THE STORY OF THE
CHURCH

FROM PENTECOST TO MODERN TIMES

Phillip Campbell

TAN

Cover and illustrations by Chris Pelicano

ISBN: 978-1-5051-1319-8

Published in the United States by
TAN Books
PO Box 269
Gastonia, NC 28053
www.TANBooks.com

Printed and bound in India

CONTENTS

The History of the Church

What do you think about when you walk into your church each Sunday? Do you pay much attention to the statues and symbols you see? Do you give a lot of thought to the words you hear and the prayers you pray? It's easy for Catholics to get into a routine when we go to Mass—to just focus on practical things like being on time, finding a place to sit, or getting wild kids to behave.

But when you go to Mass, you may not realize that your Church is built on over two thousand years of history, not to mention thousands more years from the Old Testament. The Mass you are taking part in—celebrating—plugs you into a religious tradition that goes all the way back through the centuries to the time of Christ and the apostles, and even beyond to the days of the Israelite kingdom, the teachings of Moses, and the wanderings of Abraham.

This book tells the story of the Catholic Church, the

family of God established by Jesus Christ when he came to earth over two thousand years ago. The Church is a supernatural reality founded through God's divine plan for the eternal salvation of the human race and is protected and guided by the Holy Spirit. But it is also a very human thing, made up of millions of men and women throughout time, each with their own ideas, personalities, and gifts they bring to the Church. This book tells the story of these people throughout the ages and how they each, in their own way, contributed to the building up of the kingdom of God. We will encounter many saints—as well as many villains—in this magnificent story.

We'll revisit a lot of your favorite stories as well as introduce you to some tales you've probably never heard. For example, did you know St. Peter was crucified upside down? Did you know the Desert Fathers lived in caves and battled the devil? Did you know Byzantine imperial soldiers once went on a mission to paint over religious images across the East? Or that St. Benedict of Aniane was once a Frankish warrior named Witiza? Did you know a pope once dug up the body of a deceased pope and put his corpse on trial? Have you heard of St. Hildegard, the marvelous visions she had, or the beautiful music she composed? Did you know the Carmelites once lived in the Holy Land until they had to flee from the Muslims? Or that one time there were three separate men all claiming to be the pope? Or that Pius VII was held captive by Napoleon? Did you know St. Thérèse of Lisieux met Pope Leo as a young girl and wept in his presence? Did you know Pope John Paul II was nearly assassinated, or that Pope Benedict XVI was the first pope to resign from the papacy in over five hundred years?

There are so many things to learn about the Church's history! We could spend our whole lives studying it and not exhaust the rich stories and marvelous lessons. We couldn't hope to uncover the entire treasury of history in this little book. For that reason, we have had to pick and choose which saints, stories, and events from history to include, so please forgive us if one of your favorite saints or stories didn't make it in!

Whether you are an expert in Church history or new to the study of it, one thing that should be clear from this book is how the Catholic Church shaped the world we live in. More importantly, it is like a ship that keeps us safe through the tumults of history, carrying us securely to heaven across the rocky seas of the world. It is our hope that you will be inspired by the stories in this book to strive to reach those heavenly shores.

CHAPTER 1

Christ and the Apostles

Searching for Hidden Meaning

Everywhere we look, life is full of meaning. Think of something like a birthday cake. On the surface, it looks very simple. It's a soft, sweet food made from a mixture of flour, eggs, sugar, and other ingredients, baked and often decorated with candles. But, of course, there's much more to a birthday cake than what it's made of. A birthday cake calls to mind a person's life and their achievements and celebrates their presence with us. It conjures up all sorts of emotions.

Our whole world is like this. Familiar places, people, a beautiful sunset, a lovely flower—anything can be meaningful in one way or another. Part of what it means to be human is to find meaning in things. Sometimes the meaning comes from our own experiences with things, like a toy that's special because you've had it for a long time. Other times, something is meaningful because of a hidden value or quality it has, like a simple rock that looks plain on the outside but contains a gold nugget within.

In short, things are often more than what they seem. And to be human is to seek and discover the truth and meaning behind things.

This book is about the history of the Catholic Church, an institution that is definitely more than what it seems. On the outside, the Church looks like any other human organization, with all its buildings and property and people who run things. And like other religions, it has sacred books, candles, vestments, ministers, altars, and all sorts of rituals. But the Catholic Church is not like other human institutions. It is much, much more. Why?

Because it comes from God.

In this way, the Church resembles its founder, Jesus Christ. Imagine standing in the stable of Bethlehem on the first Christmas morning and looking at the child Jesus. What would we see? We'd see a little baby, not much different than any other baby boy. But there is so much more to Jesus than we can see with just our eyes! He is God who became flesh, the fullness of divinity dwelling in bodily form, as the Bible says. In that little baby are all the treasures of grace available to mankind.

The Church is called the Body of Christ. Just as the divine and human natures come together in the person of Christ, so Christ is present in the Church through the Holy Spirit, whom Pope Leo XIII called the "soul of the Church." Like Jesus, the Church is both human and divine.

Pentecost

With this background, let's dive into the actual *story* of the Church.

After the resurrection of Jesus Christ from the dead,

our Lord commanded his disciples to wait for the coming of the Holy Spirit in Jerusalem, after which they would be empowered to go out and preach the Gospel to the world. The beginning of the Catholic Church goes back to the building in Jerusalem where the disciples faithfully carried out the will of Jesus, waiting in expectant prayer for the promised Holy Spirit.

Let's pause for a moment to enter that room to see what this historic moment was like:

————————

The large upper room was crowded with men and women huddled in prayer. Numbering about one hundred and twenty in all, this room full of people was all that remained of the followers of Jesus of Nazareth, who had been crucified a little over a month ago. But that same Jesus had risen from the dead and appeared triumphantly, urging his followers to wait for the coming of the Spirit in Jerusalem.

The people stood, heads lifted and arms held aloft, for such was the ancient posture of prayer. Some recited the psalms, some prayed the prophecies of the Old Testament, others called out to God in their own words from the depths of their heart.

At the center of this gathering were the apostles of Christ, those men chosen to be special witnesses of his resurrection and lead the Christian community. The word *apostle* means "one who is sent"; the leaders of the disciples were called the apostles because they had been sent by Christ to preach and to teach. Joining the apostles were also the Blessed Virgin Mary and other women.

It was still morning when suddenly a great wind rushed through the room! The people cried out, not in fear, but in ecstasy, for it felt as if their very hearts had been filled with a kind of holy fire. Any lingering fears or doubts they may have still had melted away as their spirits were strengthened in faith, hope, and love. Joy welled up and overflowed. Many began laughing or weeping. This, however, soon turned to awe as little flares of light appeared over people's heads.

"They look like . . . little tongues," someone said. "Tongues of fire!"

It was a marvelous sight as the very air seemed saturated with the glory of God. Praise welled up in the hearts of these men and women, and they began to open their mouths to call forth God's glory. But to their astonishment, it was not their everyday speech that came forth but strange and unknown words. The apostles cried out their praise to God in languages never taught to them.

The ruckus in the room was so loud that Jews throughout the streets of Jerusalem began to gather about the house. It was the solemn festival of Pentecost, and the city was crowded with devout Jews from all over the world, Jews who all spoke different languages.

"Strange," a Parthian traveler said, "they are speaking my language. I didn't think anyone spoke Parthian here."

"What do you mean?" another asked incredulously. "It's obvious they're speaking Coptic."

"I hear them speaking Latin," said another.

Those who had gathered around went on arguing over what language was being spoken. Finally, an elderly man, a rabbi, calmed the crowd and said, "All those people up there are Galileans. But how is it that each of us hears them in our own language? We are from all over the earth—Parthians, Medes, Greeks, Cretans, Arabs, Judeans, and more—and yet, we all hear them in our own tongue, praising the mighty works of God. What can this mean?"

A grizzled old Jew scoffed, "Bah! I'll tell you what it means. It means they're all drunk!"

Upon hearing the discussion and the accusation of drunkenness, Peter came to the window and called out, "You people of Jerusalem, listen, for these men are not drunk! It's only nine o'clock in the morning. Rather, they are speaking that which was foretold by the prophet Joel, who said, 'In the last days it shall be, God declares, that I will pour out my Spirit upon all flesh, and your sons and your daughters shall prophesy. And I will show wonders in the heaven above and signs on the earth beneath. And it shall be that whoever calls on the name of the Lord shall be saved.'"

Some of the onlookers scoffed at Peter's words, but his fiery conviction and the passion in his voice had caused many to take pause and be attentive. Some of the pilgrims well versed in the Scriptures nodded at Peter's citation of Joel.

"It does say so in Scripture," they said. "The Lord will pour out his Spirit on all flesh."

"Don't pay him any heed," another man said. "He is one of the followers of that Jesus of Nazareth."

"Yes!" cried Peter. "I do speak of Jesus, and I will speak of him boldly. Men of Israel, hear me: Jesus of Nazareth, a man attested to you by God with mighty works and wonders and signs which God did through him in your midst—this Jesus you crucified and killed by the hands of lawless men. But God raised him up, having loosed the pangs of death, because it was not possible for him to be held by it."

"How are we all hearing and understanding this man in our own languages?" the people cried.

Many others had come to listen to Peter, to hear the

man who was somehow speaking to everyone in their own tongue simultaneously.

"A miracle!" they began to call out. "God is working a great miracle through these people. Speak God's words to us!"

The crowd had swelled to thousands.

"You want the word of God?" asked Peter. "It is this: Let all the house of Israel therefore know assuredly that God has made him both Lord and Christ, this Jesus whom you crucified."

A murmur swept over the crowd. Many were deeply

moved by Peter's words. Those who lived in Jerusalem wept at the memory of the recent crucifixion of Jesus.

"What shall we do?" they called to Peter.

Peter cried out, "Repent, and be baptized every one of you in the name of Jesus Christ for the forgiveness of your sins, and you shall receive the gift of the Holy Spirit."

———

The miracle of tongues and the preaching of St. Peter brought three thousand souls into the Church that day. The miracle of tongues was a sign of the coming of the Holy Spirit.

And do you remember the story of the Tower of Babel from the Old Testament, when men, in their pride, sought to build a tower that reached the heavens? As a punishment, God scattered mankind into many tribes, and suddenly, they were each speaking different tongues, or languages. What was done at the Tower of Babel was undone on Pentecost. Through the power of the Holy Spirit, God had brought the human family back together; at Pentecost, the grace of God called men of many tribes and tongues together into the unity of the Church, which is the true structure that leads us to heaven.

After the day of Pentecost, the apostles were emboldened in the Holy Spirit to preach the Gospel of Jesus fearlessly. Miracles accompanied their preaching, and everywhere the apostles went, great wonders were done. St. Peter and St. John cured a lame man in the temple; St. Philip worked miracles in Samaria; people were even healed by the shadow of St. Peter crossing them.

The Church began to grow. In fact, it grew so fast the apostles needed to ordain more men to help them in their ministry. The New Testament book of Acts tells us that the office of *deacon* was created to help minister to the

needs of the sick and poor. The apostles would also ordain other men known as *presbyters*—sometimes called
"elders" in the Bible—to help them in their sacramental
ministry. These presbyters would become the first priests.
With apostles (the first bishops), along with their presbyters and deacons, we see the basic structure of the Catholic Church was already in place.

Paul

But the early Church suffered persecution from the hands
of the Jews. The same Jewish priests and elders who had
rejected Christ took offense at the preaching of the apostles. The Sadducees once threw the apostles into prison,
but an angel opened the doors and let them escape.

One of the most ardent persecutors of the Church was
a Pharisee named Saul. When a group of Sadducees captured and condemned the deacon St. Stephen to death,
Saul looked on with approval as Stephen was stoned to
death. He even was given letters from the Sanhedrin (the
Jewish high council) of Jerusalem to travel to Damascus
and arrest Christians there.

Yet on the way, Jesus appeared to Saul in a blaze of
glory and asked him, "Saul, why are you persecuting me?"

"Who are you, Lord?" replied a terrified Saul.

"I am Jesus, whom you are persecuting."

This truth must have overwhelmed Saul. He had not
believed what Christians said about Jesus. But now he was
encountering the risen Christ on the road to Damascus!

Saul left the encounter blind, but Jesus commanded
him to visit the house of a Christian in Damascus and
he would be healed. It happened just as Jesus had said.
Saul received his sight back, accepted baptism, and took
the Christian name Paul. For the rest of his life, St. Paul
would work tirelessly to bring people all over the Roman

world to Christ. We will talk a little bit more about St. Paul's journeys in our next chapter.

While the apostles had initially preached only to the Jews, St. Paul brought the Gospel to the Gentiles. In the Bible, a *Gentile* refers to a non-Jewish person. The first converts to Christianity were all Jewish, but what happened when a Gentile wanted to join the Church? Did they have to also accept the customs of Judaism? Or were they free from having to observe things like the Sabbath, the Jewish dietary law, and circumcision?

This became such a heated debate in the early Church that the apostles summoned a council in the city of Jerusalem. The Council of Jerusalem met around AD 48 and addressed the question of whether Gentile converts had to keep any Jewish observances. All the apostles spoke their mind, and St. Paul told of his experiences preaching to the Gentiles. The apostles agreed that Christians did not need to observe the Jewish law.

The Martyrdom of the Apostles

It is beyond the scope of this chapter to document all the journeys and deeds of the apostles. They spent the better part of the first century traversing the Roman world preaching, teaching, and working wonders in the name of Christ. By the middle of the first century, there were Christian communities all over the Roman world, from Mesopotamia in the east to Spain and Britain in the remote west.

Since Christ had made St. Peter the chief of the apostles, the churches founded by Peter would always hold a special aura of authority. St. Peter was the first bishop of Antioch, in Syria, and it was here, the Bible tells us, that followers of Jesus were first called Christians. Antioch would be one of the most important Christian Churches in the coming centuries.

However, it is not Antioch, but Rome, that is forever connected with the name of St. Peter. He founded the Church in the city of Rome, the capital of the Roman Empire. He would labor there as its bishop, building up a community renowned for its great faith. "Your faith is proclaimed through all the world!" St. Paul wrote to the Christians of Rome. We will speak more about St. Peter and Rome in the coming chapters.

Though we do not know everything about the apostles' lives, we do know how some of them died. For example, the book of Acts tells us that St. James the Greater was slain by King Herod Agrippa. The Jewish historian Josephus tells us that St. James the Less was killed by the priests of Jerusalem—thrown from the temple and beaten to death.

While we do not know for certain about the rest, tradition tells us that St. Matthew preached in Judea and was martyred there, and St. Andrew preached among the Greeks and Thracians and was eventually crucified in the Greek city of Patras. Meanwhile, Saints Philip and Bartholomew were tortured and executed in the Phrygian city of Hierapolis, while a very strong tradition says that St. Thomas made it all the way to India where he was speared to death. For their part, Saints Simon and Jude spread the Gospel together throughout Persia and Armenia; Simon was killed by being sawn in half while St. Jude was killed with an ax. The Gospel writer St. Mark was killed by being dragged behind a chariot in the city of Alexandria, Egypt.

Finally, St. Peter and St. Paul both suffered martyrdom in Rome during the time of Emperor Nero, around AD 68. Not long before, the city of Rome had suffered

from a terrible fire. Much of the city was destroyed and thousands perished. Many Romans murmured that the deranged Emperor Nero had himself started the fire in order to make room to expand his palace.

We do not know if these rumors were true. But it is certain that Nero wanted to find someone else to blame the fire on. He declared the Christians of Rome guilty of the fire and had them rounded up and put to death in hideous ways. Some were torn apart by wild beasts; others were burned alive or crucified. St. Peter was still bishop of Rome at this time and was apprehended and sentenced to be crucified. St. Peter told his Roman captors, "I am not worthy to suffer in the same manner as my Lord." They thus crucified him upside down instead, and so perished the first bishop of Rome and prince of the apostles.

St. Paul was also in Rome at the time on one of his missionary journeys. Because he was a Roman citizen, St. Paul was granted the relatively painless death of beheading.

Tradition tells us an interesting story about the death of St. John. Allegedly, John was sentenced to be boiled in oil by the Roman emperor—some say Emperor Nero, others say Domitian. But the stories agree that, to the astonishment of the Romans, St. John miraculously survived the ordeal unharmed and was sent into exile on the island of Patmos. There, he experienced the visions that make up the New Testament book of Revelation. St. John would become the bishop of Ephesus in Asia Minor and die of old age around the year AD 100. He was the only apostle to die naturally.

Though some apostles died earlier and some, like St. John, died later, by around AD 100 all of the original Christian generation was passing away. The people who had seen and walked with Christ were no more. They were followed by others who would continue to boldly proclaim the Gospel of Jesus Christ to the world.

But we have not yet left the apostles behind. In the next chapter, we will look at what has been called the Apostolic Age.

CHAPTER 2

The Apostolic Age

Sacred Scripture and Sacred Tradition

How do we know about the lives of the apostles? For that matter, how do we even know about the life and teachings of Jesus?

The history, teachings, and traditions of the very early Church come down to us through several ways. Primarily, we read about them in the New Testament of the Bible. As part of the Bible, the twenty-seven books of the New Testament are considered *Sacred Scripture*. This means they were inspired by God. The Holy Spirit inspired human authors to write those things—and *only* those things—which God wanted written down. He did this so that we might know the truth about his Son and come to find salvation in him.

The life of Christ was written by men known as the four Evangelists. Evangelist comes from the Greek word *evangel*, meaning "good news"; thus, an *evangelist* is one who brings the Good News of Jesus to others. The four Evangelists are Saints Matthew, Mark, Luke, and John. Their writings are the four Gospels, which are our records for the life and sayings of Jesus Christ; in short, they are the heart of the New Testament.

The Gospels are considered eyewitness accounts of Christ's life. St. Matthew and St. John were apostles of Jesus, St. Luke was the secretary of St. Paul, and St. Mark was the secretary of St. Peter. Besides the Gospels, St. Luke wrote an account of the history of the early Church and the travels of St. Paul. This is the book of Acts, or the Acts of the Apostles.

Much of the New Testament was written by St. Paul. His writings take the form of letters written to various local churches (such as the Romans or Philippians) or to individual people (such as Timothy or Titus). The New Testament also contains letters from St. Peter, St. John, St. James, and St. Jude. The New Testament concludes with a book of vivid prophecy and symbolism known as the Revelation (or sometimes the Apocalypse) to St. John.

Most of the New Testament was compiled before AD 70, save for the writings of St. John, which came later. By AD 100, the New Testament was complete. But it was not compiled in a single book like we have it today. Rather, individual copies of particular books of the New Testament were copied and circulated. Many churches did not possess the entire New Testament. For example, the church in Carthage might have the letters of St. Paul but not the Letter of St. James; the church in Milan might possess the letters of John but not his Apocalypse. It took time for *all* of the books to reach *all* of the churches—and for *all* of the churches to accept *all* of the books. We will talk about that process more in coming chapters.

But this raises an important question: if not every local

church had a complete New Testament, how did early Christians know what to believe?

In his second letter to the Thessalonians, St. Paul told the Christians of Thessalonica, "Stand firm and hold to the traditions which you were taught by us, either by word of mouth or by letter" (2 Thes 2:15). From this, we see that the early Church also held to that which was passed on "by word of mouth"; that is, the preaching of the apostles and their successors, the bishops. Those teachings that were passed on by the preaching and example of the apostles and their successors we call *Sacred Tradition*. How the early Christians lived, believed, and worshiped was guided by Sacred Scripture *and* Sacred Tradition.

Successors of the Apostles

By the middle of the first century, there were Christian communities all over the Roman world. How did these Christian communities form so far away from Jerusalem? Let's find out!

In our last chapter, we introduced St. Paul. He had been called by Jesus specifically to bring the Gospel to the Gentiles. For most of his life, St. Paul traveled about the Mediterranean founding Christian churches.

Typically, St. Paul would come to a city and find the local synagogue. A *synagogue* is the place where Jews read from the Scriptures and worshiped God. St. Paul would talk to the Jews and try to convince them that Christ was the Messiah prophesied in Jewish Scripture. If he was rejected by the elders of the synagogue, he would preach in the streets to the Gentiles. Sometimes, by the power of God, he would perform great miracles: he cast out demons, healed the sick, and even raised a dead boy to life who had fallen from a window.

Everywhere Paul went, he founded churches. He
traveled through Syria and the cities of Asia Minor. He
went to Greece and visited many of the Greek islands.
He visited Malta, Sicily, and Italy, spending some time
in Rome. Some traditions say he even made it as far as
Spain. By the time St. Paul was beheaded by Nero in AD
68, there were Christian churches in most of the major
cities around the Mediterranean. These churches would
continue to thrive and grow after the deaths of St. Paul
and the rest of the apostles.

However, the apostles had ensured that the churches would continue being taught, governed, and sanctified by worthy leaders. St. Paul told his disciple Timothy, "What you have heard from me before many witnesses entrust to faithful men who will be able to teach others also" (2 Tm 2:2). The apostles laid hands on other men, commissioning these men with the same directive Christ had given to them. These men who would govern the churches after the deaths of the apostles were known as *bishops. Bishop* comes from the Greek word *episkopos*, which means "overseer." The bishops were to oversee the local churches with the power and mandate received from the apostles, who received their power from Christ, who was sent by God the Father.

For this reason, even to this day, bishops are known as "successors of the apostles." The passing on of the powers of the apostles to each successive generation of bishops is known as *apostolic succession*. This means that the authority of the apostles continues in the Church through the line of bishops. Through apostolic succession, Christ continues his ministry to the Church and the world throughout all time.

Famous Bishops
The end of the first century and the beginning of the second are often known as the Apostolic Age because the bishops who governed the Church during this time had been disciples of the apostles themselves.

For example, St. Ignatius was the bishop of Antioch. The church there was very important and very old; St. Peter himself had once been bishop there. Ignatius was a disciple of St. John the Apostle. Around the year 108, he was arrested and sent to Rome to be devoured by wild beasts.

While on the way to Rome, he wrote six letters to various churches. These beautiful letters encouraged Christians to stand strong in the face of hardship. In his *Letter to the Romans*, St. Ignatius reminds Christians that service to God is more important than any earthly gain. "All the pleasures of the world," he wrote, "and all the kingdoms of this earth, shall profit me nothing. It is better for me to die on behalf of Jesus Christ, than to reign over all the ends of the earth."

In another one of his letters to the church at Smyrna, St. Ignatius encourages Christians to stay close to their bishop: "Wherever the bishop appears, there let the people be; as wherever Jesus Christ is, there is the Catholic Church." Did you notice how he called the Church "Catholic"? This is actually the first time in history we know of anybody using the word *catholic* to describe the Church. *Catholic* means "universal." The Church is universal because Christ calls all men to it, but also because all the local churches share the same universal faith and sacraments. From the time of St. Ignatius on, the Church founded by Jesus would be known as the Catholic Church.

One of St. Ignatius's most well-known sayings comes from his Letter to the Romans. Facing certain death at the mouths of the wild beasts, Ignatius wrote that he thought of himself as the bread of God: "I am God's wheat and shall be ground by their teeth so that I may become Christ's pure bread. Pray to Christ for me that the animals will be the means of making me a sacrificial victim for God." St. Ignatius was indeed ground between the teeth of the beasts, suffering death for Christ in the arena at Rome around the year 108.

Speaking of Rome, another of the great bishops of the Apostolic Age was St. Clement—or rather Pope St. Clement I, as history remembers him. Clement had been a disciple of St. Paul, who mentions him in one of his letters, calling him a "fellow worker" whose "name is written in the book of life" (Phil 4:3). At some point, St. Clement made his way to Rome and was ordained by St. Peter himself and eventually became the second pope after St. Peter, reigning from around AD 88 to 99.

As pope, Clement worked hard to strengthen the Church during difficult times. He also used his authority as successor of St. Peter to maintain order and justice in the Church. When the Christians of Corinth, in Greece, expelled their bishop and presbyters, Pope St. Clement wrote them a letter strongly admonishing them to restore their clergy and obey them. He commanded them to love each other, saying, "You see, beloved, how great and wonderful a thing is love! Let us pray, therefore, and implore of God's mercy, that we may live blameless in love, free from all human partialities for one over the other."

Like St. Ignatius, St. Clement would also suffer martyrdom. The exact details of his death are unknown, but an old legend says he was tied to an anchor and drowned in the ocean. To this day, St. Clement is often depicted holding an anchor.

We must also mention another famous bishop, St. Polycarp of Smyrna, in Asia Minor. St. Polycarp had been a disciple of St. John and in his youth had learned the Christian faith from the lips of St. John himself. Like his mentor St. John, St. Polycarp's preaching stressed the unity and love Christians must show for each other. When disagreements were starting to arise between the church of Rome and the churches of the East over the date Christians should celebrate Easter, St. Polycarp traveled all the way to Rome to discuss the matter with Pope Anicetus. Anicetus and Polycarp agreed that each local church should be faithful to their own customs.

A Martyr's Death

As a young man, St. Polycarp had known St. Ignatius. In fact, Polycarp had kissed the chains of Ignatius when he passed through Smyrna on his way to Rome. Years later, when he was an old man, St. Polycarp himself would also suffer martyrdom. When persecution broke out in Smyrna around 155, St. Polycarp was sought after. A servant betrayed Polycarp to the Roman authorities, who came and arrested him as he was lying down for bed one night. They dragged him off to be killed in the city's amphitheater. Let's see what happened next, according to those Christians who were there to witness it:

———

"I thought we were going to see the ringleader of the local sect of Christians!" demanded Demetrius, one of the members of the crowd gathered in the city amphitheater. "But this Polycarp doesn't look anything like a criminal."

"What did you expect?" shrugged his companion, Leander, munching a piece of flat bread and washing it down with a swig of wine. "That's him, and he's going to meet his end!"

"I don't know," responded Demetrius. "I expected someone who looks like a criminal. After all, they say the Christians are an evil sect of blasphemers and atheists. But this . . . ; he just looks like a venerable old man."

Indeed, the old man, Polycarp, who stood before the people of Smyrna, looked calm and dignified. Clad in a flowing white tunic with a fluffy gray beard tumbling down on to his chest, the man looked rather grandfatherly. The magistrate could see that the crowd was interested in this old man and was anxious to get on with the proceedings.

"Polycarp!" he cried out. "You stand accused of

professing the abominable sect of the Christians. Yet even now, if you will but deny Christ and swear by the fortune of Caesar, I will set you at liberty."

Polycarp shook his head and said, "Eighty-six years have I served him, and he never did me any injury: how then can I blaspheme my King and my Savior?"

The crowd roared. "Did you hear that?" chuckled Leander. "He's definitely getting fed to the beasts now!"

"I fail to see how you find this amusing," replied Demetrius. "This old man is about to suffer a horrendous death just because he confesses belief in this Christ."

The magistrate scoffed at Polycarp's obstinacy. "I have wild beasts at hand; to these will I cast you, unless you repent."

"Call them, then," Polycarp shrugged, "for we are not accustomed to repent of what is good in order to adopt that which is evil."

The crowds jeered, as if daring the magistrate to call Polycarp's bluff.

The magistrate shifted about uncomfortably in his seat. "Very well, then; I will cause you to be consumed by fire, seeing you despise the wild beasts, if you will not repent."

Polycarp was unmoved. "You threaten me with fire which burns for an hour, and after a little is extinguished, but are ignorant of the fire of the coming judgment and of eternal punishment, reserved for the ungodly. But why do you wait? Bring forth what you will."

"Look at his face!" cried Demetrius. "He looks so . . . serene. Happy, even!"

"Agreed," said Leander, taking another drink of wine. "He's mad. Burn him!" Leander shouted.

"Burn him! Burn him!" the crowd began chanting. "Burn the over-thrower of our gods!"

The people were so eager to see the spectacle that many

of them leaped up from their seats to help gather wood for the fire from the nearby shops.

As they heaped the wood into bundles, the magistrate ordered Polycarp to be tied up and nailed to the stake standing in the midst of the wood. "That won't be necessary," said the old man. "He that gives me strength to endure the fire, will also enable me to remain without moving in the pile without your nails."

The magistrate agreed and merely tied his arms behind his back. Polycarp took his position in the midst of the wood pile, praying intensely and awaiting his moment of glory. "I give you thanks that you have counted me worthy of this day and this hour, that I should have a part in

the number of your martyrs, in the cup of your Christ, to the resurrection of eternal life, both of soul and body. Amen."

When Polycarp finished his prayer, the wood was lit and the flames blazed forth. Yet to the astonishment of all present, the flames did not touch him. Though they roared and crackled, they separated themselves and surrounded the body of Polycarp like a great arch or sail. Instead of burning, he seemed bronze, as if bread were being baked in an oven. Instead of the smell of roasting flesh, the sweet smell of incense wafted into the air.

"By the gods!" shouted Leander standing up and pointing. "Do you see this?"

"It's miraculous!" cried Demetrius. Many in the crowd were standing up and shouting similar things.

Seeing this, the magistrate summoned the executioner. "Finish him," he growled.

The executioner approached the body of Polycarp, a glistening dagger in his hand. The man plunged the long blade into the breast of the old man. Polycarp wheezed, his head dropping down into unconsciousness.

But the greatest wonder was still yet to come, for when the executioner drew forth his dagger, a great gush of blood came pouring from the wound, spilling down onto the flames and extinguishing them. Along with the blood, a small white dove appeared, flying up into the bright afternoon sky.

"Where did that dove come from?" cried Leander.

"It came from the wound! I saw it!" shouted Demetrius. "The God of the Christians is powerful and mysterious!"

———

The pagans had Polycarp's body burned to ash, but the Christians of Smyrna lovingly gathered his bones and buried them. They would gather at the site of St. Polycarp's tomb every year on the anniversary of his death to celebrate Mass in his honor.

Speaking of Mass, what did Mass look like in the second century? How did Christians explain their worship and doctrines to outsiders? How did they respond to increasing persecution from the Roman government? We will answer those questions in our next chapter when we look at the apologists of the second century.

CHAPTER 3

The Apologists

Defending the Faith

In our last chapter, we talked about the age of the Apostolic Fathers. In this chapter, we will be talking about the Christian apologists of the second century.

At first glance, the words *apostle* and *apologist* might sound similar, but they are very different. The apostles were the principal followers of Jesus, witnesses of his resurrection, governors of the Church, and charged with preaching and teaching the Gospel to everyone.

Apologists, on the other hand, were Christians who took it upon themselves to defend the Christian faith in writing against their accusers. Apologist is related to the world *apology*. The writings of the apologists were known as *apologies*. Now, that might sound funny to us—as if the apologists went around saying sorry for being Christians! That's not the idea at all. In the old days, the word *apology* had a different meaning than it does now. To apologize did not necessarily mean to say sorry; rather, it meant to offer an answer or explanation. St. Peter had written, "Always be prepared to make a defense to any one who calls you to account for the hope that is in you" (1 Pt 3:15). The early apologists took this to heart, writing passionate defenses of the Christian faith.

Sometimes the apologists wrote to help non-believers understand the faith in order that they might convert. But often the apologists were writing not to persuade non-believers to accept the Christian faith but to demonstrate to the authorities that Christians posed no danger to the Roman state and should be treated better.

Enemies of the Church

Thousands of people, both Jew and Gentile, were embracing the Christian faith. But the Church also had many enemies who sought to hinder its growth, sometimes violently. The Roman authorities were one such enemy. They were always suspicious of Christians, who would not worship the official gods of Rome. This made them suspects of treason in the government's eyes. We will speak much more about the Roman persecutions in our next chapter.

Usually the Roman authorities left Christians alone, but every now and then if an anti-Christian edict was passed by an emperor (or simply if the mob demanded it), Christians could be arrested and executed, as we saw in our last chapter regarding St. Polycarp.

Sometimes pagans dragged Christians to the authorities and demanded they be punished; other times mobs themselves might attack Christians directly. For example, a mob of angry pagans attacked and killed the young man St. Tarcisius while he was carrying the Blessed Sacrament to Christians in prison. The mob wanted Tarcisius to reveal what he was holding and the saint preferred to die rather than hand over the sacrament to the pagans.

The pagan populace at large mistrusted the Christians. Because Christians met in secret and kept to themselves, the pagans imagined all sorts of horrible stories about them. They accused them of being immoral and of lying and plotting to harm their neighbors. They even made up wild stories about Christians killing people and eating them. This may have been a misunderstanding of the practice of receiving the Eucharist, which the Church believes is the true Body and Blood of Christ under sacramental signs. Of course, none of these things were true about Christians. But it goes to show that it's easy to imagine bad things about people who are different and whose customs one may not understand.

Another group who opposed the Christians were the Jews. In the ancient world, Jews were always hostile to the message of the Church; in fact, it was the Jewish priests who had conspired to put Jesus to death. Why were Jews hostile to Christians?

The Church taught that the Jewish law had passed away with the coming of Jesus—that the Old Testament Law of Moses was only temporary and no longer binding. This idea was very offensive to pious Jews, who taught that the Law of Moses was binding forever. Furthermore, the very idea that Jesus Christ was the Jewish Messiah was very troubling to Jews. If the Church's teaching was true, it meant that the Jews had not only failed to recognize their Messiah but that their leaders had actually conspired to put him to death.

Furthermore, the Church called all people, Jew and Gentile, into her flock. "There is neither Jew nor Greek . . . you are all one in Christ Jesus," St. Paul had taught (Gal 3:28). The call of salvation to all men made it irrelevant whether one was Jew or Gentile. But the Jews had always prided themselves on keeping a strict separation from the Gentiles. After all, the word of God had been revealed through the people of Israel. Why should it now come to the Gentiles?

St. Justin Martyr

Some of the earliest apologies were written to address these Jewish objections. One of these was written by St. Justin Martyr, who lived from around AD 100 to 165. He was trained as a philosopher and used his philosophical knowledge to argue for the Christian faith.

One of St. Justin's most well-known apologies was his *Dialogue with Trypho the Jew*. The *Dialogue* was written in the form of a conversation between St. Justin and a Jewish scholar named Trypho. Here's a little example of how this conversation went:

The sun was setting across the sea as two men walked along the beach. These men looked very different: one was wrapped in the cloak of a philosopher, the other the robes of a Jewish scribe. The philosopher had his curly hair cropped short and had a thin beard, as was the style of the day. This was Justin, the Christian philosopher. The Jew wore a thick black beard that tumbled down upon his chest. Upon the sides of his head were the curled side-locks that identified the man as a member of the Jewish faith. This was Trypho, the scribe.

Despite their differing appearances, they both shared a love of the Scriptures and had a zeal for the truth. On this late afternoon, Justin and Trypho were discussing the Old Testament Scriptures and having a friendly argument about their proper interpretation.

"The thing I do not understand about you Christians," said Trypho, "is that you deny that sacrifices are needed for the remission of sins. How can you say this? The Law of Moses is very clear that he who would be pious and pleasing in God's sight must offer the sacrifices according to the Law!"

"Ah," replied Justin, pointing his finger, "but what is written in the prophets? The prophet Isaiah says 'What to me is the multitude of your sacrifices? says the Lord; I have had enough of burnt offerings of rams. . . . I do not delight in the blood of bulls, or of lambs, or goats. . . . Wash yourselves; make yourselves clean; remove the evil of your doings from before my eyes; cease to do evil, learn to do good.' The Lord no longer requires sacrifices of those whose hearts have been washed in the cleansing waters of baptism."

"If the sacrifices of the Law are not necessary, then why did God command them?" asked Trypho.

"God truly commanded these sacrifices," explained Justin, "but they were only for a time. It was because of the hardness of your hearts that God commanded such things, because you were not ready for the truth that the Messiah would reveal in the fullness of time. When Jesus died on the cross, he became the one sacrifice for sin—the perfect lamb of God whose blood atones for all sin."

The two men continued on down the beach, going on like this for many hours as the sun dropped below the sea's horizon. Shadows spread out over the land and the air grew chilly as Justin and Trypho continued talking. Trypho stroked his long beard as Justin spoke quickly, waving his arms in the air as he spoke.

Eventually Trypho said, "It appears we are nearing the city and you must take your leave. I have been very pleased with this discussion, Justin. We should do this again if we are to ever cross paths once more. But, in the meantime, I hope you will remember me as a friend."

"I will remember you fondly," answered Justin. "Hopefully we can talk again, but I pray you to think on the things I have said. Perhaps you, too, will find salvation in Christ."

The two embraced and parted ways.

As Justin paced off the beach and back to the city, he thought to himself, *Hmm . . . that was a wonderfully engaging conversation. I should write it down!*

———

St. Justin did indeed turn his conversation with Trypho

into a book, as we mentioned already. But that was not the only apology he wrote. He also composed a lengthy letter to the Roman emperor Antoninus Pius begging him to lighten the laws against the Christians. Remember, the Romans believed Christians did evil things when they gathered together. St. Justin told the emperor it was quite the opposite. He described what Christians did in their secret gatherings, writing:

> And on the day called Sunday, all who live in cities or in the country gather together to one place, and the memoirs of the apostles or the writings of the prophets are read, as long as time permits; then, when the reader has ceased, the presider speaks, and encourages to the imitation of these good things. Then we all rise together and pray, and, as we before said, when our prayer is ended, bread and wine and water are brought, and the presider in like manner offers prayers and thanksgivings, and the people assent, saying Amen. Then they who are able, and willing, give what each thinks fit; and what is collected is deposited with the presider, who uses it to help the orphans and widows and those who, through sickness or any other cause, are needy.

When he penned these words, St. Justin was giving the first written record of the Catholic Mass. Does his description of Sunday worship sound familiar? It should. He describes the readings, the homily, the Eucharist, and even the taking up of the collection. The Mass has certainly changed over the centuries, but it is amazing how we can still recognize its basic structure in the words of St. Justin written almost two thousand years ago.

St. Justin came to Rome to open up a school. Unfortunately, his pleas for tolerance went unheeded by the Romans. He was soon arrested and brought to trial and asked to worship the gods of Rome. When he refused, he was scourged and beheaded in the year 165, becoming a martyr for the Faith. And that is why he is remembered by the name St. Justin Martyr.

Tertullian
Another notable apologist was Tertullian, who lived from around 155 to 240. He was from the city of Carthage in the Roman province of Africa. Tertullian was trained as a lawyer and was a gifted speaker and writer. Shortly before the year 200, he converted to Christianity and was ordained a priest. He began using his talents to defend his new faith, writing many letters on a wide variety of topics.

The Church was being persecuted in North Africa during Tertullian's day. Like St. Justin, Tertullian composed writings defending Christians against their accusers. But Tertullian realized that the more the Romans persecuted the Christians, the more the Church would grow.

"The blood of the martyrs is the seed of the Church," Tertullian wrote. And he was correct. The more the Romans persecuted the Church, the more people converted to the Faith.

But Tertullian had little sympathy for weak, lazy Christians. He sometimes thought Christians could be too insincere in the practice of their faith. He was angry and scandalized when Christians wavered in their faith or abandoned it in the face of persecution. Around the year 207, he came under the influence of a group known as the Montanists. The Montanists were named for a man named Montanus, their founder. Montanus taught that the Holy Spirit continued to give new revelation to the Church. The Montanists also were much stricter than regular Catholics; they fasted more, had more rules about how Christians should dress and behave, and generally looked down on Catholics whose practice of the Faith was less than perfect.

These Montanists were later considered heretics by the Church. A *heretic* is someone who stubbornly denies some truth of the Catholic faith. The Montanists denied that the Bible and the Tradition of the Church were the ultimate authority for Christians; they believed the prophecies of Montanus were just as important as the sayings of Jesus or the writings of the apostles. Because Tertullian joined this heresy, he has never been considered a saint, although his writings have always been admired.

Clement of Alexandria

Another great apologist was Clement of Alexandria. Clement came from a pagan family and was educated in the classical literature of Greece and Rome. He later converted to Christianity and traveled all around the eastern Roman Empire studying philosophy and theology. He eventually opened up a catechetical school in Alexandria, Egypt. A *catechetical school* was a place where priests and theologians came to study theology. Some of the most famous Christian teachers of the East studied under Clement of Alexandria.

Clement wrote to the Greek speaking pagans of the empire urging them to embrace Christianity. He argued that the Christian faith was superior to the philosophy and mythology of the Greeks. While St. Justin's *Dialogue with Trypho* was meant to show Jews how Christianity was the fulfillment of Judaism, Clement's book *Exhortation* attempted to show pagans how Christianity completed Greek philosophy.

Late in Clement's life, a persecution caused him to flee

Alexandria. He died in exile around 215, though nobody knows how. Some think he was martyred; others are not so certain.

We've mentioned persecution a lot in this chapter. In our next chapter, we will learn more about the Roman persecutions and how this affected the Church.

CHAPTER 4

Roman Persecutions

A Time of Hostility

In our last chapter, we mentioned that the pagans of the Roman Empire mistrusted Christians and believed them to be troublemakers. We've also noted throughout previous chapters how the Roman emperors themselves would lash out against the Christian community. For example, in chapter 1, we saw how the Emperor Nero blamed Christians for the great fire of Rome and had many of them put to death, including St. Peter, while in chapter 2, we saw how both St. Ignatius and St. Polycarp were executed by the Roman authorities. In this chapter, we will examine the motivations of the Romans in their attacks on the Church as well as learn about some of the larger Roman persecutions.

Before we go any further, we should define persecution. *Persecution* means hostility and ill-treatment of a group of people by the government—in this context, because of their religious beliefs. We have already talked about why pagans disliked Christians in general, but what caused the Roman authorities to actually strike out and attack the Christian Church, often inflicting torment and death on peaceful Christians?

For the Roman authorities, the problem with the Christians was that they refused to worship the state gods of Rome. In ancient Rome, as in most ancient cultures, religion was not something private. It was a very public thing. The Romans had "official" gods and goddesses of the state that were to be worshiped by all Roman citizens. The Romans believed that the official worship of these gods would secure their blessing on the empire. To not pray to these gods and goddesses was the equivalent to wishing ill on the empire.

Beginning in the mid-first century AD, one of the gods Romans were expected to pray to was the "genius" of the emperor. The genius was like a guardian spirit of a Roman household; praying to the genius of the emperor was like praying for his personal health and success. Refusal to pray to the genius of the emperor was like wishing harm to him.

Throughout the first and second centuries, emperors would occasionally institute edicts of persecution based on their whims. Nero persecuted Christians after the Great Fire of AD 64, while during the reign of Trajan (98–117), there was a sporadic persecution of Christians in Asia Minor. Trajan wrote that a person suspected of being a Christian should be summoned before the local judges and ordered to sacrifice to the state gods. If Christians refused to pray to the Roman gods or the genius of the emperor, they were, in effect, committing treason against the Roman state. This was a charge leveled again and again against Christians: "They refuse to worship our gods!" the Romans screamed out in horror.

Sometimes, faced with punishment, a Christian would abandon his faith and *apostatize*, which means to denounce your faith publicly. To prove he had done so, he would be expected to pinch grains of incense in front of the statue of the emperor. If a Christian did so, he would be released. If not, he would be punished, sometimes with death. This procedure, established by Trajan, would become common when the Roman judges dealt with Christians.

A New Kind of Persecution

Despite the persecutions, Christianity continued to grow steadily throughout the second and third centuries. By the year 200, there were thriving Christian communities in every Roman province and most major cities had Christian churches. In some cities in the East, Christians were even the majority. The Catholic Church was flourishing.

But things were not going so well for the Roman Empire. Beginning in 235, the empire entered a period of civil war and chaos that would last for fifty years. It is beyond the scope of this book to discuss the reasons for this; our study is of the Church, not the empire. For now, it's enough to know that for five decades Roman armies clashed with each other for control of the empire. Emperors were proclaimed after bloody battles, only to be assassinated shortly thereafter. Over twenty-five men held the imperial throne during this time, most of them forgettable since they only held power for less than two years. The mighty Roman Empire seemed to be breaking apart and average Romans wondered why this was happening to them.

In the year 249, a stern general and former senator

named Decius was proclaimed emperor after killing a rival. Decius believed the reason the Roman Empire was suffering was because Romans were increasingly abandoning the worship of the official gods for newer faiths like Christianity. He thought the gods were punishing Rome for this.

Therefore, Decius announced that every citizen of the empire would have to offer worship to the Roman gods. Those who did not would be punished with imprisonment, exile, or death. Those who did would be given a certificate called a *libellus*, which proved they had sacrificed.

The persecution of Decius was something new. There had been persecutions before, but they had always been local. This was the first empire-wide persecution; every single Roman was compelled to sacrifice. It was also the first persecution where the government issued certificates to people to prove they had complied.

Many Christians suffered death rather than sacrifice. One of the first and most eminent martyrs was Pope St. Fabian. He was arrested and beheaded when he refused to sacrifice. Another famous martyr was St. Agatha of Sicily. A Roman magistrate had fallen in love with St. Agatha, but Agatha had taken a vow of virginity and spurned his advances. In anger, the magistrate denounced Agatha as a Christian in hopes that the threat of death would encourage her to change her mind and marry him. But St. Agatha refused. She was scourged, burned, and suffered various tortures until dying in prison in 251.

These are some martyrs we know by name, but there are many we do not know. Let's pause for a moment to see how several ordinary people may have been subjected to trials and persecution.

―――――

"Next!" growled Urbanus, the Roman prefect. He was the local judge in charge of enforcing the law in the city.

Urbanus was in a foul mood. He had spent his entire Saturday afternoon enforcing the new imperial edict, ordering all Romans to sacrifice to the state gods. He would've rather been at his villa tending his grapes.

A roughly dressed man was escorted into the hall by burly guards. He was brought before a pedestal upon which sat a *bust* of the emperor—that is, a statue of the emperor's head. Next to the bust was a small bowl of incense and a bronze dish with some hot coals sizzling upon it.

"State your name, age, and occupation," Urbanus commanded.

"Marialus, age thirty-two, stone mason," replied the man. His answers were scribbled down by a city notary—a record keeper—seated on a stool next to the prefect.

"Well, Marialus," said Urbanus, "do you swear that you are a faithful worshiper of the gods of Rome, and are you prepared to do so now here in my presence?"

"Yes," mumbled Marialus. "I have always worshiped the gods."

"Show me," said Urbanus, gesturing to the pedestal with the statue and incense. Marialus shambled forward, grabbed a bit of incense between his thumb and forefinger and sprinkled it on the hot coals. A tiny wisp of scented smoke wafted into the air.

"Good," said Urbanus. Then, turning to the notary, "Give the man his libellus."

The notary handed Marialus a scrap of paper. On it was written Marialus's name and information, the oath he had sworn, the record of his sacrifice, and the date. Marialus stared dumbfounded at the note. He was illiterate.

"You've got your paper, now get out!" barked Urbanus. Marialus was hustled out. "Next!"

A middle-aged woman was ushered in. Her dress and mannerisms suggested she was a woman of some means.

"Identify yourself," growled Urbanus.

"Julia, age forty-six, widow," replied the woman.

"You know the routine. Swear loyalty to the gods of Rome and prove your fidelity by sacrificing to them in my presence."

Julia huffed. "My dear prefect, surely you recall my late husband, Horatianus. He was an acquaintance of yours when you both were in the legions. Is this any way to treat the widow of a friend?"

"The emperor's orders allow no exceptions," responded Urbanus, seeming bored. "Pinch your incense and you can get your paper and go."

Julia shuffled and fidgeted her hands. "Prefect, my late husband was a man of some means." She produced a small pouch that jangled with the sound of coins. "Perhaps you could give me my libellus without making me pinch the incense?"

Urbanus laughed. "This is too good! My dear Julia, you've become a Christian, haven't you? Only you've got no interest in dying for your religion if you can just bribe your way out of the imperial decree? That's the funniest thing I've heard all day."

Julia was indignant. "Yes, I am a Christian! But not all of us have the fortitude to endure rack and beast!" She threw the sack of money at the prefect. It fell into his lap. "Ten pieces of silver! Will you take my offer?"

"Notary, write her a libellus," Urbanus said, still chuckling. The notary handed a note to Julia, which falsely said she'd sacrificed. She bowed and quickly left the room.

"Bring the next one in," said Urbanus, counting the coins.

A young boy and girl were brought in.

"Name, age, occupation?" asked Urbanus.

"Quintus, age eighteen, metalsmith's apprentice. This is my sister, Tertia, sixteen. Our father and mother are deceased."

"Quintus, Tertia," said Urbanus, "do you swear that you are a faithful worshiper of the gods of Rome and are you prepared to do so now here in my presence?"

"Good prefect," the girl said softly, "we are worshipers of the true God who was made known to us through his Son, Jesus Christ. We will not pledge fealty to your gods, nor will we pinch incense to this idol."

Her brother Quintus nodded his assent.

Urbanus's mouth hung open as the guards looked at each other in dismay. "Notary," whispered Urbanus. "What do we do now?"

"I'm not sure," answered the notary. "We haven't had anyone refuse yet. I mean . . . other than those who pay you off."

Urbanus scowled and the notary lowered his head.

"What does the law say?" asked Urbanus. He and the notary fumbled about some scrolls. "Ah . . . please excuse us for a moment," he said to Quintus and Tertia awkwardly.

After some time reading the imperial decree and discussing the matter amongst themselves, Urbanus stood up, cleared his throat, and said, "According to the decree, those who refuse to sacrifice to our gods in my presence are to be taken out forthwith and put to death. You don't want that, do you?"

"We would rather die than betray the Lord Jesus," replied Quintus resolutely.

"Are you insane, son? It's not a quick death, Quintus. I beg thee, reconsider."

"Send us to the executioner," said Quintus stoically.

"What about you, girl? You're so young and lovely! You have your whole life ahead of you! Don't throw it away!"

"I'd rather throw away the life of the flesh than forfeit my soul by apostasy," said Tertia. "Your words are of no avail. Send us away."

A dark frown fell over Urbanus's face. "Notary, let it be recorded that Quintus and Tertia refused to worship the gods of Rome in my presence. Thus, by the decree of the Divine Emperor Decius, they are sentenced to be taken from my presence and tortured until they worship the gods of Rome. If they should persist in their stubbornness, let them be sent to the amphitheater and suffer the death of common criminals by sword, by fire, and by beast."

"Praise God," said Quintus, raising his hands aloft. "We have been counted worthy to suffer death for the sake of he who suffered for us!"

"May Jesus be glorified by our death!" said Tertia.

The guards led them out.

"I don't understand," said Urbanus. "Why would they sacrifice themselves over such a silly thing?"

"Their religion must be extraordinary," said the notary, more to himself than to Urbanus.

"Maybe so," replied Urbanus thoughtfully. After a pause, he continued, "We still have a job to do." He returned to his chair and sat down. "Next!"

———

Fortunately for the Christians, Decius was not long in charge of Rome. He was killed in battle in 251. With his death, the first empire-wide persecution of Christians came to an end.

The Persecution of Valerian

Persecution again struck, however, in the year 257. This time the persecutor was Emperor Valerian. The occasion of this persecution was a war against the Persians. While away on campaign, Valerian sent letters to the Senate directing them to compel Christian clergy to sacrifice to the Roman gods or face punishment. The following year, he intensified the persecution by ordering the execution of Christian leaders and the confiscation of prominent Christians' wealth. Among those who suffered under Valerian were Pope St. Sixtus, St. Cyprian of Carthage, and perhaps most famously, St. Lawrence, a Roman deacon who was roasted to death on a giant gridiron when he refused to hand over the Church's wealth to a greedy judge.

Valerian hoped these actions would win him assistance from the Roman gods to defeat the Persians. However, quite the opposite unfolded. Valerian was captured in battle by the Persians and was made a servant to King Shapur, who regularly humiliated him. Whenever the king wanted to get onto his horse, he would call Valerian, order him to kneel, and then step on his back to mount his steed. According to legend, after Valerian died in exile, Shapur had the dead emperor stuffed and set up on display in his palace, much as a hunter would do with a deer or bear that he had shot. The unpleasant deaths of persecutors like Decius and Valerian were noticed by Christians, who said that those who persecuted the Church always came to no good end.

After the captivity of Valerian in 260, the persecution came to an end and the Church would enjoy an entire generation of growth and prosperity. However, Rome still had one great persecution left in her before the ultimate triumph of Christianity. We will have to save that for another chapter. For now, we will leave the persecutions from without to learn about some of the Church's struggles happening within.

CHAPTER 5

Dissent and Heresy

Attacks From Within

Despite the efforts of the Roman emperors to destroy the Christian faith, the Church not only survived but thrived. Pagans continued to convert to Christianity even as the imperial authorities threw Christians into prison, sent them into exile, or killed them. It seemed the more the Romans attacked Christianity, the more it grew. Christians believed the intercessions of those who suffered for their faith were bearing fruit and winning more souls for Christ. As the Church Father Tertullian said, "The blood of the martyrs is the seed of the Church."

But the Roman authorities were not the only threat to the Church. The devil, having seen that his attempts to destroy the Church from without were not working, decided to try to attack the Church from within. This was accomplished by the spread of destructive heresies.

Let's go back to the Bible to learn what a heresy is. In

the New Testament, St. Paul had warned, "For the time is coming when people will not endure sound teaching, but having itching ears they will accumulate for themselves teachers to suit their own likings, and will turn away from listening to the truth and wander into myths" (2 Tm 4:3). He also said, "I know that after my departure fierce wolves will come in among you, not sparing the flock; and from among your own selves will arise men speaking perverse things, to draw away the disciples after them" (Acts 20:29–30). There are many warnings against such false teachings in the New Testament. A *heresy* is a false teaching about Jesus Christ and the truths he revealed. Heretics are baptized Christians who adopt these false teachings and teach them stubbornly.

As the Church spread, heresies began popping up. Christ founded *one* Church which preached *one* Gospel, but heretics preached a different message than that which was handed on by the apostles, spreading confusion and division within the Christian faithful.

One of the earliest heretics was a man named Marcion. Marcion lived in Asia Minor, which is modern day Turkey. When he read the Old Testament, he thought the God of ancient Israel seemed too different from the God that Jesus spoke of. He taught that the God of the Old Testament was a different God from the God of the New Testament. According to Marcion, this God of the Old Testament was evil, while the heavenly Father spoken of by Jesus was good and loving.

The Church strongly objected to this. Christians had always understood that the God who appeared to Abraham and who led Moses and the Israelites out of Egypt was the same God who was the Father of Jesus Christ. If the God of the Old Testament sometimes seemed more fearsome or distant, it was only because Jesus had revealed much more about the Father than the people of the Old Testament had known. The Old Testament Israelites had known his power, but now Jesus had revealed his compassion. Marcion was rejected as a heretic.

Another group of early heretics were the Docetists. The Docetists did not believe the Son of God had truly taken flesh in the womb of Mary. They believed Jesus's body was not real; rather, it was more like an illusion or a ghost. This was a very troubling teaching. If Jesus was not really a man, he could not have died on the cross, and if he did not die on the cross, then how could the sins of mankind be forgiven? Many Church Fathers wrote against the Docetists. The Church understood that for man and God to be reconciled, the Son of God actually had to become a man—not simply *look* like a man, but actually be one.

One of the most prevalent heresies of the early Church was a group of teachings known as Gnosticism. Gnostics took their name from the Greek word *gnosis*, which means "knowledge." The Gnostics believed that the stories of Christianity were only myths that concealed deeper, more "spiritual" secrets, which only a special inner circle of believers could understand. But their spiritual secrets were often absurd fables, including the claim that there are divine beings called Aeons who emanate out of God and live in a spiritual realm called the Pleroma, among other such oddities.

Another common belief of the Gnostics was that matter and the whole material world were evil, and only spiritual things were good. Therefore God, because he is good, could not have created the material world. They said the world was created by a different evil being called the Demiurge. One was saved by learning this secret knowledge.

Gnosticism was a recurring problem in the early

Church. Because it was complex and secret, it attracted elites and intellectuals who wanted to feel like they were part of something special. But the Church never ceased preaching against the outlandish fables of the Gnostics. The truths of salvation were not a secret only for the few; rather, Christ had come to make them known to all mankind. And regarding the material world being evil, had God not pronounced each thing "good" at creation when he called it into being? And had not Jesus Christ himself taken on matter when he became flesh?

One of the more outlandish heretical movements were the Montanists. Named for Montanus, their founder, the Montanists believed that God uttered new revelations through the mouths of Montanus and a group of women. This group said a lot of wild things, like that the heavenly Jerusalem would descend on a plain in Phrygia in Asia Minor. Many Christians who were taken in by the Montanists left their homes and went to Phrygia to await the coming of the heavenly Jerusalem. Needless to say, the prophecies did not come to pass and eventually this group died out.

Some heretical groups were known for their strictness. One such group were the Donatists. The Donatists thought most Christians and Christian clergy were too lazy. They envisioned a Church of the perfect. They taught that a priest had to be faultless for their prayers and sacraments to be effective. They also believed that some sins were unforgivable, such as murder, apostasy, and adultery. The Donatists were very strong in Africa, but they were opposed by the popes, as well as one of the most famous bishops, St. Augustine of Hippo, who lived from 354 to 430. We will learn more about St. Augustine in a coming chapter.

A Most Dangerous Heresy

We've just run through some of the most prominent heresies, but the most dangerous heresy of the ancient Church was Arianism, named after Arius, a priest of Alexandria in Egypt. What did Arius teach? Why don't we let two Christians of the early fourth century explain it for us?

————————

Fortunatus and his companion Rusticus walked along the wharves by the sea in the city of Alexandria. Fortunatus was a priest and well-known preacher in the Christian community here, while Rusticus was a fellow Christian and old friend. Today, the face of Fortunatus was heavy with anxiety.

"This heresy of Arius is spreading like a fire," said Fortunatus. "Word has just come that several of the churches along the coast have gone over to Arianism. Every day more souls fall for his smooth words and deceptive teaching."

"It is a great concern," said Rusticus, "but I am no theologian. Tell me, exactly what does Arius teach?"

"I can hardly make myself say it," replied Fortunatus grimly. "The man teaches that the Son of God was not of the same substance as God the Father. They say he is wholly different from God, less than him."

"This puzzles me, Fortunatus. If he has always existed alongside God the Father, how can he be less than him since they are equally eternal?"

"Oh, this is the worst part," scoffed Fortunatus. "They do not admit that the Son of God has always existed. They say he was created like the angels."

"The Son of God, a mere creature?" asked Rusticus in disbelief.

"I know! The blasphemy is appalling! But his teaching

has all the fascination that fads often do. It is new, and people will run after any new thing that tickles their ears."

As the two men walked beside the docks, they noticed some of the dock workers were singing while they loaded and unloaded ships.

"Wait!" said Fortunatus. "Rusticus, do you hear what those men are singing?"

Rusticus paused and gave heed to what the men were singing. "It's a common workingman's tune. I've heard the laborers in the brickyard singing it as well."

"Listen not to the tune, friend, listen to the words!"

Rusticus strained his ears to hear the words of the men's song.

Ho dee ho, what hath God wrought?
There was a time when the Son was not
All faiths except this one rot
There was a time when the Son was not

"Good heavens, Rusticus! They're singing Arius's heresy!"

"Impious heretic! It is bad enough that he should spread this nonsense about the world, but to put his impiety to meter and teach common folk to sing his poison is doubly horrid!"

"Indeed! We must preach against this with all our strength, lest he continue to seduce the simple with these songs. But you know what is especially bad about this, Rusticus?"

"What, good father?"

"It really is a catchy tune."

———

As quirky as it sounds, it is true that Arius put his teachings to catchy songs that were sung by common people.

Arianism spread so far that by the beginning of the fourth century, hundreds of churches and many bishops had gone over to the sect. When the Arians got into power, they persecuted regular Christians by closing their churches and exiling their bishops. Sometimes it seemed like Arians had taken over the entire Church.

In Defense of Orthodoxy

We've introduced you to a bunch of different heresies against the early Church in this chapter, some of which had what probably seemed like wild and crazy ideas and teachings. You may have thought to yourself, "How did the early Christians fall for this stuff?" But remember, they didn't have all the same teachings we have today from so many saints and popes and other wise theologians, and they didn't have the technology to spread the correct teachings of the Church as far and wide as they would've liked. The early Church was still figuring things out and dealing with the shortcomings of their time, so it was easier for them to fall prey to false teachings.

The important thing is not to memorize what each of these heresies taught but to understand how heresy can hurt the Church. Believe it or not, it still happens today. For example, some say the Eucharist is only a symbol rather than the true Body, Blood, Soul and Divinity of Jesus. There are lots of heresies in these modern times that we can fall victim to if we are not careful. By recognizing teachings that run contrary to the Church's teachings, we can better defend Holy Mother Church and protect her from errors.

Speaking of defenders, one of the most heroic defenders of the Catholic faith during the time of Arianism was St. Athanasius, bishop of Alexandria. Athanasius was driven from his diocese multiple times for preaching against the Arians. St. Athanasius composed many beautiful works on the incarnation of Jesus Christ that are still read and studied today. Eventually, St. Athanasius was restored to his diocese.

The true Faith as preached by St. Athanasius and other Catholics is known as *orthodoxy*; *orthodoxy* is a Greek word that means "correct thinking." St. Athanasius was a champion of orthodoxy, defending it against the errors of the Arian heretics.

The Arian heresy would continue into the middle of the fourth century, by which time the Roman Empire had become Christian and many things changed. But we are getting ahead of ourselves. Before we discuss that, we must turn to the deserts of Egypt and Syria where something new was happening.

CHAPTER 6

Christian Monasticism

Desert Fathers

In the middle of the third century, while Roman generals were battling each other for control of the empire and Christian theologians were debating with heretics, something was happening in the deserts of Egypt and Syria that would change the face of Christianity forever.

The year was AD 250, the time of the persecution of Decius, which we learned about in chapter 4. In Egypt, there was a young man named Paul who dwelt in the city of Thebes. Paul had been turned over to the Roman authorities and fled the city into the desert to hide from his persecutors, taking refuge in a cave on the side of a mountain. While this might sound like a harsh place to live, it was not so terrible a place, as there were palm trees nearby and a clear spring from which he could drink. Paul decided to stay in that cave and focus on praying and growing closer to God.

How long did he stay there? For quite a while! Paul lived there for about one hundred years, praying, fasting, and becoming a friend of God. When his clothes rotted away, he used the leaves of the palm trees to cover him- self, and his beard grew long and wild. He drank from the spring, ate the fruit of the palm trees, and was occasionally brought food by the birds. It was a difficult life, but a rewarding one. Paul was perfectly content.

Eventually, local people heard of Paul and how he chose to live. He was later known as St. Paul the Hermit. A *hermit* is a person who lives completely on his own, seeking a closer relationship with God by living in solitude.

St. Paul is known as the first Christian hermit as well as one of the first Desert Fathers. But it would be another man who would popularize the idea. This man was St. Anthony. Like St. Paul the Hermit, Anthony was an Egyptian. Anthony was the son of rich parents. Around the year 269, when Anthony was eighteen years old, his parents died, leaving him a fortune to inherit as well as the obligation to care for his younger sister.

Being a faithful Christian, Anthony wondered what he could do with his inheritance that would bring honor to God. He went to Mass to pray about it. While at Mass, he heard the reading from the Gospel where Jesus tells the rich young man, "If you would be perfect, go, sell what you possess and give to the poor, and you will have treasure in heaven; and come, follow me" (Mt 19:21).

In the Gospel story, the rich young man did not listen to Jesus. He chose to keep his wealth and walked away sad. Anthony did not want to be like that young man. He went out immediately and gave away all his possessions to the poor and entrusted the care of his sister to others. Then he went off into the desert to seek God.

He went out some way from the town and found the

broken-down ruins of an old fortress. Here, Anthony began his life of penance and prayer. The devil was not happy with this decision, however, and there are many stories about how the evil one antagonized Anthony in those early days. Let's check in on the holy youth out at the abandoned fortress to see just how the devil attacked him:

The holy man Anthony knelt, praying in the dirt as the noonday sun beat down upon his brow.

"Lord, grant me the grace to persevere unto the end," Anthony whispered.

Suddenly, Anthony felt that he was not alone. A black, eerie shadow fell over him. The heat of the sun was replaced with a damp chill. Anthony shivered and tried to remain focused on his prayers.

"Anthony," came a smooth, persuasive voice, though he heard it not with his ears but within his mind. "Anthony, what are you doing wasting your time out here? Don't you care for your sister, who is back home and misses you? You have property and wealth enough at home. Go back to her and live a comfortable life at home with your family."

"Get thee behind me, Satan," Anthony growled without opening his eyes.

The voice took the sound of Anthony's friends from childhood. "Anthony, why are you spending your youth out here? Do you want to spend your whole life this way? Don't you know how long that is? How can you be happy like this?"

Anthony made the sign of the cross and continued with his prayers. The shadow lifted, and presently things returned to normal.

But the evil one was not through with the saint yet.

That night, as Anthony reclined behind a broken stone wall to sleep, the devil made horrific noises, sometimes screeching like a pack of jackals, other times crashing about him with simulated thunder, and still other times groaning like some foul ghost of the abyss.

Anthony could not sleep. He got up, knelt upon weary knees, and prayed the Our Father. As the devil continued to make noise, Anthony would only pray louder.

A few days later, some companions from town came to bring Anthony bread and water. Anthony came walking up to greet them, his hair disheveled and his eyes sunken.

"It looks like he hasn't slept in a week!" one of them noted.

"Greetings, friends!" said Anthony, raising his hand in salute. But the devil was close by. As Anthony greeted his companions, an invisible force knocked his legs out from under him. He fell face down in the dirt. "Confound that

fiend!" grumbled Anthony as his friends lifted him to his feet. "He's been bothering me non-stop all week! But we won't give in to his wiles, will we brethren? Let us pray ever more fervently that his plots will be overthrown."

Anthony led the group in prayer. As he did, a small stone lifted itself up and flung itself through the air, striking the holy man on the crown of the head. Anthony grunted and rubbed his head, but without stopping his prayers.

Later that night, the devil took out his full rage upon Anthony. As he knelt by the old stone wall praying his evening prayers, a horde of creeping demons came skulking towards him out of the sand. Anthony made the sign of the cross, unsure whether what he was seeing was real or a vision. The demons swarmed around Anthony, knocking him to the earth. They clawed his flesh and tore his beard, beating him ruthlessly and snarling in his face. All the while, Anthony could sense the dark presence of the devil, who had taken the form of a small African boy standing some distance off. "There's nothing for you here, Anthony. Go back to the city," he mocked.

Anthony cried out, "Christ defend me! The Lord is my helper, and I shall look down on my enemies!"

At the name of Christ, the demonic horde evaporated like mist in the morning sun. Only the devil remained, still in the form of the small African boy. "You are very despicable," Anthony said, struggling to his feet. "That form suits you, for you are evil-hearted and certainly weak as a child. Henceforth I shall have no trouble from you."

With a flash of pale light in his eyes, the child hissed and vanished. After that, Anthony was not troubled any longer by the devil.

———

People from far and wide eventually came to gawk at the strange but holy man living in the ruins. He withdrew and went further out into the desert, but no matter where he went, people found him—sometimes they just wanted to look at him, other times they wanted to ask his prayers; many of these people received miracles from the prayers of Anthony.

But there were some who came to find Anthony because they wanted to join him. Anthony allowed young men who wished to live as he did to set up their own little huts nearby him, called *cells*. Cell comes from the Latin word *celare*, which means "to hide or conceal." This was a perfect name for these little huts, for within them, the hermits concealed themselves from the world to seek God.

The Last Days of Paul and Anthony

Eventually, there were so many men living with Anthony that he found himself to be the head of a little community. He decided his disciples needed some basic rules to live by and stay organized, so he gave them instructions on the best way to succeed in their vocation. Anthony and his followers became the first monks. *Monk* comes from the Greek word *monachi*, which means "alone." Monks, like hermits, live alone, but with one important difference—while a hermit lives completely on his or her own, monks live alone in cells but come together as a community to pray, eat, and work. Monks also have rules that govern how their community is structured.

Like St. Paul, St. Anthony lived to a very old age. He became known as St. Anthony the Great, but he is also called St. Anthony of Egypt, or sometimes St. Anthony the Abbot—*abbot* is a word that means "father"—because Anthony was like a father to his monks. It would eventually be used to describe the head of a monastery. By the time St. Anthony was old, there were thousands of monks living in the Egyptian desert.

Eventually, St. Anthony learned that there was another holy man, even older than himself, living out in the desert. This was St. Paul. Though he was very old, Anthony made the long trek to visit St. Paul in his cave. The two met each other and shared a meal. By that time, St. Paul was 113 years old! A great friendship blossomed from this meal shared by two old men.

When St. Anthony again went to visit St. Paul, he found Paul dead in his cave. St. Anthony lovingly buried him and returned home with the old tunic of woven palm leaves worn by St. Paul. Anthony held this tunic in such high esteem that he only dared wear it twice a year, on Easter and Pentecost.

St. Anthony would live on for another fourteen years. By that time, he himself was 105 years old and was worn by a life of penance in the hot Egyptian sun. As death drew near, he called his followers and gave them the only two possessions he had—a staff and a sheepskin cloak. Then he died peacefully surrounded by his monks in January of 356.

Leaving Behind a Legacy

Have you stopped to wonder how we know about all these things St. Anthony did and said if he lived alone for so long? If so, that's a good question!

St. Anthony had a young disciple from Alexandria named Athanasius, who we touched on in the last chapter. Athanasius took care to write down all the sayings of St. Anthony and all the great deeds he had done. These writings became a book called *The Life of St. Anthony*. Athanasius would go on to become bishop of Alexandria and later a great saint. His book on St. Anthony was extremely popular. People all over the Roman Empire read it and were inspired to live like St. Anthony.

Monks and hermits were beginning to pop up in other places too. In Syria, there were a group of hermits called *stylites* who lived on top of great pillars. Unlike Egypt, Syria was crowded with large cities, so it was difficult for hermits to find places to live by themselves. Since they could not go out to the wilderness, these stylites went up by living on the tops of pillars. Known as "pillar saints," stylites like St. Simeon and St. Daniel spent years on top of pillars that could be as tall as sixty feet.

Others experimented with different forms of community life. Around 314, a Roman soldier named Pachomius converted to Christianity and decided to take up the life of a monk in Egypt. Many other men joined him, and Pachomius decided to organize his followers in large barracks, similar to how the Roman army was organized. These became the first *monasteries*, buildings where monks lived in common to pray and seek God. The monasteries of Pachomius could be huge, sometimes housing over a thousand monks. Pachomius would later be venerated as a saint.

Women also took up the monastic life, living in communities of their own or sometimes as hermits. All across the Christian East, from Egypt to Syria to Palestine to Greece, holy men and women were taking up Christ's call to leave everything for the sake of the kingdom of heaven.

St. Paul, St. Anthony, and St. Pachomius left behind a great legacy. They are considered the founders of Christian monasticism—*monasticism* means a way of life where people give up worldly pursuits to focus on seeking God. In the beginning, monasticism was confined to the East, but it would gradually spread into the West in the following decades. We will learn about that in chapter 7, but for now we must return to the affairs of the Roman Empire, for important changes were afoot that would have monumental consequences for the Catholic Church.

CHAPTER 7

The Triumph of the Church

A Time of Growth

We have traced the growth of the Church for several centuries now, up until the fourth century, which was a very dramatic period. During this time, the Church suffered its last great persecution, saw the rise of the first Christian emperor, fought off one of the most dangerous heresies, and convened its first ecumenical council. These changes in the Church and society laid the groundwork for the establishment of Christendom in the Middle Ages. Christendom was a time, lasting over a thousand years, when culture and politics were shaped by the Catholic faith.

In chapter 4, we learned about the Roman persecutions. By the late third century, the Church had enjoyed many years of peace. After the death of Emperor Valerian in 260, no emperor attempted a whole scale persecution of the Church. Thus, Christianity grew in peace. People attended Mass, theologians wrote and argued, monks prayed, and church buildings were constructed, all without much protest from the Roman authorities. It was not a bad time to be Christian.

It wasn't that the Roman's hatred of Christians lessened or that they didn't care about religious conformity anymore. Rather, the Roman Empire was going through a time of great turmoil. We mentioned this in chapter 4 when, around AD 235, the empire entered a long period of civil war that went on for about fifty years. Rival generals killed each other and proclaimed themselves emperor, only to be deposed and killed by another not long after. Whole provinces of the empire broke off and became independent, and the economy suffered. The Roman authorities were much too busy with these problems to worry about the Christians or how and who people were worshiping in private.

Augustus Diocletian

It took an extraordinary man to bring order to this chaos. That man was Diocletian, a Roman soldier from the province of Dalmatia, on the Adriatic. He came from humble origins but rose through the ranks of the army to become an important commander. In 285, he was proclaimed emperor upon the death of the previous ruler. Diocletian immediately went about fixing the empire's problems.

One of the things Diocletian did was split the empire into a western half and an eastern half. He appointed a co-emperor named Galerius to rule the West, while Diocletian ruled the East. He and Galerius each called themselves *Augustus*, then each *Augustus* nominated a successor (meaning someone to take power after him), called a *Caesar*. This was meant to make it easier to govern the sprawling Roman Empire as well as solve the problem of who would rule by creating a stable plan of succession.

Diocletian's plan worked. The civil wars came to an end and peace was gradually restored.

But not all was well. When Diocletian tried to make sacrifices in his palace, his *augurs*—the pagan Roman seers who offered sacrifices and interpreted the will of the gods—told him they could not read the messages of the gods in the sacrifices. They told Diocletian this was because there were Christians working in the imperial palace and the gods were displeased. Diocletian dismissed all the Christians who lived or worked in the imperial palace.

The palace caught fire shortly after this. Though it would eventually be put out, the emperor suspected somebody had started the fire rather than assuming it started by accidental means. His augurs and his co-emperor Galerius blamed the Christians. Galerius suggested they persecute the Church, but Diocletian had never had problems with the Church; in fact, there was a Christian church across the street from his palace. But eventually Diocletian decided in favor of attacking the Church, issuing a decree of persecution in 303.

Diocletian ordered churches closed and all copies of the Scriptures to be handed over and burned. He ordered all clergy to sacrifice to the Roman gods on pain of exile or death. While the persecution was ordered throughout the entire empire, it was carried on with greater severity in certain places. Rome particularly had many great martyrs, including St. Sebastian, a captain of the imperial bodyguard who was famously shot to death with arrows. Another famous martyr of Diocletian was St. Agnes of Rome. Agnes was a very young girl, no more than twelve or thirteen years of age, who had pledged her virginity to Christ and was slain with the sword.

The persecution of Diocletian was the most widespread

and vicious of all the Roman persecutions—as well as the longest; it raged for ten years, from 303 to 313. It's difficult to know how many Christians suffered death under Diocletian; a likely number is between 3,500 and 15,000, with others being exiled or punished in other ways.

Emperor Constantine

Diocletian himself would not stick around to see the conclusion of the persecution. He resigned from being emperor in 305, as did his co-emperor Galerius. They each left the imperial throne to their designated successors, who in turn appointed new successors. However, the succession did not go as smoothly as Diocletian had hoped. The new *Augusti* and their *Caesars* began fighting with one another. To make matters worse, other generals who were not designated successors also got into the struggle for power.

One of the most important generals was a man named Constantine, the son of Constantius Chlorus, who was the Caesar of the West. Constantine's father was a pagan, but his mother, Helen, was a Christian. For his part, Constantine had always been a follower of the sun god, Sol Invictus. Constantine was a daring commander, popular with his men and experienced in government. He had the energy and support to rule the West.

But Italy was under the control of a rival named Maxentius, who had sacked Rome. Constantine knew he would never be able to rule the West unless he secured control of Rome. So he marched his army down into Italy but found Maxentius's army was entrenched in a well-defended position.

That night, as Constantine debated what to do, he had a dream in which he saw a Christian symbol, the *Chi-Rho*, floating in the sky, along with the Latin words, "In

hoc signo vinces," which means, "In this sign, conquer." When he awoke, Constantine ordered his men to paint the Christian symbol on their shields before attacking Maxentius. The battle was a great victory for Constantine, as Maxentius was defeated and killed. Constantine took control of Rome and was proclaimed emperor of the West.

He believed the God of the Christians was responsible for his victory. He converted to the Christian faith and began supporting the Church. One of the first things he did upon becoming emperor was proclaiming the Edict of Milan in 313. This was an agreement between Constantine and Licinius—the new co-emperor of the East—that agreed to end Diocletian's persecution and grant Christians religious freedom throughout the empire. Constantine and Licinius would eventually go to war, with Constantine coming out victorious in 324, making him the sole ruler of the whole Roman Empire.

One of Constantine's first acts was to move the capital

of the empire to the East. There were several reasons for this. For one, the eastern provinces were wealthier and more heavily populated, and it made sense that the capital should be closer to them. But also, as the first Christian emperor, Constantine wanted to start fresh with a city untainted by the deep pagan history of Rome. He chose an easily defensible location on the Bosphorus Straits between Greece and Asia Minor and constructed his new capital, called Constantinople. He built a marvelous church there, the Church of the Holy Apostles.

With the capital of the empire moving to Constantinople, the bishops of Constantinople became important leaders in the Church. But the recognized leader of the Christian people was still the bishop of Rome, the pope. This would lead to struggles between the churches of Rome and Constantinople in the future, as we shall eventually see.

The Council of Nicaea

At the time Constantine became emperor, the Church was being torn apart by the Arian heresy, which we learned about in the last chapter. Constantine had just spent years waging war to bring unity to the empire, only to see this strife. When he realized there was disunity in the Church, he wanted it stopped. He suggested that the Church summon a gathering of bishops and theologians to discuss the problem of Arianism and come to a conclusion about it.

The bishops of the Church gathered at a place called Nicaea in Asia Minor. This was the Church's first ecumenical council. An ecumenical council is a solemn gathering of bishops from across the universal Church, in union with the pope, to discuss matters of doctrine.

The Church had always been used to emperors

opposing the Church, or else paying no heed to it. Constantine not only cared about the Church, he wanted very much to be involved in matters of Church government and planned on attending the Council of Nicaea. Having a Christian emperor who supported the Church was unprecedented. How would Constantine interact with the Christian bishops? How would the bishops at the council receive him? Let's go back to the opening day of the Council of Nicaea on May 20, 325 to get an idea:

———————

The palace hall was abuzz with the conversations of bishops and priests. Seats had been arranged all about the hall, everyone with an assigned place. The bishops, clad in their heavy robes and carrying their episcopal staves, the sign of their office, clambered about looking for their assigned seats.

"Why am I way back here?" asked Potitius, bishop of an obscure diocese in rural Gaul, to his deacon Perfectus.

"The assigned seating isn't random," replied Perfectus. "Everybody is seated according to rank. The bishops of the older, more important dioceses are seated towards the front, closer to the emperor."

Once everyone was seated, a silence fell over the hall. Word had come that Emperor Constantine had arrived.

Three individuals entered the hall in a line and ascended the steps to the dais—a raised platform—where the chairs draped in purple were set out for the imperial family.

"Who are they?" asked Perfectus quietly.

"The young man is probably Crispus, son of the emperor. And those other children are his younger sons, Constantius and Constans."

The children of the emperor took their seats on the dais.

A train of theologians and bishops followed, marching in solemn procession. "Why are these clergy so honored?" asked Bishop Potitius, straining his eyes from the back to see who the men were.

"These are the personal friends of the emperor," answered Perfectus. "For example, that man there is Eusebius of Caesarea, a close acquaintance of Constantine and one of his instructors in the faith. And there is Hosius of Cordoba, representing Pope Sylvester of Rome."

Their conversation was cut off by the blare of a trumpet announcing the arrival of the emperor. All the bishops rose. Constantine himself entered the hall, clothed in robes glittering with golden embroidery. The emperor's entrance had been meticulously timed so that at this precise moment, he walked in the rays of the rising sun flooding through the windows. His purple robe seemed to be illuminated and the gold and precious stones of his jewelry flashed.

"He glows like an angelic messenger!" one bishop exclaimed. Many bishops muttered similar praises of the bearing and splendor of the emperor. Constantine did not look at any of them. He kept his head slightly downcast, though he did blush at the compliments he could hear from the assembly.

"Well, he has an excellent stature and beauty of form," admitted Potitius as he sized up the emperor from the back of the room.

"I agree," said Perfectus. "He displays a majestic dignity, and strength and vigor too!"

When he arrived at the dais, he remained standing. Attendants emerged from the side of the hall carrying a special chair wrought in gold which had been prepared

for him. The chair was set down on the dais, and the bishops near him beckoned for him to take his seat among them. The emperor bowed graciously and sat; only then did the entire assembly sit as well.

The Council of Nicaea had officially begun.

———

Though Constantine was present at the opening of the Council of Nicaea, most of the council proceedings were dominated by the arguments of the bishops about Arianism. Arius attended and tried to argue that God the Son was not divine, but the majority of bishops vehemently opposed him. According to one legend, St. Nicholas became so angry at Arius's blasphemy that he punched him!

In the end, the bishops of Nicaea voted to condemn Arius's heresy. Many of the orthodox bishops had been influenced by the powerful arguments of St. Athanasius, who was also present. Athanasius had spent years writing and preaching against Arius and was a notable defender of the Faith.

The Council of Nicaea promulgated the Nicene Creed, which we recite every Sunday at Mass. A *creed* is a statement of what Christians believe. The Nicene Creed states the Church's belief that God the Son and God the Father are both divine—"God from God, light from light, true God from true God, begotten not made."

The Flowering of Christian Civilization

By the time Constantine died in 337, many more people had converted to Christianity, perhaps as many as a third or more of the people within the empire. There would still be several decades of religious discord, however. Constantine's son and successor, Constantius II, favored the Arians and actually exiled St. Athanasius; another successor of Constantine, Julian, returned to paganism and tried to undo the influence of the Church.

But despite these setbacks, by the latter part of the century, it was clear that the Church was triumphing over both paganism and the various heresies. A series of Catholic emperors instituted laws favoring the Church and discouraging heresy, pagan temples were gradually abandoned, and Arianism withered away. In the year 380, the Catholic emperor Theodosius passed a law making Christianity the official religion of the Roman Empire. He wrote, "It is our desire that all the various nations which are subject to our clemency and moderation, should continue to profess that religion which was delivered to the Romans by the divine Apostle Peter."

Throughout the reign of Theodosius (379–395), pagan temples were closed, pagan rituals abolished, and Christianity exalted throughout the empire. The long, dark night of paganism was over. The flowering of Christian civilization was about to begin.

CHAPTER 8

The Benedictines

Barbarian Invasions

After the advent of the Christian Roman emperors, paganism gradually died out throughout the empire. Temples were abandoned or shut down, pagan sacrifices disappeared, and games honoring the pagan gods—such as the gladiatorial fights or the Olympic competitions in Greece—were outlawed. Thousands became Christians. Some did so because they sincerely believed, others to gain political advantage, and still others just shrugged and went along with the crowd. However it happened, by the middle of the fifth century, most of the old Roman Empire was solidly Christian.

This was a good thing for the spiritual and moral life of the Roman people. But it did not mean Rome's political problems went away. After the death of Theodosius in 395, the empire was again split into an eastern and western half, ruled by two emperors. This divided Roman power. Barbarian tribes from across the German frontiers migrated into Roman lands, taking huge chunks of territory away from Roman control. Generals continued to fight against each other and emperors often died violently, especially in the West.

In the year 410, a barbarian chieftain named Alaric sacked the city of Rome. It was the first time Rome had been overrun by a foreign army in centuries. Pagans mocked Christians, asking, "If your God is all powerful, why is he letting these bad things happen to you?" Christians asked similar questions: "If we have converted to the true Faith, shouldn't God bless us by protecting his kingdom?" Their faith was shaken by the bad things happening in the world.

St. Augustine: Doctor of the Church

These doubts were answered by a brilliant African bishop and theologian named St. Augustine of Hippo. St. Augustine, who lived from 354 to 430, was from the Roman province of Numidia in northern Africa. He was a very studious man, passing through various different philosophies before converting to Christianity, due in part to the prayers of his mother, St. Monica, and one of his mentors, the bishop St. Ambrose of Milan.

St. Augustine was a gifted theologian and wrote a book to answer the question of why God would permit Christian Rome to suffer. In his book, *City of God*, St. Augustine warned Christians that they should not think of Rome as "God's kingdom." There were ultimately only two kingdoms—or cities—as Augustine says in his book: the city of God and the city of man. The former is comprised of the Church who follows God's will, and the latter is those outside the Church who ultimately do the works of the devil. Even if Rome falls, God's kingdom

has not been destroyed because God's kingdom is greater than any worldly kingdom.

St. Augustine's writings would have a profound influence on how Christians viewed the Church in its relation to the world. He would become a Doctor of the Church. A *Doctor of the Church* is a person whose contributions to theology have been so important that they are recommended by the Church as a sure guide to understanding Catholic teachings.

St. Benedict of Nursia

The Roman Empire did indeed fall, at least in the West. In the year 476, the last Roman emperor, Romulus Augustulus, was deposed by the barbarian chief Odoacer. Odoacer packed up the imperial insignia, sent them to Constantinople, and said the West did not need an emperor anymore. And just like that, centuries of Roman rule in the West came to an end.

The years after the fall of the Roman Empire were chaotic for western Europe. Pagan barbarian tribes such as the Visigoths, Ostrogoths, Anglo-Saxons, and Franks set up their own kingdoms in former Roman territories. Cities shrank as people fled to the countryside for safety, roads deteriorated, and education suffered.

Nevertheless, there were still many holy men and women dedicated to the service of God. One of these was an Italian man named St. Benedict of Nursia, who was born in 480 to a family of Italian nobles, only four years after the last Roman emperor was deposed. Italy at that time was under the control of the Ostrogothic barbarians. Benedict's parents sent him to Rome for his education, but while in Rome, he decided that a life of study and worldly concern was not for him. He wanted to retire from the world to take up the life of a hermit.

St. Benedict left Rome and wandered about searching for a place of solitude to pursue his desire to live a prayerful life. This brought him into the region of Subiaco, outside of Rome. Here, he famously encountered another hermit who helped him begin his monastic life. Let's pause for a moment to take witness to this encounter:

Benedict threw himself down upon the soft earth beside the bubbling spring. He had been walking all day through the wilderness and was hot and tired. Now, by this spring near the base of a great mountain, he quenched his thirst.

"My soul thirsteth after thee, as in a parched and weary land," Benedict said as he drank the cool, flowing water and splashed some of it on his head.

After he had drunk, he reclined on the ground and looked about him. The place immediately surrounding the spring was crowded with brambles and wild cypress bushes. A little way distant, the ground began to slope up, turning suddenly into a jagged cliff and eventually a hulking mountain. No sound could be heard save the chirping of birds and the light breeze that rustled the bushes.

"What a desolate but glorious place," he marveled.

His rest was interrupted by the sound of footsteps crunching through the underbrush. Benedict leapt up and stood on guard, for lonely places like this were frequently inhabited by robbers and criminals in hiding. But the man who emerged from the bushes did not look threatening. He was clothed in a drab tunic and had wild, unkempt hair and a beard, and a wooden cross hung about his neck. The man was obviously some kind of hermit.

"Who are you, and what are you doing in this lonely place?" asked the man in a raspy voice.

Benedict smiled and bowed. "I am Benedict of Nursia, a follower of Christ who has come seeking solitude."

A wide grin spread across the hermit's face. "Ah, another hermit," he said, his eyes gleaming. "Peace and grace in our Lord Jesus. My name is Romanus. For five years I have lived in this place seeking God in the wilderness. My home is this mountain," he said, gesturing to the looming slope of rock behind him. "I live in a hut at the top."

"Romanus, what do you call this place?" asked Benedict.

"It is called Subiaco, my friend, and if you seek the life of a hermit, there is no better place than this. In fact, I can show you an excellent place.

"Please," said Benedict.

Romanus led Benedict through some dense underbrush to the base of Subiaco's cliff side. "How do we ascend?" asked Benedict. "The cliff face looks impassable."

"Only to the untrained eye," replied Romanus, smiling. "A few paces to the west of here are some footholds by which we can make our way up."

The hermit struggled along the cliff, fighting back thickets and tree branches. More than once Benedict was whacked in the face with a branch as he followed Romanus. "Love is patient," he said to himself, sighing and making the sign of the cross. He trudged along behind Romanus for several minutes, the brambles getting thicker by the moment. Benedict began to wonder if the hermit knew where he was going or if he was just crazy.

But soon enough, Romanus cried out, "Here we are!" Benedict saw a very narrow ledge winding up the side of the cliff, so narrow indeed that only one person could move along it at a time and only while pressing one's body to the rock face. The two men began the painstaking climb up the cliff.

The ledge wound up for about fifty feet before it came to an abrupt end. "What now?" asked Benedict.

"We climb," said Romanus. The hermit tested the cliff in several places with his foot before scrambling up. Benedict followed behind, though more slowly, carefully feeling out each foothold before moving.

About twenty feet up, the two men arrived at a short ledge concealing a dark cave opening. "As promised!" laughed Romanus as the wiry man pulled himself up onto the ledge, dangling his feet in the air while Benedict came slowly behind.

Benedict clambered up onto the ledge and looked at the cave. It was not large, but it was big enough for him to sleep and pray in and was very secluded. He doubted whether anyone from the ground would even see it.

"It seems just right, Romanus," he said, "but in this desolate spot, how will I get food and water?"

"Good question," replied Romanus thoughtfully. "I know! I live above you. I can lower a basket of food from a rope. Would that work?"

"That's very thoughtful of you," said Benedict. "I think it just might. But not too much food. I don't want to trouble you or wither your food supply."

Romanus chuckled and pointed at his bony arms. "Do I look like I have a lot of food to spare?"

———

St. Benedict lived in that cave for many years. He became so shaggy that people who passed by and caught

a glimpse of him thought a wild beast was living in the area. Although Benedict looked wild on the outside, his life of prayer, penance, and solitude was bringing him closer to God. He became famous for his sanctity.

The Rule of St. Benedict

A group of monks came to St. Benedict and asked him to become their abbot. Benedict warned them he would be too strict for them, but the monks insisted, so Benedict went with them. However, it soon became apparent Benedict's warnings would prove true. The other monks tired of the difficult lifestyle he placed them under and regretted making him abbot. In order to get rid of him, they tried to poison his drink at meal time. But when St. Benedict made the sign of the cross over the cup to bless it, the cup shattered in his hands, revealing the monks' evil plot. It was clear God was protecting him! Needless to say, St. Benedict left these monks.

He would go on to found his own monastery at a place called Monte Cassino, atop a mountain where the locals had once worshiped Apollo. Benedict's sanctity and experience gave him great insight into how a monastery of monks should be governed. On the one hand, many monks were too lazy and lacked discipline, like the ones who had tried to poison him. On the other hand, there were some monks whose lifestyles were so hard that they discouraged people from taking up the monastic life at all—such as some of the Desert Fathers or the pillar saints. St. Benedict believed people needed a monastic rule that appealed to the common man, something that would allow average people to become holy while not being so challenging that it discouraged them.

He composed a rule known as the *Rule of St. Benedict,* or the Benedictine Rule. St. Benedict's rule divided the day into periods of prayer, study, work, and rest. His motto was *ora et labora*, "prayer and work," which summarizes the spirit of St. Benedict's rule. Benedict believed monks should keep busy with their hands, whether copying manuscripts or working in the monastery's orchard or some other form of work.

The *Rule of St. Benedict* said many things about how a monastery ought to be run. For example, it explained what kind of man the abbot should be and how he should be selected. It also told the monks what times of day to pray and what psalms to pray, and it made recommendations for what foods to eat and how to keep discipline in the monastery.

St. Benedict's rule became a very popular way to organize monasteries. He would found twelve monasteries during his life. And because St. Benedict was such a holy man and worked so many miracles, his fame and the fame of his rule spread abroad.

Though St. Benedict died in 547, monks continued to organize monasteries according to his rule. Soon there were thousands of Benedictine monks throughout western Europe. Besides carrying on the important work of prayer and sanctification, these monks made important contributions to civilization. Their monks worked hard copying manuscripts, preserving much of the writings of the ancient world. As they cleared forests and drained marshes to turn to farmland, they helped settle the wildernesses of Europe. They brought Christianity to the barbarian kingdoms and became missionaries.

In our next chapter, we will learn about how men and women who had devoted themselves to the Rule of St. Benedict became instrumental in converting the barbarians of Europe to the Christian faith.

CHAPTER 9

A Time of Missionaries

Spreading the Faith

As the old Roman Empire broke apart, barbarian tribes migrated into the old Roman provinces and set up their own petty kingdoms. Some of these tribes came out of central Asia, others from the forests of northern Germany, and still others from Scandinavia. But though they came from different places, these tribes were all pagan.

When they settled throughout Europe, however, these tribes came into contact with the older Christian culture left behind by the Roman Empire. Gradually, Christian missionaries won these pagan tribes over to the Catholic faith. By the eighth century, almost all of Europe had embraced the Christian faith. The old Roman populations intermingled with the newer barbarian settlers creating new peoples: the French, Spanish, English, and so on.

As we shall see, many of these early missionaries were monks. Sometimes they were followers of St. Benedict's rule, like St. Augustine of Canterbury; other times, they practiced a different form of monasticism, such as St. Patrick. But wherever they came from or whatever their manner of living, Europe was won over to the Faith by the patient, humble example of holy men and women seeking to serve God and win souls for Christ.

Since we've talked mostly about the Roman Empire so far, we've spent a lot of time learning about the conversion of those peoples and places that had been under Roman control. But even before the conversion of Constantine, the Catholic faith was spreading outside of the empire.

For example, in the third century, the entire nation of the Armenians, in western Asia, converted to the Christian faith under the influence of the great miracle worker St. Gregory Thaumaturgus (d. 270). Armenia holds the distinction of being the first Christian nation.

In the next century, a Roman Christian boy named Frumentius was sold into slavery in the far-off Kingdom of Ethiopia, in eastern Africa. Frumentius served in the royal court and befriended the prince, Ezana, winning him to the Christian faith. When Ezana became king, Frumentius went to visit St. Athanasius and was ordained bishop during the reign of Constantine. Frumentius returned to Ethiopia, spreading the Faith in Ezana's kingdom for almost fifty years and translating the Scriptures into Ge'ez, the language of the Ethiopians. Today, St. Frumentius is venerated by Ethiopian Christians as the Apostle of Ethiopia.

Irish Missionaries

Following the Christianization of Rome, the Catholic faith continued to spread into realms Rome had never touched, sometimes through unexpected means. A great example of this is the story of St. Patrick.

Patrick was a Roman Briton who lived in the Roman province of Britannia. As a boy, he was kidnapped by Irish pirates who sold him as a slave in Ireland, which at that time was a wild place ruled by warring tribes and under the dominion of the feared pagan Druids.

Patrick served as a slave for six years in Ireland keeping sheep on a mountain. During this time, he prayed fervently and grew in holiness, until one day a dream from God told him to escape and take a ship to Gaul (modern-day France). Patrick was able to escape and made his way to Rome. Soon thereafter, he was ordained a bishop and, believe it or not, returned to Ireland to convert the very people who had formerly been his captors.

For the next several decades, St. Patrick went about Ireland converting people to the Catholic faith and founding monasteries. Others would continue his holy work, such as St. Brigid of Kildare, who founded the first convent in Ireland. St. Enda founded a monastic school on the island of Aran that formed other Irish monks as missionaries, and St. Columba ventured over to Scotland to convert the pagan Picts. For three centuries, Irish missionaries journeyed about the European continent establishing monasteries and preaching Christ.

The Eldest Daughter of the Church
The old Roman provinces of Gaul had been invaded and settled by a Germanic tribe called the Franks. This pagan tribe was split into various warring factions, but they eventually were united by a powerful warrior king named Clovis. Though he was a pagan, Clovis was married to a Christian princess of Burgundy named St. Clotilde. St. Clotilde wanted to have their son baptized a Christian, but when the baby was baptized, it fell sick and died soon afterward. Clovis was furious and blamed Clotilde and

her Christian faith. When she became pregnant again, he was hesitant to let the new child be baptized, but eventually he was won over by the persuasions of St. Clotilde and St. Remigius, the bishop of Rheims. His baby son was baptized, and this time, he survived.

Clovis converted to the Catholic faith in 497 in a manner very similar to the conversion of Constantine. Engaged in a desperate battle against a rival tribe, Clovis cried out to the Christian God for help and promised to worship him in exchange for victory. The tide of the battle suddenly turned, and Clovis was victorious. He attributed his victory to the power of Jesus Christ. He was soon after baptized by St. Remigius, along with thousands of his

warriors. The Kingdom of the Franks—or France as we call it today—was now a Catholic kingdom. We thus call France the "Eldest Daughter of the Church" because it was the first pagan kingdom within the boundaries of the old Roman Empire to embrace the Catholic faith.

More European Conversions

As the Roman Empire was falling in the West, the peninsula of Spain was overrun by a barbarian tribe called the Visigoths. Once pagan, the Visigoths had been converted to the Arian heresy by an Arian bishop. Once in Spain, they established a barbarian kingdom there and professed Arianism.

Yet that would not be the end of their story. They were slowly won over to the Catholic faith by the preaching of two saintly brothers, St. Isidore of Seville and St. Leander. In 587, the Visigothic king Reccared I renounced Arianism and embraced Catholic Christianity. Most Visigothic nobles followed his example. Zealous bishops held local councils reforming the life of the clergy and laity throughout Spain. For the next century and a half, Visigothic Spanish culture would flourish under the government of pious Catholic kings and disciplined clergy.

The popes, too, took a lively interest in the conversion of the pagan barbarians. The first Benedictine monk to take the Chair of St. Peter was Pope St. Gregory the Great, who was pope from 590 to 604. One day, when Pope Gregory was walking about Rome, he saw some pale-skinned boys being sold as slaves. He asked to what tribe the boys belonged, and they told him, "We are Angles." Pope Gregory responded, "Not Angles, but angels, if they were Christian!" The Angles were a tribe that had settled on the far-off island of Britain; they were also known as the English. Pope Gregory resolved to send a missionary to this distant land to win its pale-skinned inhabitants for the Church of God.

Consequently, he dispatched St. Augustine, who was a Benedictine monk, and a few companions to the island of Britannia. There, they would preach the Catholic faith to the pagan Angles and Saxons who lived there (this St. Augustine should not be confused with St. Augustine of Hippo, whom we met in chapter 8).

In 597, St. Augustine and his companions landed on the Isle of Thanet off the coast of the Anglo-Saxon kingdom of Kent in the southeast of Britain. There, they were given an audience with the pagan king Ethelbert. Let us see what this first encounter was like:

————

Augustine and his companions waited pensively on the rugged turf of the Isle of Thanet. The monks' habits flapped loudly in the strong sea wind. Some ways off in the distance, near the beach, the entourage of Anglo-Saxon king Ethelbert of Kent approached over the tumbled, chalky stones and beach grasses. The king, dressed in a long blue tunic and garbed in a cloak of fur, led the way, followed by a large train of counselors and attendants.

"He certainly has brought a crowd to talk to some humble monks," said Brother Laurence. "Do you think he means to do us harm?"

"God forbid," said Augustine. "King Ethelbert is not a stranger to the Faith. His wife, Bertha, is a Christian princess of the Franks. Still, let us pray to the good Lord that he will give us a welcome reception."

"Hail, men of God!" Ethelbert called out, raising his hand in the air from some distance.

"Long life and strength to you, O great king!" called Augustine, bowing.

"Now!" hissed Brother Laurence to the monks. Immediately, the brothers began chanting a litany for the eternal salvation of themselves and the Anglo-Saxon people.

King Ethelbert and Augustine drew near each other. The two men walked up to each other and embraced while the Latin chants of the monks were carried in the wind.

The king's attendants came afterward, carrying a heavy wooden chair of solid oak. "Your throne, O king," an attendant said, placing the chair firmly in the grass. The king sat himself upon the throne. It was an odd sight, a king sitting upon a throne in the middle of a windy field and surrounded by monks.

"You will forgive the peculiarity of this meeting," said King Ethelbert, "but the sages of our gods told me I should not meet with you indoors. They say you are magicians, but that your magic has no power out in the open."

"Gracious king," said Augustine, "we are no magicians. We are servants of the Triune God—Father, Son, and Holy Spirit—who is adored by your wife, Bertha of

the Franks. We come to you to tell you of the salvation offered through Jesus Christ our Lord."

At the mention of the name of Christ, all the monks made the sign of the cross. Brother Laurence showed the king an image of Christ painted upon a board.

"Indeed," said the king, observing the image, "she has told me much about this God. But I want to hear it from your own lips."

At this, all the king's counselors, warriors, and attendants sat down in the grass, quiet and attentive.

Augustine nodded to Laurence. Brother Laurence motioned with his hand, and the monks all sat down cross-legged in the grass as well. Augustine, leaning upon his episcopal staff, stood before the king alone. He cleared his throat.

"In the beginning, God created the race of men to dwell upon this earth, to live in harmony with him and each other, and to serve him in purity. However, in the time of our first parents, the old tempter, the devil, seduced man to sin against God . . ."

Augustine went on in this manner for some time as the sun sank low and long shadows stretched out upon the turf. As he concluded, St. Augustine took his place among the monks and sat down cross-legged in the grass.

After a moment or two in thought, Ethelbert said, "Your words and promises are fair indeed, yet they are new and uncertain, and I cannot accept them and abandon the age-old beliefs that I have held together with the whole English nation. But since you have traveled far, and I can see that you are sincere in your desire to impart to us what you believe to be true and excellent, we will not harm you. We will receive you hospitably and take care to supply you with all that you need; nor will we forbid you to preach and win any people you can to your religion."

"*Deo gratias*," replied Augustine, bowing his head and making the sign of the cross.

────────

Though King Ethelbert was not ready to accept Christianity that day, he allowed Augustine to preach freely and gave him some land at Canterbury to build a church. Augustine set up the first English diocese at Canterbury; today, he is remembered as St. Augustine of Canterbury. Ethelbert's wife, Bertha, is also a saint—St. Bertha of Kent.

Eventually, the Anglo-Saxons accepted Christianity and King Ethelbert himself was baptized in the year 600. Other Anglo-Saxon kingdoms followed. For many years there was war between the Christian Anglo-Saxons and the pagan Anglo-Saxons; sometimes one kingdom would prevail, sometimes another. But Christianity gradually spread so that within a century almost all of England was Christian.

There would be many more missionaries who pushed into Europe's more remote regions, such as Scandinavia, Germany, and the Balkans. But for now, we must pause and look at some political developments in western Europe that would change the balance of power on the continent—and the development of Christianity—in profound ways.

CHAPTER 10

Rome and the Byzantines

A Divided Empire

In our last chapter, we took a very broad look at some of the missionary efforts of the Church throughout Europe and even as far abroad as Asia and Africa. Indeed, with every passing decade, pious monks and zealous bishops were pushing Christianity into new lands, carrying the saving message of Jesus Christ. Monasteries and convents were founded, becoming not only centers of spirituality and learning but often the origins of towns which would spring up around them.

But now, let us return to Italy. When we last spoke of the Italian peninsula, the western Roman Empire had just collapsed and was replaced by a barbarian kingdom ruled by the Ostrogoths. It was in this age that the holy St. Benedict emerged to pioneer the monastic movement that would transform religious life in the West.

The eastern Roman Empire, however, had continued

on, and the emperors at Constantinople had never accepted Ostrogothic rule in Italy. During the sixth century,
the eastern Roman Empire—which we shall hereafter
refer to as the Byzantine Empire—fought a long war to
retake Italy from the Ostrogoths. By the seventh century,
the Byzantines maintained a very loose hold on Italy from
their capital at Ravenna in the North. They were in control, but barely.

Yet central Rome came increasingly under control of
the popes. Following the end of the Roman Empire in the
West, the most powerful figure left in Rome was the successor of St. Peter. The popes gradually began to assume
control over more matters of government—repairing the
roads, keeping the water flowing, and maintaining law
and order. The lands around Rome became known as the
"Patrimony of St. Peter." However, the emperor in Constantinople was still nominally in charge, and in times of
war or great danger, it was to the court of Constantinople
that the popes and the people of Italy would turn.

Pope St. Gregory I

One of the most important popes of this time was Pope
St. Gregory I. He sat on the Chair of Peter from 590
to 604, but he began his religious life as a Benedictine
monk. Gregory was so devoted to St. Benedict that he
wrote the first biography of the saint; it is from Pope
Gregory's writings that we know much about the life of
St. Benedict.

Gregory had also served as the ambassador of the pope
to the imperial court in Constantinople, and later founded
a Benedictine monastery in Rome. He was known for his
wisdom, humility, and excellent gifts for organization
and government. When the previous pope died suddenly

from a plague in 590, the clergy of Rome unanimously acclaimed Gregory to be pope.

Gregory did much to build up the Church and papacy during his reign. As we saw in our last chapter, he sent St. Augustine to Britain to convert the English. But he also wrote a book on how to be a good bishop called the *Regula Pastoralis*; for over a thousand years, a copy of St. Gregory's book was given to all new bishops. He worked tirelessly to organize the Church in Italy and kept in contact with bishops and Christians from around the Christian world by his tireless letter writing. Gregorian Chant, the official music of the Catholic Church, is also named after Pope Gregory, since it was this pope who collected and organized the various different chants being used by the Church.

By the time St. Gregory died in 604, the Church in Italy was much better organized and the pope was a much stronger and well-respected figure, seen now as the natural leader of Italy. Pope Gregory would eventually be known as St. Gregory the Great.

The Rise of Islam

Shortly after the death of Pope St. Gregory, a new danger to the Christian Church emerged: the rise of Islam. Islam was a religion founded by the merchant Mohammed from the Arabian city of Mecca. In the year 610, Mohammed claimed he had a revelation from an angel, and he would claim many more revelations in the coming years. According to Mohammed, the angel told him that there was only one God, called *Allah* in Arabic, and all the other religions in the world were false or incomplete. Mohammed said that the Arabs should worship only Allah and submit themselves to him.

Mohammed's teaching was called Islam, which means "submission." Those who followed Islam became known as Muslims. Mohammed converted his family to the new faith, but the Arabs disliked Mohammed's teaching and drove him into exile. While in exile, he made more converts and raised an army, returning and conquering Mecca. Once in power, he compelled the Arabs to stop worshiping idols and accept Islam. Many did, and by the time Mohammed died in 632, much of Arabia was under Islamic power.

The Muslim armies began to spread out and take away Byzantine lands, like Jerusalem in the year 637. Meanwhile, Arab Muslim armies swept westward across North Africa, extinguishing ancient Christian communities that had existed there since the early Church. In 711, the Islamic armies poured across the Straits of Gibraltar into Spain, defeating the Christian armies of King Roderic and putting most of the peninsula under Islamic rule, leading to the end of the Christian Visigothic Kingdom of Spain.

The Arab armies then tried to press north into France but were halted only by the might of the Frankish warlord Charles Martel, whom we shall learn about shortly.

Persecution From the Iconoclasts
With the coming of Islam and the fall of Christian Palestine, North Africa, and Spain to the Arabs, Christianity was in grave danger. Another problem was that, as time wore on, the imperial court at Constantinople became less and less reliable. Civil war rent the empire in the early 700s, making it hard for the Byzantines to exercise any influence in the West.

In addition to this, the Byzantine Empire was falling prey to a new heresy called iconoclasm. Pushed by Emperor Leo III, *iconoclasm* was a heresy that said Christians should not venerate images. Since the very early Church, Christians had always paid special homage to holy images, called *icons*, of Christ, Mary, and the saints. Churches in the East and West were decorated with colorful mosaics and paintings depicting scenes from the Bible or the lives of the saints.

But Emperor Leo wanted to forbid the veneration of any images, except those of the emperor. He sent soldiers to the churches of the empire to destroy their holy images. This, as we shall see, was often carried out with violence:

––––––––

"You have no business here!" Deacon Gennadios cried out, trying to shove the imperial soldier back through the door.

"We're here on the emperor's orders," grunted the captain. He shoved the deacon aside with his burly arm and tromped into the chapel. A squad of armed guards entered behind him.

"You know the routine, men. Take care of the images," ordered the captain.

The soldiers were coldly efficient in their work. One brought in a large wooden bucket filled with white paint and plopped it on the floor of the chapel. Another came behind him with a large mop attached to a long handle. He dunked it in the paint and crudely slopped the dripping mop against the wall of the chapel, smearing white paint across an image of St. John the Apostle. Other teams of soldiers did likewise to the other images painted on the walls of the church.

Deacon Gennadios wept.

"I'll take care of the icons," growled the captain, striding towards the front of the chapel while carrying a thick club. He came to the *iconostasis*, the large wall dividing the sanctuary from the nave. The iconostasis was decorated with dozens of icons representing the communion of saints.

"Wait!" came a trembling voice from the sanctuary. It was the old priest Andronikos. The white-bearded priest shuffled through the gates of the iconostasis and fell on his knees before the captain. "Please captain, these icons have been in this chapel since the days of the emperor Justinian. Have reverence for God and for our heritage!"

"I have my orders," the captain said gruffly.

"In the name of God and the Holy Virgin," said the priest, clutching the captain's arm.

"Don't touch me!" the captain barked, thumping the old priest upside the head with his club. Father Andronikos wheezed and tumbled over. Deacon Gennadios rushed to his aid. The captain swung his club and began breaking the icons one-by-one. Gennadios winced at each thwack of the club against the icons.

It was all over in a few moments. The centuries-old icons had been broken to pieces and all the images on the chapel walls hastily whitewashed. The soldiers had packed up their mops and were already heading off to the next church. Andronikos, still being held by Gennadios on the ground, yelled, "God forgive you for your sacrilege!"

"You'll keep silent if you know what's good for you!" said the captain menacingly, pointing his club at the priest. He smiled, then turned and left, his booted feet crunching over the shards of smashed icons littering the floor.

————

A story like this was far too common during this time. Emperor Leo tried to intimidate the popes into carrying out his policies in Italy and in the West as well, but the popes refused. In fact, Pope Gregory III summoned a synod and excommunicated the iconoclasts as heretics. To be *excommunicated* means to be removed from the Church and deprived of the sacraments.

Leo retaliated by taking control of several dioceses away from the pope and transferring them to the control of Constantinople. But Leo's iconoclasm was very unpopular, both in the West and the East. Revolts broke out against him in Greece and Ravenna. He tried to subdue Italy, but a storm destroyed his imperial fleet. By the time Leo died in 741, most of Italy had been completely detached from Byzantine control.

Fortunately, orthodoxy returned to Constantinople with the accession of the empress Irene in 775. Irene restored the veneration of holy images and convened the

Nicaea

Second Council of ~~Constantinople~~ in 787, which taught that when a Christian venerates a holy image, they do not venerate the image itself *but the reality represented by the image*. A person praying in front of an icon or statue of Jesus is not worshiping a painted board or a piece of stone; rather, he gives honor to Jesus himself, whose image is represented on the icon or in stone.

By the middle of the 700s, Christianity was at a crossroads. On the one hand, the Christian faith was spreading into new lands and many peoples were embracing the Gospel, and the papacy was becoming stronger and better organized. But on the other hand, there was a growing division between Rome and Constantinople, both politically and religiously, and the rise of Islam saw many ancient Christian communities swallowed up by the new Arabic Muslim conquests. In addition, the heresy of iconoclasm rent the Christian communities of the East for a generation before orthodoxy was finally restored after the Second Council of Constantinople.

All of this left the popes wondering whether it still made sense to continue looking east to Constantinople for support, and we shall see how they handled this concern in the next chapter.

CHAPTER 11

The Carolingians

The Moors Invade

In the last chapter, we briefly touched on the rise of Islam. Though Mohammed died in 632, Islamic armies swarmed across the Middle East, conquering Egypt, Palestine, and Syria from the Byzantines, before diving into North Africa, bringing those lands under Islamic dominion as well.

In the year 711, they crossed the Straits of Gibraltar and invaded the Catholic Visigothic Kingdom of Spain. Though the Visigoths fought valiantly under their king, Roderic, they were defeated and almost the entire Spanish peninsula fell under the rule of the Muslims, whom the Christians called the Moors.

With Spain under control of Muslims, the Islamic armies now turned their eyes north to the Kingdom of the Franks, France. At that time, the family of King Clovis, called the Merovingians, still ruled the Kingdom of the Franks. But the descendants of Clovis were not as powerful as he had been. The kingdom was divided and weak and the kings did not intervene much in the affairs of the realm. This did not bode well for the Franks. The Muslim armies had never been defeated and were on the verge of adding France to the Islamic empire.

The Lineage of Charles Martel

But there were still men of power and influence among the Franks. The most important Frank of the day was Charles Martel. Martel was the mayor of the palace, a kind of second-in-command to the king. But because the Merovignian kings were so weak, Martel actually wielded the *real* power within the kingdom. You might compare it to a puppet and a puppet master. Though the puppet is what you see, it's the person—the puppet master—operating the puppet who is in control. In this case, the king was the puppet and Charles Martel was the master. People saw the king and he looked like a ruler, but someone else was truly doing the ruling.

When Martel heard of the Moorish threat, he gathered together a host of hearty Frankish warriors and marched south. At a place called Tours, his bearded, battle-ax carrying Franks fought the Muslim Moors and dealt them a crushing defeat. The Moors fled back to Spain and never tried to invade France like that again.

Martel was a hero and the savior of France—and probably all of Europe. If he had not been victorious at Tours, the Muslim armies would have swept into western Europe. His fame also made him more powerful. In fact, Charles Martel was like a king in everything but name. His family, called the Carolingians, became extremely important.

This continued under Charles's son, Pepin the Short.

Pepin, like his father, ruled the Frankish kingdom in the name of the Merovingian kings. But eventually Pepin got sick of having to be second-in-command to a useless king. He thought he should be king of the Franks and wondered how he could bring this about. The Merovingians had ruled the Franks for over three hundred years; he couldn't simply take the kingship. He needed an excuse, or rather, a justification. Pepin began formulating a plan to get the pope to agree with his idea. He reached out to Pope Zachary II, asking whether it was right for a king who had no power to reign; Zachary said it was not, but that the one who had real power ought to be king.

Pope Zachary issued a papal bull to Pepin confirming this. A *bull* is a document issued by the pope about some important matter. This gave Pepin the excuse he needed to overthrow the Merovingians. Using the words of the pope to support his plan, Pepin had the last Merovingian king, Childeric III, captured. Childeric's long hair—the symbol of his royal authority—was cut off and he was sent to a monastery. Pepin had himself proclaimed king of the Franks in 751.

Pepin ruled France well and expanded the Kingdom of the Franks. He also did not forget how the pope had helped him, and soon the popes would need his help in return. The popes were being troubled by the Lombards, a powerful tribe that had set up a kingdom in northern Italy. Pepin marched into Italy and defeated the Lombards, giving much of the land in central Italy to the papacy as the Church's own territory. Pepin figured if the popes had their own territory, they would have more security and not be as prone to threats from other kingdoms. These lands were called the Papal States.

When Pepin died, his son, Charles, succeeded him. Charles proved to be an energetic and just ruler. His people called him Charlemagne, which means "Charles the Great." He was the greatest ruler the Franks ever had. At over six feet tall—large for back then—he was a mountain of a man who inspired confidence in the soldiers he led into battle. Charlemagne's long reign was full of battles and adventures that put most of western Europe under his control. He conquered Germany and compelled the pagan tribes there to accept Christianity, he beat back barbarian invaders from the East, and he extended Frankish power into Italy to protect the pope. Everywhere he went, Charlemagne was victorious.

He was also a very pious man. He had a chapel built in his palace at Aachen where he attended Mass and heard the Divine Office. He surrounded himself with monks who helped educate him and his children in the Catholic faith. He built monasteries, befriended popes, and made sure the clergy in his realm were well-educated. In short, he was a great friend of the Church.

Never was this truer than in the year 800, when the people of Rome rioted and drove Pope Leo III out of the city. Leo was forced to turn to Charlemagne for help, and Charlemagne answered the call, coming into Italy and escorting Leo back to Rome, much to the pope's appreciation. Charlemagne ended up spending that Christmas in Rome, and on December 25 of the year 800, while Charlemagne was praying at Mass, Pope Leo approached him and placed a crown on his head, declaring Charlemagne the Roman emperor. Charlemagne later said he was surprised by this, claiming he had no idea the pope was going to crown him emperor.

From the year 800 onward, Charlemagne went by the title "emperor." The Byzantine Empire still lived on in the East, but the Byzantines had not played much of a role in the West for some time. And the Byzantines had

the troubling habit of falling into heresy occasionally, as had occurred during the Iconoclast controversy. Pope Leo thought the strong and pious king of the Franks a better ally than the distant Byzantines. In crowning Charlemagne, the pope taught that the imperial power had passed from Byzantium to the Franks.

St. Benedict of Aniane

Charlemagne died in 814, but his descendants retained control of his kingdom until the year 987. The time of the Carolingians was a time of great spiritual reform for the Church.

One of the most important reformers was St. Benedict of Aniane. St. Benedict of Aniane, his birth name Witiza, was the son of a Frankish count close to the Carolingian family. Like most sons of the nobility at the time, young Witiza was destined for the life of a warrior.

But that changed one day while campaigning with the armies of Charlemagne throughout Europe in the year 773. Let's pause for a moment to check in on him:

————

"Witiza!" cried Arnulf. "Help me, brother!"

Witiza struggled through the din of the battle and the bustling of men to make his way to the river's edge near where his brother Arnulf had fallen into the water.

"Can you move?" called Witiza.

"No! I've been hit by an arrow in the leg. I can't swim. Please, help me. The armor . . . it's dragging me down."

Witiza dropped his sword and leapt into the water, still donned in his chain mail. *The water is not too deep and Arnulf is not so far out*, he thought. *So long as I don't go farther out, I should be safe in this armor.*

Witiza extended his arm. "Grab on, brother!" he called.

Arnulf struggled and thrashed, fighting as hard as he could to scramble to Witiza several feet away. A cloud of blood swirled in the water around his leg.

"I can't reach!" Arnulf called.

Witiza groaned as he stretched his arm even farther. His brother's wet hand clutched on to his, but Witiza lost his balance and went tumbling headlong into the water. The river poured into his nostrils. He suddenly could not tell which way was up.

But after several seconds of panic, Witiza got his head above water. His brother had made it to the shore and was lying on the bank groaning. Witiza found it hard to move; he was lying on his back in the river and felt the weight of his chainmail pulling him under as the current began tugging him out into deeper waters. He knew if the current got hold of him, he would not survive.

Indeed, things seemed grim. On the shore, the battle

pressed on near the riverfront. Arnulf was carried off by his Frankish comrades while arrows rained down. Some even fell in the river near Witiza as the current dragged him away. He lost his footing and felt himself being dragged farther out and farther down. It was a constant struggle to keep his mouth above water.

"Help!" he gurgled as he fought to keep the river water from swirling into his mouth. Thoughts of his death flashed through his mind, until, moments later, he disappeared beneath the dark, cold water. The raging noise of the battle faded beneath the silence of the water. Witiza stopped struggling and looked up helplessly, watching the sunlight dancing on the river's surface. *Am I ready to face God?* he wondered.

Just as Witiza was passing into unconsciousness, he felt a pair of rough hands grab him and jerk him out of the water. He began to spit and cough as he was dragged

to the bank of the river and dumped into the mud. As he struggled to regain his breath, he saw two thick peasants looming over him, peering curiously into his face with dark, beady eyes.

"You . . . you saved me!" Witiza said, choking.

"The man with the wounded leg told us to come rescue you," one of the peasants said, holding up a silver coin. "He paid us to go find your body."

"But we didn't think you'd be alive," grunted the other.

"Neither did I," admitted Witiza. "And what of the battle?"

"The battle is over. The Franks have won," said the men.

"Then take me back to my brother, my fellows," said Witiza, standing up as water poured off of him.

"God spared you today," one of the men said.

"I believe he did," replied Witiza, making the sign of the cross.

––––––––

The experience of nearly drowning changed Witiza. He began to think about what would have happened had he stood before God that day. Would his soul have been ready? How would he have been judged? Had he been faithful with the graces and good things God had given him?

Ultimately, Witiza decided to abandon the world and the life of a warrior and devote himself to the service of God and the Gospel of Jesus Christ. Witiza would join the Benedictine order and take the name Benedict, after the founder of the order. He found that many Benedictine monks were no longer keeping the *Rule of St. Benedict* with the same rigor as the early monks. He founded a monastery at a place called Aniane. There, monks kept the *Rule of St. Benedict* with great discipline and lived very holy lives. The monastery at Aniane became a model for monastic discipline throughout France. Other monasteries began imitating the practices of Benedict's monks of Aniane. The Carolingian emperor, Louis the Pious, even summoned two royal synods in which monasteries in the realm were commanded to adopt the discipline of Aniane, and St. Benedict was authorized to ensure these reforms were carried out. At the time of his death in 821, St. Benedict of Aniane was the most influential monk in the entire Carolingian empire and was responsible for the greatest reform of monastic life in the West since St. Benedict of Nursia himself.

Missionaries Who Became Saints

The Carolingians also sponsored or encouraged the sending of missionaries into the furthest reaches of Europe where the light of the Gospel had not yet penetrated. One of the famous missionaries of the time was St. Boniface. Boniface was sent by the pope to preach to various pagan tribes living in central and northern Germany. In one of his first encounters with a tribe called the Hessians, Boniface was told that they were accustomed to making sacrifices to the gods at a great oak tree. In bold defiance of their gods, St. Boniface chopped the oak tree down and taught the Hessians to honor Jesus Christ instead. He went on to build churches and became their bishop.

St. Boniface later preached to other German tribes, but he was eventually martyred, killed while holding a Bible. The Bible he died holding is preserved to this day, its hardened leather cover still marred by the sword strokes of the pagans who killed him. But the German missions did not end with Boniface's death; many other missionaries came to Germany to finish his work, especially during the time of Charlemagne.

North of Germany is the land of Scandinavia. Scandinavia was home to various tribes of pagan warriors called the Vikings. This area was first evangelized by St. Anskar, a Frankish missionary monk who spent years among the people of Scandinavia preaching the Gospel and building churches. Though only some of the Vikings accepted the Faith at first, Anskar would be followed by other missionaries and bishops. He is known as the Apostle to the North and is sometimes depicted holding a church building to signify his success at founding churches.

Continuing our tour around Europe, to the east and south of Germany is a mountainous region known as the Balkans. The Balkans open up onto the great plains of eastern Europe that lead into Asia. These regions were inhabited by a group of pagans called the Slavs, who had settled in the area around the time the Roman Empire was collapsing.

The Slavs were evangelized by two brothers called St. Cyril and St. Methodius. Both the Byzantine emperor and the pope supported the mission of the two brothers. Cyril and Methodius spent years trying to teach the Slavs the Gospel. But they found that the Slavs did not have a written language and therefore could not read. The brothers decided that the Slavs needed their own writing.

St. Cyril studied the Slavic language and invented an alphabet and writing system for the Slavs. After this, he taught this writing system to the Slavic converts. Once they could read it, Cyril and Methodius had the Scriptures and other Christian writings translated into the Slavic alphabet so the common people could learn the Faith. Various Slavic tribes began converting to the Faith, and other missionaries would follow. By the year 1000, all the peoples of the region had accepted the Faith. St. Cyril and St. Methodius are remembered as the Apostles to the Slavs.

The Carolingian Renaissance

The era of the Carolingians was a very important time in the history of Christendom. Many churches and monasteries were built throughout Europe, and there was a great reform in the morals and discipline of the Church. Additionally, learning and writing flourished. For all these reasons, this period is often called the *Carolingian Renaissance*. The word *renaissance* means "rebirth." It was called the Carolingian Renaissance because it was a rebirth of the learning and building that had disappeared since the fall of Rome.

Pepin, Charlemagne, and the Carolingians built a powerful worldly empire that would endure for over one thousand years, but they also left behind a world in which the Church was much more expansive and the Christian faith more important than ever to the well-being of society. In our next chapter, we shall see how the growth of the Church's influence became a source of conflict between the popes and the secular rulers.

CHAPTER 12

Dark Days for the Papacy

Political Popes

From the time of Charlemagne onward, the Church became much more influential in society—not just as a source of spiritual teaching and a vessel of salvation but as an institution that held significant political power. The alliance of the papacy and the Carolingians gave prestige to both the Church and the Carolingian state. This was helpful to both: the Carolingians were affirmed in their power by receiving the blessing of the Church, and the Church benefitted by winning the protection of the Carolingians.

But this relationship also had its downsides. From the year 800 on, the papacy would become even more embroiled in the politics of western Europe. Becoming pope meant not only having tremendous influence over the Church but also a lot of political power. Once the papacy acquired this prestige, power-hungry men sought to control it. Noble Roman families schemed to get their relatives elected to the papacy. If these men got elected to the papacy, they often spent their time enriching themselves and warring against rival families rather than governing the Church. It became a very dark time for the papacy.

A Bizarre Trial

During the latter part of the ninth century, there was a pope named Formosus who got mixed up in the political troubles of Italy and the Carolingian empire, encouraging one Carolingian noble to rebel against the emperor. After Formosus died, another pope, Stephen, wanted to condemn Formosus for his failures. What followed was one of the most bizarre stories in the history of the papacy:

The papal court was crowded with observers. Clerics murmured to one another about the proceedings they were witnessing. Pope Stephen paced back and forth in front of the Chair of St. Peter, thundering out accusations against the man seated in the chair.

"Is it not true that you have violated the canons of the Holy Church by taking possession of an episcopal see illegally? What do you say for yourself?"

Pope Formosus sat silently in the chair, gazing off blankly with dark, hollow eye sockets. A fly buzzed. The clerics in attendance held their noses to stave off the foul odor coming from Formosus.

"By what right do you wear those pontifical garments?" continued the angry Pope Stephen, gesturing to Formosus's vestments. Formosus was fully clad in elaborate pontifical regalia, complete with the papal ring, shoes, and papal miter upon his head. "Well, have you no answer?" demanded Pope Stephen.

A deacon standing near the chair of Formosus stood up. "Well, Your Holiness, given that Pope Formosus has been dead for over a year, it is unlikely that he can answer."

The assembled clerics chuckled.

"I know that!" Pope Stephen snapped. "I'm not expecting a year-old corpse that I dug up and dressed in pontifical clothes to reply. That's not the point. The point is that he is publicly accused of his crimes and suffers humiliation for them, even if it is only symbolic."

"Very well," said the deacon, covering his face and swatting away the flies that buzzed about Formosus's corpse. "What other charges do you bring against the late pontiff?"

Pope Stephen went on to accuse Formosus of many other crimes before turning to the assembled clerics. "What say you, clergy of Rome?"

The clerics looked at each other awkwardly before an older bishop rose to his feet. "Holy Father, these

proceedings are most . . . eh . . . unusual. But if the late Formosus is truly guilty of all the things you accuse him, then he was unworthy of the Chair of St. Peter."

"Then by the authority of that same St. Peter whose chair Formosus was unworthy to hold, I invalidate all his actions, declare his appointments null and void, and proclaim him an enemy of the Church of God."

Pope Stephen nodded to a group of acolytes standing off to the side. They came forward and threw the body of Formosus upon the ground and stripped all the pontifical garments off the corpse. Pope Stephen then knelt beside the body and, taking a knife, cut off three fingers on Formosus's right hand—the ones the dead pope had once used to bless the people.

Pope Stephen rose to his feet, holding aloft the severed fingers and waving them before the clergy. With a fire in his eye, he bellowed, "It appears Formosus will no longer be able to offer blessings to the people!"

The clergy looked at each other with grave concern.

"This is a new low," one of them muttered. "God have mercy."

But that was not the end of the bizarre trial. Stephen had Pope Formosus's body loaded down with chains and sunk in the Tiber River. The people of Rome were horrified for Pope Stephen's disrespect for the dead, and they felt bad for Pope Formosus. To make matters more complicated, the body of Formosus washed up on the banks of the Tiber and many sick people who went near it were cured.

Eventually, the Roman people rebelled against Pope Stephen. They threw him in prison and then strangled him to death. The next pope recovered the body of Pope

Formosus, had it properly buried, and voided the decrees of Pope Stephen's trial.

Otto the Great: Holy Roman Emperor

The story of the "Cadaver Synod," as it has come to be known (a cadaver is a term for a dead body), is often told to demonstrate the deplorable state of the papacy at the time. But it was not only power squabbles between the popes and the Italian families that made things so bad. There were also political problems within the Carolingian empire that would have disastrous consequences for the papacy.

The heirs to Charlemagne's empire were not as strong or wise as he had been. Within a few generations after his death, his empire was fragmented between a Germanic half to the east and the Frankish half to the west. The Germanic kingdom was plagued by civil war until it was taken over by a man named Otto the Great in 936.

But Otto's rule in Germany was not secure. There were many nobles who would have liked to overthrow him. Otto wanted to use the Church to support his reign. Mistrusting his nobles, Otto preferred to use bishops to help him govern. He appointed bishops to empty positions within his feudal hierarchy and made use of them as administrators of the government. When a new bishop was appointed, he gave them the symbols of their office— the episcopal ring and staff. This practice was known as *lay investiture* because the new bishop was invested with the symbols of his office by the ruler, who was a layman. This gave the impression that bishops were getting their office from Otto rather than the Church, which obviously made the German bishops more dependent on Otto.

All this helped Otto in his struggle against the nobles, but it got the Church's bishops involved in worldly and political affairs, which was certainly not good for the Church. Even worse, Otto would soon succeed in getting the Church further under his control.

There was an Italian nobleman named Berengar who was attacking the Papal States and proclaiming himself king of Italy. Otto marched his army down into Italy and defeated Berengar, assuming control of all his lands in northern Italy. Pope John XII was grateful for Otto's assistance. He allowed Otto to unite the kingdoms of Italy and Germany into one and granted Otto the title "Holy Roman emperor" in 962, declaring him special protector of the Church.

Otto and the pope entered into an agreement which stated that while the Roman clergy would elect the pope, a new pope had to swear an oath of allegiance to the Holy Roman emperor before he could take his office.

Pope John XII quickly regretted giving Otto so much influence over the Church and tried to undermine him by stirring up Otto's enemies against him. This enraged Otto. He marched back into Rome, declared John XII deposed, and set up a new pope. However, because the old pope was still alive and the new one was not legally elected, he was not considered a true pope; rather, he was an antipope. An *antipope* is a man who claims to be pope but is in fact not the real pope. Eventually John XII was restored, but Otto would continue to hassle and attack the papacy for the rest of his reign.

Though Otto died in 973, his successors continued to use the title Holy Roman emperor; the various kingdoms of Germany and northern Italy were known as the Holy Roman Empire. Future Holy Roman emperors would continue to assert their power over the popes, claiming the right to approve a newly elected pope. Lay investiture became the norm throughout the Holy Roman Empire.

Bishops, clergy, and even popes seemed subject to the political authorities.

Nor was this situation unique to the Holy Roman Empire. In other kingdoms, such as England, France, and the newly Christianized kingdoms of eastern Europe, kings often selected bishops, invested them with the symbols of their authority, and made use of them like officers of the state.

It's not difficult to understand how this was bad for the Church. Christ called his pastors to devote themselves to the care of souls, not seeking after political power and temporal wealth. Even though most bishops who served in the governments of their king or emperor did so out of good motives, focusing so much attention on political matters inevitably meant that it was difficult for bishops to give enough attention to the care of souls.

It was a dark time for the papacy. Even so, Christ never leaves his Church without remedy. Men and women continued going to Mass, praying, and working out their salvation. Monks and nuns continued offering their lives to God in solitude, and missionaries continued spreading into remote regions, bringing the Gospel to new peoples.

As for the captivity of the Church to the power of laymen, that would begin to change in an out-of-the-way little monastery called Cluny, as we shall learn in our next chapter.

CHAPTER 13

The Struggle Against Lay Authority

Under a Secular Thumb

By the tenth century, the Church across Christendom was well established and very influential. But because of this, it had been slowly dominated by layman—kings, lords, and even the Holy Roman emperor—intent on subverting the Church to suit their own political agendas. Bishops were usually appointed by the secular rulers and expected to attend on them at court like royal officials, and monasteries and convents were often under the patronage of a powerful secular lord to whom they owed obedience. Nobles—and even other clerics—often sold Church offices to the highest bidder, a practice known as *simony*. And as we saw in the last chapter, no new pope could take his office until he swore allegiance to the Holy Roman emperor. Being under the thumb of lay and secular authorities was a major issue for the Church.

But, as we have come to see, God never leaves his Church without divine assistance. Even in challenging times, God always raises up pious men and women eager to serve him and work for the care of souls. That would be true in the tenth century as well. In an age when lay persons dominated the concerns of the Church, it is perhaps proof of God's sense of humor that it was a lay person who helped set the events in motion that would begin to rectify this situation.

A Monastery in Cluny
In southern France, there lived a man named William who was the Duke of Aquitaine. Like most nobles of the age, William was a warrior who had fought in many battles. But he was also very devout and tried his best to be a good Christian. His love of Christ and the Church earned him the nickname Duke William the Pious.

William decided that his domain needed a monastery. In the year 910, William constructed a great Benedictine abbey at a place called Cluny and selected a holy monk named Berno to be its first abbot. Had William been like other nobles, he would have regarded Cluny as his personal property and ordered the monastery to be governed as he saw fit. But William was pious enough to know that it was not a good thing for lay people to govern monasteries. He wanted Cluny to be truly independent.

"I want you to live out your calling free to follow God however you see fit," he told Abbot Berno.

"You mean I owe you no obedience?" Berno asked.

"The only earthly individual to whom you owe obedience to is the pope," replied Duke William. "I grant Cluny complete freedom from my authority."

Duke William the Pious was right. Left to themselves, the monks of Cluny were able to serve God as they saw fit. They followed the Rule of St. Benedict without having to care about worldly problems or serving any temporal lord. Cluny became a thriving monastery, and Berno was later venerated as St. Berno of Cluny.

The independence of Cluny gave the monks the opportunity to reflect on the state of the Church throughout Christendom. Would it not be better if all churches and monasteries were independent, as Cluny was? What other problems were keeping the Church from serving God more purely?

The monks of Cluny began advocating for a series of reforms throughout the Church. They called for an end to the practice of simony and encouraged priests and religious to be more faithful to their vows of celibacy and strive more sincerely after holiness. But most importantly, they argued for an end to lay dominance over the Church. They especially objected to lay investiture, the practice whereby a new bishop was given his episcopal ring and staff by a secular lord. For the Cluniacs, lay investiture was the most potent symbol of lay domination.

"That a bishop should receive his ring and staff—which symbolize his apostolic authority and office as pastor—from a lay person is an offense to God and the Church," the Cluniacs argued. "A bishop's authority comes through his sacred ordination, not from any king or ruler."

As other monks and travelers visited Cluny, they took these ideas back to their own lands. By the end of the century, the ideals of Cluny were being discussed all over Europe. One of the most important reformers was a young monk named Hildebrand.

Pope Gregory VII versus Henry IV
In 1073, Hildebrand was elected pope and took the name Gregory VII. Pope Gregory VII immediately began

fighting back against imperial control of the Church. He rejected the Holy Roman emperor's right to select the pope; instead, he wanted the cardinals of the Church to elect the pope. Cardinals were very important clerics, often the bishops of large cities or important churches within Rome. Ever since the time of Pope Gregory VII, the College of Cardinals has been responsible for electing the pope. Gregory also summoned councils condemning the practice of investiture. He said that investiture was the means by which the emperors kept the Church in subjection and called for it to end.

The Holy Roman emperor at this time was Henry IV. As you could probably imagine, Henry thoroughly disliked Pope Gregory. When he heard about the pope's condemnations, Henry gathered a group of princes and his own bishops loyal to him and proclaimed that Gregory was not the real pope. He then called for him to be removed from office.

When Pope Gregory heard this, he excommunicated Emperor Henry. At first, Emperor Henry did not take the excommunication seriously. But soon Emperor Henry's nobles began to rebel. No Holy Roman emperor had

ever been excommunicated, and his nobles did not want to serve an emperor who was kicked out of the Church.

Things got difficult for Henry and he eventually had to try to make peace with the pope. In the winter of 1076, Emperor Henry went to speak to Pope Gregory. The pope was staying at a castle called Canossa in northern Italy. Henry wanted to speak with the pope, but Gregory refused to see him. For three days he appeared before the gates of Canossa on his knees in the snow pleading with Pope Gregory to absolve him. After three days, Pope Gregory was finally convinced of the emperor's sincerity. He absolved Henry of his sins and lifted the excommunication.

But the peace was short-lived. Henry would again anger the pope, and would even make war on Gregory and attack Rome. The controversy over investiture bled into the next century, many years after Gregory and Henry were both dead. It would not be solved until an agreement called the Concordat of Worms in 1122. A *concordat* is an agreement the Church enters into with the government of a nation. The Concordat of Worms was made between Pope Callixtus II and Emperor Henry V, the son of Henry IV. The Concordat said bishops could receive lands and castles from their lords, but they could not receive their staff and ring from them because these were the signs of their spiritual office.

The Martyrdom of Thomas Becket

England was another kingdom where the king exercised a great deal of control over the Church. Bishops were selected by the king, invested by him with their ring and staff, and expected to function as officials of the state and help pursue the king's policies. The king might choose anyone he wished to be bishop, even if he had no qualifications. For example, in 1162, the English king Henry II chose his friend Thomas Becket to be archbishop of Canterbury. Thomas Becket was not even a cleric but was the chancellor of England whom Henry chose because of his friendship.

Fortunately, Thomas Becket took his ordination to the episcopacy seriously. As soon as he was ordained, he began giving away his possessions to the poor and standing up for the rights of the Church. King Henry was trying to subvert the entire Church in England to his authority by forcing the English Church to adopt something called the Constitutions of Clarendon, a group of reforms intended to restrict the influence of the pope in England and curb the power of bishops there. They allowed the king to have access to Church revenues and gave him the power of appointing bishops, as well as forbid clerics from traveling to Rome without the king's permission. The reforms also called for priests charged with crimes to be tried in secular courts rather than Church courts.

Though most English bishops promised to observe the Constitutions of Clarendon, Becket would come to oppose them, for which he was exiled by King Henry. Becket and Henry eventually reconciled and Becket returned to England, but their conflict was far from over.

When it was time for King Henry to crown his son as heir to the throne, King Henry gave this privilege to three bishops who had been loyal to him. This angered Becket, as the right to crown a successor was always the privilege of the archbishop of Canterbury. Becket accused the three bishops of failing to stand up for the rights of the Church and excommunicated them. They fled to Normandy, where King Henry was spending the winter of 1170.

King Henry was irritated by Becket's actions and regretted making him archbishop. According to tradition, while he sat around drinking with his knights at Christmas festivities, he began lamenting his troubles with Becket and blurted out, "Won't somebody rid me of this troublesome priest?" Four of Henry's knights took this as a veiled order to have Becket killed. They departed Normandy and returned to England, finding Thomas Becket at Canterbury on the night of December 29, 1170. What happened next would become one of the most iconic events in the history of the English Church:

————

Thomas Becket left the altar where he had been preparing

to say Vespers to attend to the visitors. Four knights were standing in the doorway of the church at the side of the transept, weapons drawn.

"Shame on you for coming armed into the house of God!" Becket called out, still clad in his white surplice.

"We have only come to talk, Your Grace," greeted Sir Reginald, one of the knights. "You have no need to fear."

"If that be true, leave your weapons outside and return unarmed. Then we may talk. It is not right to enter a holy place so armed."

The knights glanced at one another and then, beginning with Sir Reginald, walked out of the doorway and dropped their weapons beneath a tree in the courtyard. Returning, Sir Reginald said, "By order of his majesty, King Henry, you are commanded to appear at Winchester to give an account of your actions in respect to the king."

Becket snorted in contempt. "The king only wishes me to come to Winchester to renew his violent pressures on me to yield to his will and offend the Church of God. I tell you, I will not go and I will never go so long as the king maintains his unjust war upon the rights of the Church and the privileges of the see of Canterbury."

"Is that your final answer?" growled William de Tracy, another of the knights.

"Definitive. Now if you will excuse me, I have to go say Vespers." Becket disappeared up the staircase leading into the choir area where he would say Vespers.

"Arrogant, insufferable man!" shouted Sir Richard. "We didn't come all this way for nothing!"

"No, we didn't," agreed Sir Reginald. "Come, brothers, let us retrieve our blades!"

The four knights returned to the courtyard and picked up their weapons. Sir Reginald carried a large ax.

Thomas, meanwhile, was entering the choir where the

Vespers liturgy was sung. "Shall we bolt the doors to keep those knights from bothering us again?" asked Brother Gervase, a monk of Canterbury.

"No," Becket shook his head. "It is not right to make a fortress out of a house of prayer. Leave them open."

Moments later, the four knights came rushing up the stairs. When they threw their cloaks, it became apparent that they were fully clad in chain mail, as if ready for battle. Their sword blades glittered in the candlelight.

"Where is Thomas Becket, traitor to king and country?" Sir Reginald demanded.

"Reginald," came the voice of Thomas from the apse. The bishop strolled calmly towards the men. "You once received favors from my hand, and now you come at me armed?"

"Absolve the bishops you excommunicated," shouted Reginald, pressing the ax against Becket's chest. "Or I will tear out your heart!"

"I'm ready to die!" Becket replied.

The tumult going on in the choir had aroused the

attention of some of the townsfolk outside the church, and a few of the more curious locals had begun to creep into the nave to see what was afoot.

"That does it!" exclaimed Reginald. He dropped his ax and seized Becket by the collar. "You're coming with us!"

Becket tore himself out of Sir Reginald's grasp. "I'm going nowhere, you detestable fellow!"

The other knights rushed upon Becket and tried to lift him off the ground and put him on their shoulders to forcibly carry him off. Becket wrestled and pressed his back up against a nearby pillar, resisting with all his might. Some of his acolytes came to help as well, and before long there was a tussle between Becket, the knights, and some of the clergy. Townspeople looked on from the shadows in horror.

Becket grasped Sir William de Tracy by his chain mail and somehow mustered the strength to throw him down on the pavement. This infuriated Sir Reginald, who drew a sword and swung at Becket. Becket ducked and the blade swiped the cap off his head.

"I commend my cause to the Church of God, St. Denis, and all the saints of the Church!" Becket yelled.

Reginald swung another blow, but one of Becket's priests leapt in the way; the blow grazed Becket's shoulder and struck the priest in the arm, wounding him. Sir William de Tracy whacked Becket upside the head from behind with the flat of his sword, knocking him down, stunned. He folded his hands in prayer, and looking off at the distant altar, said, "Into thy hands, O Lord, I commend my spirit. For the name of Jesus and the defense of the Church, I am willing to die."

Another knight, Richard Breton, loomed over Becket and said, "Receive this for the love of my lord!" He swung his sword with such violence at Becket's head that the top of Becket's skull was chopped off his head and the blade of the sword snapped in two on the marble pavement. Another of the attackers planted his foot on the neck of Becket's corpse, thrust his sword into his opened head, and scattered his brains all over the floor of the church.

"Let us go, let us go!" he said. "This traitor is dead. He will rise no more!"

The men looked at each other as a shadow of deep dread seemed to fall upon them. They were all shaking. Townspeople had begun to trickle into the choir and dip their handkerchiefs in Becket's pooling blood. "A martyr," some of them whispered, folding the handkerchiefs lovingly and carrying them off as relics.

The killers fled out the side door of the cathedral and into the night.

———————

Thomas Becket would be proclaimed a saint and martyr by Pope Alexander III in 1173. King Henry II did public penance at Becket's tomb to atone for his role in the saint's death. The shrine of St. Thomas Becket at Canterbury would become one of the most popular pilgrimage destinations in all of Europe.

Though the struggles of the tenth and eleventh centuries did not entirely free the Church from lay control, the Concordat of Worms was a major step forward. The popes of the following century would exercise much greater independence than they had previously, and the decline of lay investiture led to many flourishing reform movements, which we will talk more about in chapter 15.

But before we talk about the ideals of these monastic reforms, we must talk about another ideal that would transform Christendom: the Crusades.

CHAPTER 14

The Crusading Ideal

Tension in the West

In chapter 10, we learned how after the fall of the western Roman Empire, the eastern Roman Empire became known as the Byzantine Empire. From their well-fortified capital of Constantinople, the Byzantines continued to rule most of the eastern Mediterranean for many centuries. For much of the Middle Ages, Constantinople was the biggest and wealthiest city in the world and the Byzantine Empire was the heart of Christian civilization in the East.

But by the latter years of the Christian age's first millennium, Byzantium was in trouble. In the seventh century, Muslim armies had overrun Palestine, Syria, and Egypt, gobbling up almost half of the Byzantine Empire's territories. Millions of Christians came under Muslim domination, often facing persecution or death for their faith.

The Greek speaking Christians of Byzantium also had very bad relations with the popes and the Latin Church of the West. Ever since the fourth century, the Church of Constantinople had claimed it was more important than the Church of Rome. For many centuries, the popes and bishops of Constantinople argued about who was the supreme authority for Christians. We also saw in chapter 10 how the Byzantine emperors tried to force Iconoclasm on the West. Occasionally, the Byzantine emperors pushed other heresies, such as Monophysitism (the belief that Christ had only a single, divine nature) or Monothelitism (the idea that Christ had two natures but only a single will).

It is not important to memorize these heresies; the point is that the relationship between Constantinople and the Church of Rome was often very bad. Sometimes the Greek Churches even went into *schism*, which means they refused obedience to the pope and would not hold communion with the Churches of the West. These schisms were usually resolved—that is, until the year 1054.

Tensions between Latin and Greek Christians had been particularly bad in southern Italy. Michael Cerularius, the patriarch of Constantinople, had published a letter condemning many practices of western Christians. In response, Pope Leo IX sent papal legates to Constantinople in 1054 to try to smooth things over with Michael Cerularius and the Greeks. But when the papal legates arrived, Cerularius refused to see them. After many days, they became angry. The legates went into the Greek basilica of Hagia Sophia and left a parchment on the altar. This parchment was a decree stating that Michael Cerularius and those in communion with him were excommunicated. Michael Cerularius was so angry he issued his own decree of excommunication against the pope! Of course, the visible unity of the Church is the pope, and as the successor of St. Peter, he cannot be "kicked out" of the Church.

Theologians debate whether the East really went into schism at that point or sometime later, but the point is that by 1054 relations between Constantinople and Rome were at the worst point in centuries. The East and West had broken communion with each other, now more formally than ever before. This break is often referred to as the East-West Schism or the Schism of 1054.

A Time of Crusade

The timing of this schism was rather unfortunate because not long after this, a new wave of Islamic conquerors, the Seljuk Turks, came out of the East. The Seljuks seized Anatolia from the Byzantines and began robbing and killing Christians who were following the ancient pilgrimage routes into the Holy Land. The Byzantine emperor, Alexius Comnenus, became desperate and swallowed his pride by asking the West for help.

Pope Urban II summoned a regional synod of Clermont in France in the fall of 1095. He relayed the plight of the Christians in the East and Emperor Alexius's request for help.

The response of the Christian West was astonishing. Thousands of people, from nobles and knights down to commoners, pledged to make the dangerous trek east to liberate the Holy Land from the Muslims. This began the era of the Crusades, a period spanning several centuries when Christians from Europe attempted to maintain a Christian kingdom in the Holy Land. *Crusade* means "cross-bearer"; to go on crusade was known as "taking up the cross."

It is beyond the scope of this book to review the

political and military aspects of the Crusades (for this, one should refer to *The Story of Civilization Volume II: The Medieval World* by TAN Books). We are more concerned here with the crusading ideal and how it affected the development of the Church and practice of the Faith in the lives of average Christians.

For that, we have to turn to the city of Jerusalem, which had a very powerful hold on the imaginations of medieval Christians. As the physical site of our Lord's death and resurrection, it was the most important of all the holy places. It seemed a matter of common sense that this city in particular should be in Christian hands, and when the crusaders first came to Palestine in 1099, they did not consider the conquest of the country complete until the holy city of Jerusalem was firmly in Christian hands.

But Jerusalem also symbolized the Church herself. St. Paul called the Church the "Jerusalem from above"—the heavenly Jerusalem—and the mother of Christians (see Gal 4:26). To go on crusade to Jerusalem—whether as a warrior or a pilgrim—was seen as a very intense spiritual journey or a journey of penance and purification. The medieval popes often granted generous indulgences to go on crusade. An *indulgence* is a cancellation of penance and the temporal punishment for sins already confessed. Have you been to confession? If so, you know you receive a penance, which is usually a prayer or work of charity you are supposed to do. An indulgence was a cancellation or lightening of a heavy penance in exchange for something easier. Christians who "took up the cross" and went to the Holy Land were undertaking a considerable penance and so often had all their other penances canceled by indulgences.

To protect these travelers, military orders were formed.

A *military order* was a band of knights who took religious vows. They were known as "fighting monks." The knights of the religious orders would train and fight like knights, but when not in combat, they prayed the Divine Office like monks. They also observed vows of poverty, chastity, and obedience. The three great military orders were the Knights of the Temple (also called Templars), the Knights of St. John of Jerusalem (also called Hospitallers), and the Order of the German Brotherhood of St. Mary of Jerusalem (also called the Teutonic Knights).

The military orders combined chivalry with monastic piety and had the support of the Church. In fact, the rule of the Templars was even composed by St. Bernard of Clairvaux, the most eminent saint of the age. The Templars, Hospitallers, and Teutonic Knights protected pilgrims traveling through the Holy Land and served as the first line of defense against Muslim attacks.

A Pilgrim's Journey

From 1099 to 1187, Jerusalem and the surrounding lands were ruled by Frankish-Norman lords under a "king of Jerusalem," a lord from one of the various ruling houses. During this time of Christian governance of Palestine, tens of thousands of Christian pilgrims from all over Europe made the arduous trek east to worship at the places where our Lord lived and taught. Let us join one of these pilgrims, an Englishman named Morris, who has come to Jerusalem on a quest of spiritual purification during the reign of King Baldwin II in 1119:

———

Morris piously recited the *Pater Noster* as he pressed his way through the throngs of pilgrims crowding the dusty Via Dolorosa in Jerusalem. His voice mingled with those of hundreds of others raised in prayer, walking the same street Christ walked on his way to death.

The Palestinian sun was hot on Morris's weather-beaten brow and his coarse pilgrim habit was rough against his skin. The smell of dirt and sweat was everywhere. But it did not bother him; in fact, the smells and heat and sounds helped him focus his prayers.

"I am truly one with these Christians from all over the world who have come here to honor Christ and do penance for their sins," he thought.

The Via Dolorosa stretch through the city was a little over a half a mile. The pace was slow because of all the pilgrims crowding the street. After some time, the street opened up into a vast courtyard before the Church of the Holy Sepulchre, a massive building that dominated the surrounding neighborhood. Inside this structure were the holiest sites of Christianity—the place where Jesus was crucified, as well as the tomb in which he was buried and from which he rose from the dead.

The Church of the Holy Sepulchre was a stately old building; parts of it dated back to the time of Constantine. But among the prayers of the crowds, Morris also heard the clinging of hammers and chisels. The church was undergoing a massive renovation that had been initiated when Godfrey de Bouillon took Jerusalem twenty years earlier.

A massive crowd of pilgrims swarmed about the door to the church. "Looks like I'm not getting in there anytime soon," Morris said to himself. "Might as well take a moment to rest." He slid down against a stone wall in the shade of a portico. "Ooh," Morris groaned as he undid his sandals, shook the sand out of them, and rubbed his blistered feet.

Taking a swig of water from his flask, Morris rested his head against the wall and gazed out into the courtyard at the assortment of people. There were many pilgrims just like him, easy to identify by their coarse tunics, brown mantles, pilgrim staff, and cross about their neck. But there were also many local residents of Jerusalem. They covered their heads with wound turbans, had thick beards, and wore flowing garments. The women dressed similarly but had different head coverings. They looked strange to Morris, though he had grown accustomed to seeing them since his arrival. He wondered how many of the locals were Christian and how many were Muslim. It was not easy to tell by looks alone.

Very conspicuous were the members of the military orders, such as the Templars and Hospitallers. These warrior-monks could be seen milling about the crowds in pairs, sometimes armored, sometimes not, but always wearing the distinctive colors of their order: the white cloak with a red cross for the Templars, the white cloak with a black cross for the Teutonic Knights, and the black cloak with a white cross for the Hospitallers.

There were also monks, nuns, and clergy of all sorts, as well as the local Franco-Norman nobility. These were an interesting sight to behold. Going about in a kind of hybrid of French and Palestinian garb, these elites were often attached to the court of King Baldwin and owned estates in the countryside outside Jerusalem.

Morris eventually strapped his sandals on again and walked over to the Church of the Holy Sepulchre. The entry way was still thronged with a smelly mass of people, but Morris was quick on his feet and managed to press his way through the crowd and into the massive doorway of the church.

The interior was dark and smaller than Morris expected. *"I've been to Canterbury Cathedral back home and it was larger than this,"* he thought. The dozens of candelabra and thousands of votive candles did little to dispel the darkness, casting the entire place in shadow and a sense of holy reverence. Pilgrims in prayer crowded around the high altar, kneeling and touching something in a chamber beneath it.

"What do they touch?" asked Morris to a pilgrim beside him.

"It is the rock of Golgotha," the man said, "the very stone where the cross of our Lord once stood and upon which the salvation of mankind was procured!"

Morris made the sign of the cross and dropped to his knees, praying the *Gloria Patri* in a hushed, reverent tone.

It took some time, but Morris was gradually able to creep closer to the altar, now only a meter away. He gazed piously at the stone, smoothed and polished from millions of pilgrims kissing and touching it. Morris's heart welled up with emotion at the thought of what occurred at this very place a thousand years ago. It was hard to stay focused, as many other pilgrims pressed against Morris to get their own look at the stone.

"Make your reverence and move along for others," someone whispered to Morris. He quickly leaned in, pressed his lips to the cool, smooth stone, and then withdrew, his place being taken by others.

Morris spent an hour in the shadows after kissing the stone, kneeling in prayer. Deep in contemplation at the sacrifice of Christ and what his salvation had cost, his heart was full of pious resolutions: to pray more, to be more charitable and forgiving, to spend more time thinking about his eternal salvation, and to give more to the poor. Tears welled up in his eyes. He had not been prepared for how powerful the experience would be.

"Now I can die contented, O Lord," he prayed, as he beat his breast in the shadows of the holy place.

———

Morris was fortunate. Many Christians were not able to devote the time or resources to a Jerusalem pilgrimage. The popularity of the Crusades and of the pilgrim ideal, however, meant that Christians might also turn to closer pilgrimage sites. Catholics in France or Spain might walk the *Camino* path that led across the mountains of northern Spain to the shrine of Santiago de Compostela, where according to legend St. James was buried. French Catholics might go to Our Lady of Notre Dame or Chartres, both of which were constructed during the crusading age. For Germans, there was the cathedral of Cologne which, after 1248, boasted the largest façade and some of the tallest spires in the world and contained the relics of the Magi. English Catholics prayed at Canterbury where St. Augustine had first established Christianity on the island and where Becket was murdered. Poles went to the Sanctuary of St. Jadwiga in Trzebnica, while Irish Christians walked barefoot up Croagh Patrick, the mountain where St. Patrick once spent an entire Lent in prayer. People from all over Europe came to Rome to pray at the tombs of St. Peter and St. Paul. And there were many, many more pilgrimage sites.

Though the Crusades reinvigorated the pilgrim spirit of Christians and brought about a greater interest in the ideas and customs of the East, they ultimately failed to help reunite the Greek and Latin speaking Churches. In fact, the crusaders returned in 1204, this time attacking Constantinople itself and conquering it. The Byzantine emperor had promised the crusading army some money to help defend them but ultimately failed to pay them, so the crusaders took his capital city instead. For almost sixty years the crusaders governed Greece like feudal lords, but were finally driven out in 1261.

We have only touched on the full story of the Crusades here, but the point is, things got bad for the Byzantines, and their relationship with the Catholic West continued to deteriorate.

In our next two chapters, we will be learning about some of the reform movements within the world of monasticism that were leading to the creation of new religious orders.

CHAPTER 15

Monastic Reform Movements

The Origins of the Norbertines

Back in chapter 11, we learned about the monastic reforms of St. Benedict of Aniane during the Carolingian era. These reforms in the ninth century helped revitalize western monastic life for the next several centuries. But by the eleventh and twelfth centuries, life had changed drastically. The Cluniac movement and the struggle of the popes against the Holy Roman emperor ended with a Church more independent than in earlier centuries. Meanwhile, medieval cities were growing, the Crusades were bringing the East and West back into contact with each other, and the military orders offered an example of how monastic life could be wedded to chivalry.

With all these changes in Christendom, it's not surprising that the period from the eleventh through the thirteenth centuries was a time of great diversity among religious orders. New religious orders were founded, old religious orders reformed, and a whole new crop of holy men and women rose up to proclaim Christ to the world through the observance of poverty, chastity, and obedience.

One of the early monastic reformers of the High Middle Ages was St. Norbert of Xanten, a German monk who lived from 1075 to 1134. St. Norbert was, at least at first, not very excited about his vocation as a monk, preferring the intrigues of the imperial court. He paid someone else to take his place chanting the divine office in his monastery so he could take on a position in the court of Holy Roman emperor Henry V. The wealth from his work for the emperor enabled him to live a life of luxury. He wore fine clothes and went about looking more like a noble than a monk.

But this all changed one day when he was riding his horse near the village of Xanten. A storm erupted and a thunderbolt struck the ground just beside him. St. Norbert was thrown from his horse and wounded. This brush with death made him rethink the way he was leading his life. He resolved to do penance and take his monastic vocation much more seriously.

St. Norbert used his wealth to found a monastery and was ordained a priest shortly thereafter. He gave the remainder of his wealth to the poor and went about begging. In time, he became a well-known preacher, and eventually the pope asked him to found a religious order in Laon, France. The bishop welcomed St. Norbert, who selected a lonely, marshy valley called Prémontré to begin his order. Disciples soon flocked to Norbert, both men and women. A monastery was built and St. Norbert's order was called the Premonstratensians—or the Norbertines for short. The Premonstratensians used a version of the monastic rule written by St. Augustine of Hippo.

Premonstratensian monasteries were unique in that they were double monasteries; a *double monastery* is a monastery in which monks and nuns live together under the same roof, though in two separate wings.

Though St. Norbert died in 1134, his order spread throughout Europe and a Third Order was eventually founded for lay people; a *Third Order* is a branch of a religious order open to lay persons. The lay members participate in the prayers and activities of the order but remain in the world rather than living in the monastery.

The Origins of the Cistercians

In the generation after St. Norbert, there was a movement among the Benedictines of France to improve the way St. Benedict's rule was observed. There were many arguments in the medieval Church over the best way to observe Benedict's rule. Many monks no longer did manual labor, as St. Benedict had taught. Was this good or bad? Even though monks couldn't own private property, should monasteries own things collectively? And how much involvement should a monastery have in worldly affairs? These debates led to the creation of several new religious orders.

One of those who thought Benedict's rule could be observed more closely was named Robert of Molesme. Around 1070, Robert was made the abbot of a Benedictine monastery, but he found the monks quarrelsome and disobedient, and so he left. A few other holy men came to Robert and asked him to be their superior. The little group went to the Valley of Langres in France and founded the small abbey of Molesme, dedicating it to the Holy Trinity. Soon, other monks came to Molesme to join them.

Robert's abbey had a reputation for holiness and

discipline. It attracted many pious monks, and a convent for women was founded as well. But the success of Molesme proved a burden. The wealthy made so many donations that the monks were no longer poor. This led to nobles trying to influence the affairs of the monastery. Robert was disappointed when monastic life became lax.

In 1098, he and a group of his monks left Molesme to found a new monastery, one where wealth and privilege would have no place. They founded their new monastery at a place called Cîteaux, where it flourished. Robert's monks became known as Cistercians after the Cîteaux monastery. Eventually, the monks of Molesme apologized to Robert and asked him to return, promising to reform their lives and obey him. Robert returned and governed Molesme until his death in 1111. Though he founded the Cistercians at Cîteaux, he is remembered as St. Robert of Molesme.

One of the members of the new Cistercian order was St. Bernard of Clairvaux. Bernard had arrived at Cîteaux in 1112 with thirty-five of his relatives whom he had persuaded to join the order. St. Bernard was eloquent and strong willed, and he was a pious mystic. He quickly became one of the leading members of the new order. In 1115, St. Bernard was given land in Champagne upon which to found another Cistercian monastery. He and several companions founded the Abbey of Clairvaux. This would be St. Bernard's home for the rest of his life and forever associated with him.

St. Bernard went on to found many Cistercian monasteries. He was a gifted writer and very wise; so wise, in fact, that he was consulted by popes, kings, and theologians to solve difficult problems. He wrote the rule for the Templar Knights and was a supporter of the military orders. Bernard had a reputation as a holy man and worked many miracles throughout his life. By the time he died in 1153, the Cistercian Order was the fastest growing religious order in Europe, boasting thousands of monks across hundreds of monasteries, and much of this success was because of Bernard.

The Origins of the Carthusians

Another effort at monastic reform came from the German monk St. Bruno of Cologne. Bruno came from a noble family and, as a young man, studied at the cathedral school of Reims. He was ordained a priest and worked in the administration of the diocese of Reims but was shocked by the worldliness he saw there. He left to seek solitude and spent time with St. Robert at Molesme. He soon found his vocation was not with the Cistercians, however, and with a few companions, he went to seek out Bishop Hugh of the French diocese of Grenoble. Bruno wanted to get the bishop's blessing to settle down as a hermit in his territory.

It's worth stopping here for a moment to hear an interesting story of how Bishop Hugh came to recognize St. Bruno's unique sanctity:

———————

Bishop Hugh of Grenoble tossed and turned on his bed. It was one of those nights. No matter what he did, the bishop could not rest. He tussled his blankets restlessly, fluffed his pillow, and flipped it to rest his sweaty head on the cool side. But nothing worked. He finally flopped on to his back, eyes wide open, staring at the vaulted stone ceiling of his bed chamber. A gentle breeze blew through his window as a cricket chirped in a dark corner of his bedroom.

"Ah, if I can't sleep, I might as well take it to the Lord!"

Bishop Hugh swung his legs out of bed and groaned as he got up. Wrapping himself in a night robe, he slogged across the flagstone floor of his chambers to a rough stone altar at the far end of his room. Bishop Hugh struck a flint and lit several candles. The gentle glow revealed a wooden crucifix hanging on the wall above the altar.

Hugh slumped down upon the kneeler and made the sign of the cross. He took out a worn little book from his robe pocket, a psalter, and began praying through the psalms. *"Venite laudemus Dominum iubilemus petrae Iesu nostro,"* he began. *"Praeoccupemus vultum eius in actione gratiarum in canticis iubilemus ei."* But, as so often happens to people on such sleepless nights, as soon as Hugh had resolved to get out of bed and do something else, drowsiness began to overcome him. He stumbled over the Latin phrases, his eyelids drooped, words slurred, and his lips felt like rubber. A moment later, his head slumped down into his chest and he was snoring soundly.

But though he slept, Hugh's mind was alert, for a powerful dream came upon him. He seemed to be standing upon a broad plain of grass, clothed in his episcopal garments. Suddenly, a great darkness began to circle the bishop, closing in on him. Hugh was afraid and cried out to God. "Save me, Lord!"

Just then, a bright light shone down upon him. It was so brilliant he had to cover his eyes. The darkness retreated. Was it an angel, he wondered? Hugh uncovered his eyes and attempted to gaze at the source of the light. It appeared to be coming from the sky.

"A star!" Hugh cried.

But this was no ordinary star, for it appeared to be moving, getting closer. As it did, Bishop Hugh could see that the light was not a single star, but seven stars arranged in a line. The stars drew closer until they seemed to float overhead. The bishop was bathed in the radiant, warm light. The stars then arranged themselves into a circle and began spinning. The entire field was illuminated as heavenly music swelled all about him.

"Your grace!"

Hugh awoke with a start. It was morning. Birds were chirping outside his window. In the streets below, he could hear the sounds of people going about their daily work.

"Your grace!" rang the voice again. It was Brother Robert, a canon of the cathedral and Hugh's personal attendant. "You have visitors requesting an audience."

"Oh . . . um . . . yes, Brother Robert," Hugh called through the heavy oaken door. "I will be down momentarily. Bid the visitors to wait, please."

As Hugh changed from his night robe into his tunic,

he pondered the dream. "What could those seven stars symbolize? The seven sacraments? Seven virtues? The seven gifts of the Holy Spirit?"

He continued to contemplate the strange dream as he donned his red episcopal zucchetto cap and opened the doors of his chamber. Brother Robert was waiting outside the door.

"Good morning, your grace," he said, kissing Bishop Hugh's ring.

"Tell me about our visitors," said Hugh as the two men began to walk toward the audience hall.

"Well, they are seven hermits seeking installation with your diocese. They are led by a man named Bruno, a man of Cologne, who–"

"Wait just a moment," interrupted Hugh. "Say again?"

"Bruno of Cologne?"

"No, not that. Did you say *seven* hermits?"

"Yes," replied Robert, puzzled. "Seven hermits."

Bishop Hugh smiled and made the sign of the cross.

"Your grace, is there something you're not telling me?"

"Let's just say I love it when God makes it easy," chuckled Bishop Hugh.

———

St. Bruno eventually settled in a place called Chartreuse. The group of monks who lived with him became known as the Carthusians. The early Carthusians lived in small cells at a distance from one another, coming together for the Divine Office. They dedicated much of their time to copying religious manuscripts.

Eventually, St. Bruno's order grew and other monasteries were founded. One of St. Bruno's pupils, Eudes of Chatillon, was elected pope in 1088, taking the name Urban II (the same pope who summoned the First

Crusade). Urban II summoned St. Bruno to Rome to help him reform the Church. St. Bruno spent the remainder of his life as an advisor to the pope, dying in the year 1101. Like St. Norbert and St. Robert, St. Bruno had become the founder of a sprawling new religious order that would revitalize religious life in Germany and Italy.

St. Hildegard

Though she didn't found a religious order, we must mention the German mystic St. Hildegard of Bingen in this chapter, who lived from 1098 to 1179. St. Hildegard came from a large family and entered the convent at the young age of eighteen. Ever since she was young, St. Hildegard had received visions, which her confessor commanded her to write down. The visions portrayed the drama of salvation in intense, colorful terms: she saw that humans were living sparks of God's love, that the harmony of God's creation is destroyed by sin, and that our daily lives are the scenes of intense battles between the powers of light and darkness.

Her visions were read by none other than Pope Eugene III himself, who was deeply moved by them and encouraged Hildegard to continue writing. She became well known and wrote over three hundred letters to bishops, holy people, popes, and princes on all matter of subjects. She also created art, wrote poetry, taught on subjects of medicine and physiology, preached to the faithful, and authored marvelous works of music still sung today. On top of all this, she served as abbess of the convent of Bingen.

Venerated as a saint even while alive, St. Hildergard was made a Doctor of the Church by Pope Benedict XVI in 2012. Pope Benedict thought Hildegard was a model all Catholic women could follow. He said, "Let us always invoke the Holy Spirit, so that he may inspire in the

Church holy and courageous women like Saint Hildegard of Bingen who, developing the gifts they have received from God, make their own special and valuable contribution to the spiritual development of our communities and of the Church in our time."[1]

Lay Saints

This was also a time of many great lay saints too, especially among the nobility. For example, in Scotland reigned good King Malcolm and his wife, St. Margaret. Malcolm was a generous man but a bit rough around the edges. His wife, St. Margaret, helped to soften his heart and grow in virtue. She took on a very active role in governing the kingdom with her husband. She was exceptionally generous, establishing churches around the kingdom and attending to the relief of the poor and the education of the young, and she corrected abuses within the Church throughout her realm. It is said that she never sat down to eat without first feeding nine orphans. In her private life, she spent much time devoted to reading and prayer and attended midnight Mass regularly. She had a happy marriage with King Malcolm, bearing six children. When she died in 1093, she was sorely missed by her people, who already revered her as a saint.

Another saintly queen of the time was St. Elizabeth of Hungary. St. Elizabeth was born in 1207 and had a very rough childhood. Her mother, the Queen of Hungary, was murdered in a squabble between rival political factions when Elizabeth was only six years old. Her father sent her away when she was still young to a powerful kingdom in Germany. There, she married Count Ludwig of Thuringia in 1221. The two had three children

---

[1] https://www.franciscanmedia.org/saint-hildegard-of-bingen/.

together and Elizabeth lived a life of austerity, serving the poor and building up the Church in Thuringia. Ludwig supported his wife in all her works; in fact, Ludwig himself would be called Ludwig the Saint.

Unfortunately, Ludwig died of an illness, leaving St. Elizabeth a widow. She was heartbroken, but devoted herself even more to God. She joined the Third Order of the new Franciscans—whom we will discuss in our next chapter—and spent the remainder of her life working with the poor. According to legend, a leper whom she let sleep in one of the royal beds was cured of his leprosy after sleeping in a bed St. Elizabeth had slept in.

Elizabeth died in 1231 and many miracles continued to be reported at her grave. She was canonized by Pope Gregory IX in 1235.

There were many more holy men and women of the twelfth and thirteenth centuries, more than we could possibly have time to cover here. But the important point is to know that this was a time of intense spiritual zeal in which holy men and women—both religious and lay persons—wanted to reform the way Christians lived their faith. Monastic reform movements brought about new orders such as the Premonstratensians (Norbertines), Cistercians, and Carthusians; meanwhile, holy monarchs like St. Margaret of Scotland, St. Elizabeth of Hungary, and many others worked to improve the lives of the poor and the condition of the Church within their domains.

This spirit of renewal would continue on into the next century when it led to a whole different kind of religious order—the Mendicants.

CHAPTER 16

The Mendicant Orders

Far From Perfect

By the year 1200, Christendom was in a good spot. Cities and towns were growing. People were living longer and having more children. The average peasant farmer was healthier and lived better than his ancestors. More people could read and were getting educated than ever before. There was more wealth to go around. The Church was thriving. New religious orders were springing up as beacons of holiness. The papacy was well organized, independent, and largely governed by pious and capable men. And all across Christendom, beautiful churches in the new Gothic style were being built. It seemed to be a golden age.

Of course, no place or time is perfect, and the thirteenth century was far from perfect. Men are men, and as long as life goes on under the sun, there will always be sin. Rulers were often more concerned about growing their own wealth than helping their people.

The Church, too, was not immune to the corruptions of the age. Though bishops no longer received their offices from laymen, they could still get wrapped up in worldly and political problems and ignore their flocks. Far too many powerful kings still tried to manipulate the Church. And in some places, the education and spiritual formation of priests was poor. Among many people there was a sense that the Church was not attending to the spiritual needs of average Christians. Additionally, wandering preachers were beginning to spread dangerous heresies. Even though things were going well overall, common people thought they could be much better, and it seemed God agreed.

In our last chapter, we saw how vibrant new orders like the Premonstratensians, Cistercians, and Carthusians were founded in the eleventh and twelfth centuries to reform monastic life. In this chapter, we will see how God raised up two very important religious orders to combat the errors of the age.

St. Francis of Assisi

Assisi is a quaint town nestled in the shadow of the Apennine Mountains in central Italy. In the early thirteenth century, it was a prosperous city that had grown rich from trade, but it was often at war with the cities around it.

Francis di Bernadone was the son of a wealthy cloth merchant of Assisi. Young Francis lived a carefree life of feasting, drinking, and having parties with his friends. But more than anything, Francis wanted to be a knight and do brave deeds in battle. When Assisi went to war with the neighboring city of Perugia in 1201, Francis was excited to take part in the battle.

But he soon found that war was not as glorious as he thought. Assisi lost the battle and Francis spent a year in a Perugian prison. Another attempt to go off to war a few years later was cut short by sickness. Francis's dreams of becoming a knight seemed to be fading, and it became clear that God had other plans for him. He made a pilgrimage to Rome, after which he decided to live in poverty. When he returned to Assisi, he gave up the life of feasting and began preaching a life of simplicity in the streets. His family and former friends were taken aback by the new Francis.

One day, Francis was praying in the old, ruined chapel of San Damiano near Assisi. As he prayed deeply, the crucifix above the altar began to speak to him.

"Francis," our Lord said, "go and rebuild my Church which, as you can see, is crumbling."

Francis thought our Lord meant to rebuild San Damiano, so he went about gathering stones to restore the ruined chapel. But soon Francis realized that our Lord meant for Francis to rebuild the Church not with stone but by his example. Francis's devotion to poverty and simplicity would be the medicine to counteract the worldliness of the Church in his age.

Francis began by giving away all his possessions. His father thought he had gone mad and brought him to the bishop to set him straight. But that didn't work. Francis eventually forfeited his right to his family's estate and chose instead to live in absolute poverty.

In time, he gathered other followers, men devoted to simplicity. Francis called his group the Order of the Friars Minor. *Friar* is a Latin word that means "brother." But the Friars Minor were known as Franciscans, after their founder. The Franciscans were very different than the Benedictine monks. For one, they did not live in

monasteries but instead wandered about. They also did not perform manual labor but begged for their food. Because they begged, they are called a mendicant order. *Mendicant* comes from a Latin word for begging, and a *mendicant order* is a religious order that survives from begging.

Everywhere Francis went, he preached that people should place love of God above love of material possessions. This was a good message for Catholics at this time to hear. Many people joined Francis's order, and even those who did not were deeply moved by his preaching. People who met him were inspired to change their way of living.

But not everybody was sure about Francis. It was

uncommon for people to voluntarily live in poverty at that time and some were suspicious of him; some even suspected he was leading people into heresy with new and strange teachings. Francis decided to go to Rome to meet Pope Innocent III, seeking approval for his way of life. At first, Pope Innocent thought Francis's idea of living in absolute poverty was impractical. He sent Francis away without approving his order. But according to legend, after sending Francis away, the pope dreamed of a mighty church teetering, about to fall over, but then a man in a little brown habit came and held the church up, preventing its collapse. Innocent recognized the man in the dream as Francis. After another audience together, Innocent approved Francis's way of life in 1209.

The Franciscan order grew quickly from there. Scores of men joined throughout Italy and the rest of Christendom. Within a few years, the Franciscans were sending missionaries abroad to the Crusades—Francis himself made the journey to Egypt in 1219 to try to convert the Islamic sultan to Christianity. And everywhere the order spread, miracles worked by the hand of Francis occurred. Healings, exorcisms, the taming of wild beasts—it seemed that God would withhold no gift from the beloved little poor man from Assisi. You can still read many of these marvelous tales today in a book called the *Fioretti*, which means the "Little Flowers" of St. Francis.

Women, too, were moved to take up Francis's way of life. A young girl of Assisi named Clare was inspired to found an order of nuns based on the example of Francis. Francis was pleased with Clare's devotion to his ideas. Clare's order is commonly referred to as the Poor Clares in her honor. To this day, they remain devoted to St. Clare's vision of poverty and simplicity.

Francis lived a very difficult life full of fasting and

penance. By the 1220s, he was worn out from his work, preaching, and hard penances. Shortly before his death, Francis was praying in a cave on Mount La Verna in Italy. Brother Leo, one of Francis's most trusted friars, described what happened next: "Suddenly he saw a vision of a seraph, a six-winged angel on a cross. This angel gave him the gift of the five wounds of Christ." This was the stigmata, the wounds of Christ miraculously imprinted on the body of Francis. He bore these wounds on his hands, feet, and side for the rest of his life.

Francis died on October 3, 1226 at the age of forty-four. As he lay dying, he asked to be stripped of his habit and laid naked on the dirt floor so he could die the way he had come into the world, with nothing. By the time of his death, his followers numbered in the thousands and the spirituality of the Church had been renewed. He was canonized as a saint only two years later, one of the quickest canonizations in history. The Franciscans are still around today and are currently the largest religious order in the world.

St. Dominic and the Order of Preachers

St. Francis and his Franciscans are the best-known medieval mendicants, but they were certainly not the only ones.

Around the same time St. Francis was growing up, a young Spaniard named Dominic de Guzman was also feeling the call of poverty. Like St. Francis, Dominic's parents were wealthy. Dominic studied theology, but during the course of his studies, Spain was desolated by a famine. He sold his clothes, possessions, and even his manuscripts to feed the hungry. His fellow students were astonished, but Dominic said, "How can I spend my time studying when people are dying of hunger?" Soon after,

Dominic became a canon; a *canon* was a kind of monk attached to the service of a bishop.

As a canon, Dominic spent time in France trying to convert heretics. (We will learn about them in chapter 23.) Dominic saw that the Church's efforts at converting the heretics were being hindered because the preachers sent to them were not practicing what they preached. He believed that heretics could only be won back to the Faith by men who showed real holiness, simplicity, and discipline.

Upon the approval of the pope, Dominic founded a mendicant order called the Order of Preachers, but they were called Dominicans, after Dominic. Like the Franciscans, the Dominicans were committed to a life of simplicity and begging. Unlike the Franciscans, Dominic wanted all his friars to study theology so they could preach to the heretics.

He also promoted the practice of saying what was then called Our Lady's Psalter, a series of Our Fathers and Hail Marys said while meditating on the mysteries of Christ's life and while using beads on a string to keep track of the prayers. If you think this sounds like the Rosary, you're right! These are the origins of this beloved prayer prayed by millions today. The Rosary had been prayed for many years by monks, but St. Dominic thought it should be taught to lay people as well as a means of keeping them from heresy and sanctifying them. St. Dominic spent a great deal of time promoting the Rosary. According to tradition, the Blessed Virgin herself appeared to St. Dominic and put this grand idea into his mind. Many heretics were converted through St. Dominic's preaching and his use of the Rosary.

The efforts of the Dominicans were very successful. Though Dominic himself did not live long enough to see it (he died in 1221 only five years after founding his order), within a few years, the greatest teachers and preachers in Christendom were Dominicans. Dominic was canonized shortly after his death. Today, the Dominican order, made up of simple friars and nuns, continues to live the ideals of St. Dominic.

The Carmelites
The Carmelites were another mendicant order that originated in the early 1200s. The Carmelites have an interesting history because their origin takes us far from Europe, east across the Mediterranean to Palestine and the Holy

Land. There is a mountain called Carmel in northern Palestine. If the name of Mt. Carmel sounds familiar, that's because it is mentioned in the Bible. Mt. Carmel is the place where the prophet Elijah had his famous showdown with the pagan prophets of Baal, which you can read about in the eighteenth chapter of the Old Testament book of First Kings. God sent fire from heaven to burn up the sacrifice offered by Elijah to prove his power.

Ever since that miracle, which took place in the ninth century BC, there was a community of Jewish hermits who lived on the slopes of Mt. Carmel, dedicating their lives to God in prayer at the spot where he once so powerfully manifested his power. With the coming of Christ and the founding of the Church, Christian hermits also began living on Mt. Carmel. When the Crusaders seized the Holy Land in the late eleventh century, some hermits from the West took up residence there. These hermits organized themselves into an order around 1150. They more or less followed the monastic practices based on the Rule of St. Augustine and were known as Carmelites.

The Carmelites spread outside Carmel and had other foundations throughout the Holy Land. But after 1187— the year Jerusalem was retaken by the Muslims—the situation of the Carmelites in the Holy Land became dangerous. Their abbeys were frequently raided or destroyed by the Muslims. More than once they were driven from the slopes of Mt. Carmel itself. The Carmelites realized it was no longer safe to stay in the Holy Land, so between 1238 and 1254, groups of them began migrating to Europe. They settled in Sicily and France, but a great many came to England. Some also chose to stay behind and brave the dangers of living among the Muslims. In 1291, the Muslim armies returned to Mt. Carmel. The remaining Carmelites were slaughtered while they prayed the "Salve Regina" and the abbey burned.

The Carmelites held their first European general chapter in Aylesford, England in 1247. A *general chapter* is an assembly of monks, where representatives of all the monasteries in an order gather to make important decisions on how the order is managed and to elect new superiors. The Carmelites elected an Englishman named Simon Stock to be the general of the Carmelites. Simon, though already advanced in age, did much to promote the mission of the Carmelites and founded many chapters in England.

Do you wear the brown scapular or know someone who does? If so, you can thank Simon Stock, for it was he who promulgated the devotion of the brown scapular—according to tradition, at the behest of the Blessed Virgin Mary herself. Here is how that story unfolded:

————

Simon's feet ached. He had been walking over a bumpy road across the English countryside for five hours. This was what it meant to be general of the Carmelites. The various chapters of the order needed to be visited to ensure they were living faithfully to the rule of the order.

"How long until we reach Oxford, Father Simon?" asked Brother Jonas, one of a handful of brothers Simon had brought along.

"Not until sunset, Brother Jonas," old Simon said, wheezing. "Let us pray for continued good weather until we shall arrive."

"Holy Mary, Mother of God, grant us fair weather and safe travels!" said Brother Jonas, crossing himself.

Good, have recourse to Mary, thought Simon. *She is a sure refuge to those who have recourse to her.* Simon's mind became occupied with pious thoughts about the Blessed

Virgin Mary. He forgot about his aching feet and thought only about the grace of Christ obtained through Mary's prayers.

Suddenly, a great light shone all about Simon. Before him stood the Virgin Mary herself, radiant and powerful. Nor was she alone; behind and above her floated throngs of angels and the spirits of the blessed.

Simon trembled and fell to his knees. "Oh, good Lady, what brings you to the aid of a poor sinner such as I?" he asked, clutching his hands in prayer. He scarcely dared to raise his eyes to the magnificent sight.

Mary smiled at Simon. She held out her hand to him, in which she held a brown garment. It was a scapular, a kind of smock worn by monks. Simon took the scapular from her hands.

"A brown scapular? What am I to do with this?"

"This shall be the privilege for you and for all the Carmelites," she said gently, "that anyone wearing this habit shall be saved."

"Oh, Blessed Mother, your goodness is boundless! You have filled this old man with joy!"

Tears welled in his eyes as he bowed. When he opened his eyes again, she was gone.

"Father, are you well?" called Brother Jonas. "You fell to the ground and have neither moved nor spoken for the past ten minutes!"

"Did you not see the light? The angels? Our Lady?" stammered Simon, rising to his feet.

"No, Father, none of it. But what is that in your hand?"

Simon looked. The scapular Mary handed him was still in his hand, as real and substantial as the road beneath his feet.

"This? *This* is a gift!" he shouted, making the sign of the cross.

————

Simon promoted the brown scapular for the remainder of his life. Wearing it was a sign of devotion to Mary, and those who wore it piously had Mary's promise that they would never lack the grace of eternal salvation. The brown scapular became a very popular devotion; even King Edward II of England would wear it, as did many other important people. The brown scapular is still one of the most popular Catholic devotions today. The original scapular would have been larger, more like a smock. But eventually, scapulars were made smaller, a little bigger than a stamp, as you probably know them today. As for Simon, he died in 1265 while visiting a monastery in France. He was canonized two centuries later and today is venerated as St. Simon Stock.

A Lasting Legacy
By the mid-thirteenth century, the Dominicans, Franciscans, and Carmelites had changed Christendom. Because of the example of the Franciscans, Catholics were reminded of the importance of valuing spiritual things above material wealth. The Dominicans stressed learning and helped the Christian clergy become more educated, as well as graced the Church with the gift of the Rosary. Both orders gifted the Church preachers such as St. Anthony of Padua and St. Albert the Great. Meanwhile, the Carmelites became models of a vibrant, contemplative spirituality and promoted Marian devotion through the wearing of the brown scapular.

The mendicant orders helped to reconnect the average Christian with the spirit of the Gospel. Rather than live tucked away in monasteries, they went about preaching and teaching and doing good, reforming the morals of

Christians with their good example and changing peoples' ideas about what the ideal Christian clergyman should look like. Christians began to expect a higher degree of learning and sanctity out of their priests.

In our next chapter, we will shift from the spiritual to the academic as we learn about the philosophy known as Scholasticism and how it influenced the Church of the thirteenth century.

CHAPTER 17

Scholasticism

Education in the Middle Ages

From the very beginning of Christianity, the study of theology had always been central to the Church's intellectual life. From the earliest Greco-Roman apologists up to our own day, theologians have studied the revealed Word of God to gain knowledge about who God is, what he asks of us, and how we should live.

But there are other things that can help us understand God as well. For example, in the first chapter of the New Testament book of Romans, St. Paul says that we can learn about who God is by observing nature. This idea brings us into the realm of philosophy. In this chapter, we will learn about how the introduction of classical philosophy—specifically the writings of Aristotle—gave birth to something called Scholasticism, one of the most important and enduring schools of thought in the history of Christendom. Scholasticism comes from the Latin word for school; it essentially means "philosophy of the schoolmen."

The subject of this chapter has a lot to do with what was going on in medieval schools. Unfortunately, we do not have the time here for a full discussion of education in the Middle Ages; for that, we recommend chapter 22 in *The Story of Civilization Volume 2: The Medieval World*.

But we can go over some of the main points here. After the fall of the Roman Empire, most education took place in monasteries and was reserved only for those who would enter the service of the Church. Later, around the ninth century, bishops founded schools in their cathedrals that were open not only to clerics but to the sons of the nobility as well. Students learned the seven liberal arts— grammar, logic, rhetoric, arithmetic, music, geometry, and astronomy—as well as courses in literature and other subjects. Girls could be educated as well, but they were usually taught by private tutors within the home.

The Birth of the University

But by the twelfth century, something new was happening in Christendom: the rise of the university. As cities grew in importance, many cathedral schools moved into the larger cities. Students and professors gathered together and formed universities. A *university* was a type of medieval school organized for higher learning. Unlike the cathedral schools, universities received a charter from the pope. The charter was a document giving the university independence from a bishop or lord. At the universities, students could study theology, philosophy, law, and medicine.

It's important to note that in the beginning, the word *university* did not refer to a campus or a set of buildings like it does today. The word *university* is related to the word *union*; both come from the Latin word *unus*, which means "one." The university was viewed as a kind of union of the students and professors, joined together in a single mission of education for the glory of God and the gaining of knowledge. In other words, *university* referred to the people. When somebody said, "I will attend the University of Paris," they did not mean they were going to live on a campus but that they were joining a group of scholars.

The first universities were founded in the late eleventh century, but by the thirteenth century, many major cities had thriving universities. Some of the more famous medieval universities were at Paris (France), Oxford (England), Bologna (Italy), and Salamanca (Spain), but there were many more.

Universities taught four subjects: theology, philosophy, medicine, and law. Most students at the universities were clergymen. In fact, every student at the university was required to take minor orders. This means they were considered clergymen, but in the lower levels of the clergy, such as an acolyte or porter. The most eminent professors were those of theology.

During the twelfth and thirteenth centuries, there was a great debate over the relationship between philosophy and theology. As we learned back in chapter 3, theology is the study of the revealed truths of the Christian faith. *Philosophy*, on the other hand, is the study of those general truths which can be known by reason alone.

Let's use an example to make sure you understand the difference. Suppose we're discussing the idea of the soul. If I were to ask, "What do the Bible and the Church's tradition teach about the human soul?" this would be a theological question—it is theological because it is asking about what God has revealed to us and what the Church teaches about it. However, suppose I were to ask, "What

can we know about the human soul from our own reflection and experience?" This would be a philosophical
question—it is philosophical because it is asking about
what we can know from reason alone.

However, just as in our example about the soul, philosophy and theology can both give us insights about the
same subject, just from different perspectives. Sometimes
it was and still is confusing to tell a philosophical argument apart from a theological argument. Also, what if
theology and philosophy came to different answers about
a question? Could something be false according to reason
but true according to theology, or vice versa? Many philosophers being studied at the university were pagans—
some of them were even Muslim. Was this dangerous to
the Catholic faith? Should they have been studying only
Christian philosophers? The point is that the study of
philosophy raised many questions.

Aristotle

The most popular philosopher the medieval universities
studied was an ancient Greek philosopher who lived from
384 to 322 BC. This was, of course, Aristotle. He was
certainly not new, but he was new to the Christian West.
Knowledge of Aristotle's writings had been lost in the
West after the collapse of the Roman Empire. Most western Europeans could not read Greek, and so the writings
of the Greek philosophers faded from their minds. When
the Muslims began to conquer the lands of the old Byzantine Empire, they preserved Aristotle's writings and
other Greek philosophers and wrote their own commentaries on them. When the crusaders came to the Holy
Land, they brought back the translations of Aristotle—as
well as the Islamic commentaries on his writings—and
theologians in the universities began to study him.

The introduction of Aristotle's ideas into the Latin speaking West changed the way people thought about philosophy and how it related to faith. For example, Aristotle taught that all things that existed were a union of two things: matter and form. Matter is the stuff something is made out of, like the marble used to make a statue; form is the specific characteristic, shape, or arrangement of that matter that make it what it is, the specific shape of a certain statue. Christian thinkers saw this as an excellent way to offer a rational explanation as to how Christ is truly present in the Eucharist: the form of bread and wine remain, but the matter or substance of the bread and wine is replaced with the Body and Blood of Christ. The Eucharist *is* the Body and Blood of Christ but under the forms of bread and wine.

Many more of Aristotle's insights were adapted to help explain Christian theology. Teachings about virtue, the immortality of the soul, the role of the state, the nature of sin and redemption, and much more all found in Aristotle a ready aid to explain their precepts in philosophical terms. Thus, theology was like a queen and philosophy like her maiden—ready to stand by and offer aid and support to the truths of the Faith when required. Using philosophical proofs to better explain the Christian religion helped build the faith of many, as it offered additional reasons to believe the Church's teaching by demonstrating Christianity was true according to reason as well as faith.

A whole school of thought arose around the principles of Aristotle. It was known as Scholasticism. It's difficult to give a quick and easy definition of Scholasticism. Essentially, it was a system of theology and philosophy that relied heavily on Aristotelian logic, using reasoning to draw careful distinctions and resolve contradictions.

Scholastic thinkers had a very specific way of handling

FORTNITE BATTLE PASS !!!

disputed issues. Scholastic theologians tended to first pose a question in a yes or no format. Then they brought forth arguments both in favor and against; the Scholastics thought it was very important to understand both sides of a dispute before addressing it. Then they brought forward the arguments of people who were authorities on the subject, usually Church Fathers or Doctors of the Church. Finally, they came to a conclusion, offering a rationale for their argument, answering the objections, and supporting their conclusion with citations from the proper authorities.

Traditional Catholic theologians were skeptical of what philosophy and the Scholastic method could contribute to theology. Wasn't everything God wanted us to know found in the Scriptures and the Church's tradition?

These concerns were answered by the wonderful theologians who came out of the Scholastic movement, many of whom went on to occupy the most prestigious positions at Europe's universities. These universities often produced remarkable professors famous for their wisdom and teaching. Many of these professors were Dominicans, such as St. Albert the Great. St. Albert was a professor at many universities and was a famous theologian and scientist. Others were Franciscans, such as St. Bonaventure, one of the most renowned theologians of the age.

But another saint was perhaps the greatest example of a brilliant thinker whose writings and teachings formed the medieval university. This was St. Thomas Aquinas.

St. Thomas Aquinas

St. Thomas lived in the thirteenth century. He had been destined for a career as a Benedictine abbot, but he was drawn to the new mendicant orders and joined the Dominicans. His parents were against this, even to the point that they kidnapped him and locked him in a tower until he changed his mind. But he held fast to his plans and eventually they relented, releasing him and letting him join the Dominicans. Here's the story of how St. Thomas convinced his family to release him:

―――――――

Young Thomas rubbed his hands together while he blew on the struggling fire. It had been over a year since his family confined him to this dreary room in the Aquino family castle, and it wasn't exactly the warmest room in the place. The creaky wooden shutters on the window did little to keep out the winter drafts, and the large rounded stones that made up the floor and walls were perpetually cool and clammy. There were a few fur rugs on the ground, which he presently sat upon, but they did little to vanquish the chill.

Thomas picked up a long stick and poked the fire, turning the coals. He stared into the dull orange glow of the coals.

"Lord, have mercy," he muttered.

How long would his family leave him locked up here on the fourth floor of the castle in this drafty corner room? Would they never relent? They had tried everything to get him to change his mind about joining the Dominicans. They had tried reasoning with him, arguing with him, even threatening him. Still, Thomas was resolute.

"Thy will be done, O God," he prayed.

Still, it had been over a year now, and Thomas was getting very lonely. He desired fresh air and human companionship. How long could he endure? What else would they try?

A gentle creaking of the heavy oaken door broke his gloomy thoughts. Thomas looked up curiously. He seldom had visitors, only his mother once a week. A key turned in the lock. Thomas rose. He assumed it would be one of his family members. But when a strange woman entered instead, a look of confusion fell over Thomas's face.

"You must be Thomas?" she said, closing the door behind her.

"Yes . . . I am," he stammered. "Who are you, and how did you get a key to my room?"

"I'm a friend of your brothers. They thought the two of us might enjoy getting to know each other."

"I don't need any company," Thomas said, looking at the ground.

"Come now, Thomas," she said, walking up and taking a seat beside him, "don't you want to fall in love with a woman?" She put her hand on his arm. "Don't you want to leave this silly religious calling behind?"

A flash of holy anger welled up in Thomas. He lunged away from the woman and shifted towards the fireplace. He grabbed hold of the stick he had recently tossed on the fire and plucked it from the flames. The end of the stick was hot and smoldered a fierce orange.

"Get out!" he said, waving the hot stick wildly in the air. "You will not deter me from my course! Get out!"

The woman screamed at the sight of the wild-eyed youth waving the hot stick about. "You're insane!" she shrieked, running to the door. Thomas followed her, stick in hand. She quickly unlocked the door and rushed out, disappearing down the corridor.

Thomas slammed the door shut behind her. Panting, he took the hot charred end of the stick and drew a cross on the door in ash. "No one will rob me of my purity," he cried aloud to God and anyone nearby who might be listening. "And no one will make me waver in my resolution to join the Dominicans!"

After this, St. Thomas's family realized he would not be dissuaded and agreed to release him and let him join the Dominican order.

Once a member of the Dominican order, he became a student of the great St. Albert. Thomas eventually became a professor and lectured in theology at the University of Paris. He lectured, prayed, and wrote works of theology.

One of his books is called the *Summa Theologiae*, or *Summa* for short. The *Summa* contains St. Thomas's teaching on many theological questions. It was written in the standard Scholastic question and answer format so that it would be easy for students to understand. Even though St. Thomas wrote his *Summa* for students, it became one of the most important theological books of all time. The *Summa* is still read and studied today and shapes much of the Church's theology.

St. Thomas died in 1274 while on the way to attend the Council of Lyons. He would be canonized in 1323. Many years later, Pope Leo XIII called St. Thomas's teachings

the Church's "golden wisdom" and recommend his teachings as an ideal for all Catholic theologians to follow.

By the thirteenth century, the old cathedral schools had developed into thriving universities in all of Europe's major cities. Students studied not only theology but also the newer courses in law, logic, medicine, and philosophy. The university system would continue to grow and produce some of the best educated people in Christendom for the next five hundred years. Next time you're traveling and see a college or university, think of the thirteenth century.

The Fourth Lateran Council

The Church also developed in other important ways during the thirteenth century. In 1215, Pope Innocent III summoned the Fourth Lateran Council, which was the largest council of the Middle Ages. The Fourth Lateran Council took some very important actions. Have you ever heard the word *transubstantiation*? It is the theological word the Church uses to describe how the bread and wine of the Eucharist turn into the Body and Blood of Christ at Mass. Transubstantiation means that the essential substance of the bread and wine are transformed into the Body and Blood of Christ, but the forms of bread and wine remain so that the sacrament appears to be bread and wine to the senses but is in reality the Body and Blood of Christ.

The Church used concepts borrowed from Aristotelean theology to help explain this mystery. This is an example of the relationship between philosophy and theology at its best—philosophical concepts helping to enlighten the teachings of the Faith.

Have you ever heard of the Easter obligation? This is the obligation of every Catholic to go to confession at least once a year and receive Holy Communion during the Easter season. This, too, was laid down at the Fourth Lateran Council, as were many other important decrees concerning the morals of the clergy, marriage, and much more.

By the end of the thirteenth century, the Church was better organized, its clergy better educated, and the popes more independent than ever before. The new orders of the Franciscans, Dominicans, and Carmelites were flourishing. The integration of philosophy and theology—as best represented by Scholasticism and the teachings of St. Thomas Aquinas—was aiding in the rapid development of Catholic theology.

But the Church would soon have to defend itself once again against a new and rising power, as we shall soon see.

CHAPTER 18

Kings Versus Popes

Maintaining Balance

Christians of the medieval period believed very strongly that there was a balanced, harmonious order to society. To be sure, there were many different groups in the world all jostling each other for influence—nobles and commoners, popes and kings, town and country—and though there were many groups with competing interests, people could always find a way to live in harmony if they just followed God's order for society. At least that's how the medievals tended to view things.

One of the biggest problems of the medieval world was the question of the proper relationship between the Church and the government. In a Christian society, how do the two work together to further the good of God's kingdom?

We discussed this back in chapter 13 during the disputes about lay investiture. But the problem was not unique to the Middle Ages; indeed, it went back to the very beginning of the Christian Church. Jesus had said for Christians to "render therefore to Caesar the things that are Caesar's and to God the things that are God's" (Mt 22:21). This was clear enough when the governing authorities were pagans who cared little for the Church or Christian truth, but what were Christians to do in the age of Christendom when the governing authorities were also Christians? What do we do when God and Caesar are on the same team?

Centuries later, around the time of the fall of the Roman Empire, there was a pope named Gelasius who wrote on this very question. Pope Gelasius wrote, "There are two powers by which the world is ruled: the sacred authority of priests and the royal power. Of these, the power of the priests is more important, for they are accountable to God even for kings on judgment day. While kings rule over mankind, in divine things even they must bow their heads before the clergy, from whom come the means of salvation."

Since the time of Pope Gelasius, Christians used many images to explain the relation between church and state. Some described the two powers as two swords, and Pope Innocent III famously compared them to the sun and the moon. How the relationship between the Church and the state ought to look was one of the greatest debates of the Middle Ages.

Clashes Between Church and State

In chapter 13, we discussed the relationship between the Church and the government in the Middle Ages. Pope Gregory VII and the Holy Roman emperor Henry IV had engaged in a bitter struggle called the Investiture Controversy, which was an argument concerning how much control the Holy Roman Empire should have over the Church. The controversy ended with the Church winning more independence from the empire.

But not everybody was happy about this arrangement. In 1152, a new king of Germany named Frederick Barbarossa was crowned. Frederick wanted to regain imperial control of the Church and make the Holy Roman Empire the most powerful kingdom in Christendom.

Frederick became Holy Roman emperor in 1155 because of the help he gave the papacy. The pope at this time, Adrian IV, had been run out of Rome by a rebellion. Pope Adrian did not like having to ask Frederick for help, but he had no choice. Frederick agreed to help the pope win back Rome. In return, the pope crowned him Holy Roman emperor.

This gave Frederick more power in Italy. He brought his armies into northern Italy and tried to force all the cities there to obey him. But the northern Italian cities didn't like this because they had always been independent.

The new pope, Alexander III, pressured Emperor Frederick to give up his wars. In response, Frederick tried to attack Alexander by supporting an antipope. We learned about antipopes back in chapter 12. When more than one person claims to be pope, it is terribly confusing and spreads disunity in the Church. Pope Alexander III excommunicated Emperor Frederick for his support of the antipope. But Frederick continued to wage war throughout Italy for many years. Though he had some successes, he was eventually forced to recognize Alexander III as the true pope and was reconciled with the Church.

Emperor Frederick wanted to be known as a good and chivalrous knight. When news came that the Kingdom of Jerusalem had fallen to the Muslims in 1187, Frederick called a crusade to retake the city. This was the Third

Crusade and it was a magnificent affair. Emperor Frederick was joined by King Richard of England and King Philip Augustus of France. Together, the three grand armies of France, England, and the Holy Roman Empire set out to retake Jerusalem.

How splendid it must have been to see the three greatest monarchs of Christendom, armor glistening and banners unfurled in the wind, marching towards Jerusalem! But the crusade was doomed to failure. While crossing a river in Asia Minor, Emperor Frederick fell from his horse and drowned. The imperial army came apart, and the Third Crusade was not able to recapture Jerusalem.

While the popes did not get along well with Frederick Barbarossa, they got on even worse with his grandson, Frederick II. When Frederick was a boy, he lived in Sicily, where he was king of a small Norman kingdom. Frederick II wanted to become Holy Roman emperor, but the pope was afraid he would unite Sicily and the Holy Roman Empire against him. Frederick promised that if he was crowned emperor, he would not unite Sicily and the empire. He also promised to go on a crusade. This gave the pope the assurance he sought as he relented and crowned Frederick II Holy Roman emperor in 1220.

Soon after Frederick was crowned, the pope asked him to keep his vow and go on a crusade. But Frederick put it off for too long. Eventually, the pope excommunicated him for failing to keep his vow. Frederick invaded the Papal States and did everything he could to hurt the pope. Once, he even kidnapped one hundred bishops and cardinals!

The Church called Frederick II the Antichrist and a persecutor of the Christians. Frederick wanted all the princes of Germany to help him in his struggle against the pope, but most princes stayed out of it. They knew

Frederick was called Antichrist and persecutor and they did not want to be lumped in with him.

Frederick II died suddenly in 1250. His heirs would continue to fight the Church for another generation. But the greatest medieval enemy of the Church was not a Holy Roman emperor but a French king.

An Attack on the Pope

The clash between the Church and state came to a head during the papacy of Boniface VIII, who was pope from 1294 until 1302. During that time, France was at war with England. The French king, Philip IV, wanted to tax the French Church to pay for the war. Pope Boniface wrote a letter telling King Philip he was absolutely not allowed to tax the Church without the Church's permission.

But King Philip was not afraid of Pope Boniface and refused to seek the Church's permission. Pope Boniface eventually wrote a papal bull reminding the king that he, like all other Christians, owed obedience to the pope. In this bull, called *Unam Sanctam*, Pope Boniface taught that kings were not exempt from the duty of listening to the pope. This angered King Philip so much he sent a group of thugs down to Italy to teach Boniface a lesson. What happened when they found him? Let's find out:

———

It was early September of 1307. A gentle, warm breeze blew across the gardens of the papal palace at Anagni, a city south of Rome where Pope Boniface had been staying since August. The pope was pacing about his gardens with a few attendants reading letters that were pouring in to him about the situation in France.

"This is very bad," the pope said to one of his advisors.

"King Philip is obstinate. It looks like we shall have to excommunicate him."

"Shall I draw up the bull of excommunication, your holiness?" asked Brother Guido, his secretary.

"Yes, Guido. Prepare it for publication as soon as possible."

"That won't be necessary," came a gruff voice from the garden gate.

The pope and his attendants turned.

"Who are you?" demanded Boniface of the large, burly man armed with a club.

"Long live the king of France," the man said, grinning a dirty, yellow-toothed smile. The pope could hear the sound of commotion in the streets. A papal servant ran into the garden panting.

"Your holiness, a large band of mercenaries in the pay of the French king has pushed their way into the city. They intend to carry you off!"

A gasp arose from the pope's attendants. Meanwhile, other armed men entered the garden.

"Protect the pope!" Brother Guido shouted, rushing at the armed men. "Your holiness, flee!" he cried as he lunged at the burly man with the club. A single well-placed blow from the club laid Brother Guido out on the ground. A few other clerics did the same and met similar fates. The pope, meanwhile, ran inside and barricaded himself inside his audience hall with the rest of his entourage.

For the next five hours, the pope remained locked in his audience hall while soldiers swarmed about the grounds, plundering treasures and trying to break down the massive bronze-plated doors. The pope sat upon his chair, surrounded by a handful of cardinals and servants. Sweat beaded upon his brow and he twitched every time he heard another *bang* on the door.

"I cannot believe Philip would sink to such manifest evil as to lay hands on the person of the Roman pontiff," he said more to himself than anyone else.

Soon there was the sound of smashing wood from down the hall. "They have smashed the door that connects the palace to the cathedral," yelled Francesco, the pope's nephew.

Boniface stood up and, making the sign of the cross over those with him, said, "It has been an honor serving the Church with you, gentlemen. I impart to you my apostolic blessing, and I suggest that if you do not want to be carried off along with me, that you flee now." The teary-eyed cardinals nodded and, swiftly kissing the pope's ring, fled down a corridor. "You, too, Francesco," the pope said to his nephew, patting Francesco on the head.

"But uncle," he protested.

"No foolishness! Get out of here. Now!"

Francesco nodded and scuttled off. Only a single Spanish bishop now remained.

"You're not going to flee with them?" asked the pope.

"The disciples all fled the garden," the Spaniard said. "Save St. John. Let me be your John."

Boniface smiled wryly. "Well, St. John, get me my pontifical robes and tiara."

The Spanish bishop brought the pope his pontifical vestments and the papal tiara, the large triple-crown the pope wore upon his head on ceremonial occasions. Clad in his robes and tiara, the pope sat down upon the papal throne, a large cross in his hand, and waited. A moment later, a crash rung out and the hall was quickly flooded with armed men. The pope was violently pulled from the chair, the tiara knocked off his head and his vestments ripped off. The pope was thrown to the ground as the Spanish bishop was beaten and tied up.

A tall man with a sword approached. This was Sciarra Colonna, one of the pope's greatest Italian enemies, the leader of the mercenaries, and a supporter of King Philip. He put the blade of the sword to the neck of Pope Boniface.

"I should slay you here," growled Colonna.

"Here is my head, here is my neck," responded Boniface. "I will patiently bear that I, a Catholic and lawful pontiff and Vicar of Christ, be condemned. I desire to die for Christ's faith and his Church."

"That can be arranged," replied Colonna, pressing the tip of the blade against the pope's flesh. A tiny drop of blood dripped down Boniface's neck.

"No," said a Frenchman, one of the counselors of King Philip. "Let's not make a martyr out of him. Philip wants him brought to France. Come, bring him!"

———

Boniface would never make it to France. The townspeople of Anagni fought back against the mercenaries of Colonna and Boniface was rescued and had to be hurried away to Rome under the guard of hundreds of horsemen. All this action was too much for the old pope, however, and shortly after returning to Rome, he became ill and died.

With Pope Boniface out of the way, King Philip felt powerful enough to do what he wanted with the Church. He decided to go after another group that had a lot of money: the Templar Knights. The Templars were a military order formed during the Crusades. We learned about them in chapter 14. By the time of King Philip, they had become very wealthy, and the king wanted their money. But how could he take it from them?

Eventually, King Philip came up with the idea of charging the Templars with crimes. If they were found guilty of the crimes, he could control all of their wealth. In September of 1307, Philip issued a secret order to his soldiers to arrest all the Templars on a single day.

The Grandmaster of the Templars at this time was an old knight named Jacques de Molay. De Molay was convicted of all manner of false crimes and burned at the stake, along with many other Templars. With de Molay dead and the Templars disbanded, King Philip was able to get his hands on all the Templar gold. But he did not have long to enjoy it; King Philip died within a year.

The Growing Power of Kings

Throughout the late Middle Ages, kings like Philip IV were growing in power. They had more money, stronger armies, and better organized governments. The late medieval kings started thinking that they should have a stronger say in how the Church within their kingdom was run. As we saw in the case of King Philip IV and Pope Boniface, this often got them into trouble with the popes.

In England as well, the Church was facing aggression by a hostile King Edward I, who reigned from 1272 to 1307. He passed laws making it difficult for the Church to be granted new lands. Like Philip IV, he attempted to tax the Church and plunder its goods to pay for his wars. When Pope Boniface VIII prohibited this in his papal bull *Clericos Laicos*, King Edward declared clergy who refused to pay taxes to their king outlaws, forcing many clerics to make the difficult choice between loyalty to the pope or to their king.

What we see in both the cases of King Philip IV and Edward I is the growing power of the state and its hostility to the Church. What do we mean by this? In the earlier Middle Ages, medieval kingdoms were made up of a dizzying complex of various little princedoms, duchies, towns, and other territories, some of which could have spoken different languages. The kings would rely upon the personal bonds of his feudal vassals—the knights, lords, and nobles who owed them allegiance—to govern. The kings' powers were very dependent upon the cooperation of the nobility, as well as the Church.

But by the latter part of the Middle Ages, the kings' power had grown considerably. They relied less on the fickle nobles and more on their own royal officials. While nobles squabbled with each other over lands and inheritances, kings such as Edward and Philip revised the laws of their kingdoms to make the royal power stronger and more financially secure. They also built efficient ways to administer their kingdoms without having to depend upon the nobles. Gradually, the medieval kingdom grew from a hodge-podge of different lands united by feudal bonds to the king and came more to resemble nations as we know them today. And as the kings became more powerful, they increasingly resented the influence of the Church in society and coveted its wealth and lands.

After the death of Pope Boniface VIII, things did not go well for the Church. We will learn more about it in the next chapter.

CHAPTER 19

The Babylonian Captivity

A French Pope

In our last chapter, we learned about how the growing power of national kings threatened the independence of the Church. Men like King Philip IV of France and Edward I of England sought to use their power to dominate the clergy in their kingdoms and pillage the Church's wealth to pay for their wars. Pope Boniface VIII boldly stood up to these men, declaring that the state had no authority to tax the Church and reminded kings that they, too, were subject to the pope's authority.

However, unlike earlier conflicts between the pope and a ruler, Pope Boniface VIII lost his battle. He was kidnapped by thugs working for King Philip of France and died soon after from the trauma. King Philip ruled supreme.

Pope Boniface was succeeded by another pope who did not live long. When the cardinals met again to elect a new pope in 1305, everybody was afraid of King Philip. The king worked hard behind the scenes to get a Frenchman elected. He thought if he could get a French pope sitting on the Chair of Peter, the Church would be more sympathetic to his wishes. And Philip was successful. The new pope, Clement V, was a Frenchman, who before becoming pope had been an advisor and friend of King Philip. Some claimed that Pope Clement allowed King Philip to do whatever he wished, and for the most part, this was a fair accusation. It was Pope Clement who allowed King Philip to carry out his unjust attack on the Templars, which we read about in our last chapter.

The Roman people did not know what to think of the new French pope since most popes at the time were Italians. They were suspicious of Clement and many didn't like him.

As it turned out, Clement did not like Rome either. Rome was not the nicest place to live in the Middle Ages. It was filthy, cluttered, and miserably hot in the summer. The city was torn by fighting between rival families and its fickle populace was prone to riots and violence. Once, the Basilica of St. John Lateran—the pope's own church—was set on fire and became dangerously unstable. In 1305, Pope Clement did something that rocked the Church: he moved the papal court from Rome to France, eventually settling on the city of Avignon in southern France. As you might've guessed, this was awfully convenient for King Philip.

Many Catholics strongly disapproved of the papal court moving to Avignon; after all, had not St. Peter founded his church in Rome? Whatever the pope might think of Rome as a city, it was where the popes had always lived. Plus, if the pope lived in France, would he not become a servant of the king of France rather than a servant of

God? Clement and his supporters scoffed at these concerns, returning to the claim that Rome was dangerously unsafe.

Those who did not like the move to Avignon saw many of their concerns come true. The popes continued to live at Avignon for sixty-seven years, during which time seven French popes sat on the Chair of Peter and had entire papal courts made up of Frenchman. French popes used Church money to help pay for France's wars, French kings were given special privileges other kings did not receive, and French popes were heavily involved in French politics. During this time, the popes lived in a grand palace within the city which still exists today.

Petrarch, a famous author of the time, said that Avignon was like the Babylon of the West. In the Bible, Babylon is a symbol of corruption, worldliness, and wealth. By saying this, Petrarch meant that the Avignon papacy had allowed the spiritual mission of the Church to be set aside in favor of worldly, political concerns. Since the amount of time the papacy was in Avignon would be roughly the same amount of time the Jews were exiled to Babylon in the Old Testament, the time of the Avignon papacy would later be known as the Babylonian Captivity of the popes.

This was all very troubling. Other Catholic kings took the pope less seriously because they thought he was just a lackey of the French, while average Christians worried that the Church was too caught up in political problems. The whole situation encouraged heretical groups who preached that the Church should not have any property or that it was too worldly.

Enriching the Faith Through Drama

With all this turmoil going on, we must never forget that God never abandons his Church. The Church is both divine and human: divine because of its founder Jesus and human because of the weak and sometimes sinful people who make it up. The Church can sometimes look dirty on the outside, but inside, it is from God, just like when Jesus was on earth he looked like a normal man—sometimes tired, sometimes dirty from a hard day's work—but he was actually the Son of God. He was more than he appeared.

And we also have to remember that the Church is more than just the hierarchy. So often we can think of the Church as just the popes and clergy. What about regular folks who were not bishops, priests, monks, or nuns? Medieval Christians practiced their faith in a variety of ways. Besides attending Mass on Sundays and Holy Days—of which there were many more than there are today—Christians would often make pilgrimages to local saint shrines to pray for their needs. Those who could read could go to the nearest monastic library and study the Bible or lives of the saints, and later, after the printing press was invented, they could purchase religious books and read them in their homes. They also learned the Faith from the beautiful Christian art and architecture that surrounded them. New devotions like the Rosary were becoming popular. And there were always many associations—some religious orders, some run by lay people—that dedicated themselves to taking care of the sick and poor.

One of the favorite pastimes of Christians during the 1300s was going to see plays with religious themes. These plays were often held outdoors in the town square. There were several different kinds of plays.

Mummers plays featured two characters engaged in combat, sometimes dramatic scenes like St. George versus a Turk, or Robin Hood versus an evil knight, and other times more comical ones like a fool—a silly, uneducated person—winning a war of wits with the devil himself. Whatever the pair, they might be introduced by a man dressed up as Father Christmas or even as God. Sometimes a quack doctor would show up for comic relief to restore the defeated character to life. Amidst all this, the point of mummers plays was to show the triumph of good and virtuous characters over evil ones.

Mystery plays depicted scenes from the Bible, usually accompanied by singing. They might show stories such as the creation of the world, the fall of Adam and Eve, or the Last Judgment. These plays were often performed in cycles and could go on for days, usually structured around the liturgical year. To this day, there is a famous series of mystery plays in Oberammergau, Germany held once every ten years during Holy Week that depict scenes from our Lord's passion.

Miracle plays were depictions of the lives and miracles of the saints. If the saint was a martyr, the martyrdom story would often be acted out. These originally developed around the liturgical calendar as a way of enriching the celebration of the saints' feast days. For example, on the feast of St. Lawrence on August 10, the martyrdom of St. Lawrence could be acted out in the town square outside the church, complete with a reenactment of Lawrence being barbecued alive on a makeshift grill erected for the play.

Morality plays were allegorical plays with the purpose of demonstrating the rewards of virtuous living and the miseries that befall the sinner. Actors would represent abstract ideas like justice, humanity, or death and depict the soul's journey towards God.

One of the most famous medieval morality plays was called *Everyman*, a story about a worldly man being reminded of his obligations to God through an encounter with Death. Though *Everyman* was written a bit later than the period we are studying—in the late 1400s—it is an excellent example of medieval morality plays. Let's pause to see what it might have been like to see a scene from *Everyman* in an English town during the Middle Ages:

———

The peasant Giles and his companion Baldric stood rapt in attention as the play began. It was autumn, the time of year when Christians contemplated the last things. The bishop of Coventry decided to commemorate this time of the liturgical year by bringing a troupe of actors to perform the popular morality play *Everyman* for the people of Coventry. Giles and Baldric were part of a large crowd of onlookers standing in the square as the actors took to the makeshift wooden stage erected in front of the cathedral.

"I ain't never seen this one before," said Giles.

"Me neither," agreed Baldric. "I hope they show the jaws of death swallowing up sinners!"

Giles laughed. "You're easy to entertain, ain't you? Every play can't have the jaws of death, now, can it?"

The sound of a fife playing silenced the men's chatter and announced the beginning of the play. The crowd had already listened to a lengthy introductory speech by an actor in a white robe and fake beard portraying God the Father. Now a simple looking man in a pilgrim tunic entered the stage from the left as the fife continued to play.

"Behold, Everyman!" called out the white-robed character of God from beside the stage. "He goeth about his life's journey, attending to various and sundry duties, chasing wealth and honor. But he knows not that the time of his visitation draws near!"

The tone of the music changed to a melancholy tune as a black-robed figure emerged from the right side of the stage.

"Everyman," the black-robed figure called out, "I have come to find thee."

"Fair day, good sir," replied Everyman. "I pray thee, what is your name?"

"I am Death, Everyman."

The crowd began to hoot and jeer at the sight of Death.

"Oh, good," said Baldric, rubbing his hands together. "Maybe we'll see the jaws of death now!"

"What have you come for?" asked Everyman.

"To take you away with me for judgment," answered Death.

The music turned ominous.

"I cannot go!" said Everyman. "I'm not ready!"

"You have no choice," replied Death, grasping his arm.

"Wait, can I pay someone else to go for me?"

"No, this journey must be made by you and only you. However, you may take any of your friends with you who are willing."

Everyman's face perked. He seemed comforted by this, even intrigued.

The rest of the play consisted of Everyman trying to convince a companion to go with him to the judgment with Death. He tries to take his companion Fellowship, but Fellowship refuses to come. So do Kindred and Cousin.

"We have our own accounts to settle with Death," said Kindred and Cousin. "We cannot go with you."

Everyman turns to his other friend, Possessions, but he, too, refuses to come. He says God's judgment will be even more severe if Everyman tries to cling to him. Neither Beauty nor Strength can make the journey. Everyman is panicked. He paces across the stage waving his arms and lamenting his misfortune.

"Looks like he's at his wits' end," said Giles.

"Have you found nobody to come with you?" asked Death.

"Nobody," sighed Everyman. "I shall go to the judgment alone."

"But who is that sickly, weakened person over there?" asked Death. Everyman looks. Off to the side of the stage is a woman dressed in rags, lying on the ground. "Perhaps she can come to the judgment with you."

"Who are you, my lady?" asked Everyman. "And why art thou so sickly?"

"Oh Everyman, I am Good Deeds. I am sickly because you have neglected me in life. I am weak because you have loved me so poorly."

"But . . . can you accompany me to the judgment with Death?"

"Not in this condition. I am too weak."

"But all is not lost!" boomed the sudden voice of God from the side of the stage. "For Good Deeds summons her sister, Knowledge, and together they lead Everyman to confession."

Everyman knelt down before an actor dressed as a priest, received absolution, and promised to do penance. As a symbol of his penance, he is whipped. Every time the whip strikes him, Good Deeds rises up some and grows in strength.

"Now I am strong because you have loved God and done penance," she said. "Now I am ready to accompany you to the judgment."

Everyman took Good Deeds by the hand as Death lead the two of them to the right of the stage. The fife music picked up. Then, a heavy creaking came below the stage. Two gigantic trap doors opened up. Smoke bellowed out from the opening, created by two stagehands burning wet leaves beneath the stage.

"The jaws of death!" cried Baldric. "It's about time!"

The Death character descended into the opening, and taking Everyman and Good Deeds with him, the three disappeared beneath the stage.

The crowd erupted in thunderous applause.

"Excellent play, don't you think?" said Giles. "Really makes a fellow think."

"My favorite part was when he died," said Baldric, crunching into a rutabaga he pulled from his pocket.

Giles shook his head. "You are so predictable, my dear friend."

———

Did you understand the moral of the story? Plays like this taught people that their possessions, friends, and even their family are not things they can take with them when they die. Yet good deeds *are* things they can take with them, and hopefully use to get into heaven. Just as Jesus used parables—stories—to teach lessons, so these plays tried to do the same.

St. Catherine of Siena

Medieval Christians were not perfect by any means, but they were extremely pious. It's not surprising that, despite the Church's troubles, there were many saints who emerged during the 1300s, many of them laypeople, like St. Elizabeth of Portugal or St. Bridget of Sweden.

The best-known lay saint of the 1300s, however, was St. Catherine of Siena. Siena is a city in northern Italy. St. Catherine came from a very large family of twenty-five children! Catherine was a very devout little girl and had visions of Christ when she was still young. Her parents wished her to marry, but Catherine protested, saying she wanted to serve God as a virgin.

Eventually, St. Catherine's parents allowed her to join the Third Order Dominicans. The Franciscans also had a Third Order, as did other religious orders. Now clothed in the Dominican habit, St. Catherine lived a life of prayer and good works and became famous in Siena as a mystic and holy woman. Many important people wrote her letters asking for her advice. She even helped make peace between warring cities. Perhaps the most amazing thing about St. Catherine is that, like St. Francis, she received the stigmata.

Like most holy men and women, St. Catherine wanted the clergy to be reformed and the pope to return to Rome. She wrote letters to Pope Gregory XI, the French pope at Avignon, begging him to return the papal court to Rome. She even went to Avignon in person in 1376.

We do not know what St. Catherine said to Pope Gregory, but it is a touching scene to imagine: this young, sickly girl, clothed in the habit of the Dominicans, conversing as a friend with the powerful pope in the splendid papal fortress of Avignon.

Pope Gregory XI finally agreed to return to Rome the following year, entering Rome in January 1377. The long Avignon papacy was over. It is not certain how much influence St. Catherine had on the pope's decision to return. But her work seemed accomplished. Shortly after

Pope Gregory's return, she fell ill and died in 1380 at age thirty-three. She was canonized and later made a Doctor of the Church.

The papacy had returned to Rome, but that was not the end of the Church's troubles, as we shall soon see.

CHAPTER 20

The Great Western Schism

Too Many Popes

When Pope Gregory XI returned to Rome in 1377, people assumed the papacy's troubles were over. The long residence of the popes at Avignon had finally come to an end. The successor of St. Peter was once again residing in Rome.

But the good feelings did not last long. Gregory died in 1378 shortly after his return to Rome and this led to rioting by the Roman people. Remember, for the past seventy years, the popes had all been Frenchmen and were widely seen as puppets of the French monarchy. When Gregory died, the Roman people surrounded the papal conclave and demanded the cardinals elect an Italian. The cardinals were afraid the mob would kill them if they did not comply. So they elected an Italian archbishop, Bartolomeo Prignano, who took the name Urban VI.

In a time when the Church needed unity, the selection

of Prignano was perhaps a poor choice. Pope Urban VI was honest, but he was not a gentle man. He was stubborn and easily provoked to anger and could be extremely harsh with those who worked under him. Being pope made him even worse, and he had a reputation for arrogance and wrathfulness. The cardinals soon regretted electing such a difficult man.

The French in particular were unhappy with Urban's election and began plotting against him almost immediately. Most of the cardinals fled Rome to get away from Urban and the Roman mob. A group of them met without Urban and issued a declaration that Urban's election was invalid. They claimed that they only elected him because they were afraid of the mob and that there was no pope. Then, led by the French cardinals, they elected the archbishop of Cambrai, Robert of Geneva, who took the name Clement VII. Clement and his supporters promptly moved back to Avignon and excommunicated Urban. Urban, meanwhile, claimed Clement was an antipope and took drastic measures against him, including raising money to prepare for a war.

This left the Church with two men claiming to be pope, Urban VI in Rome and Clement VII in Avignon. This dilemma was known as the Great Western Schism. One might think everyone wanted this situation resolved as quickly as possible. The Church is *one* and there can only be *one* successor of St. Peter. But it was not that easy. Each pope had been elected by the cardinals and had their own supporters. They had each nominated their own bishops and cardinals and had their own papal courts. Each pope gave orders in their name. Each wore papal vestments. They both looked like the pope, and they each had good arguments for their case. To make matters worse, after each pope died, their own cardinals each elected successors.

The Christian people were confused, to say the least. Some kingdoms supported one line of popes, some the other. Usually, a kingdom's support for a pope had political reasons. For example, France and England were at war with each other, so each kingdom supported a different pope; France supported the popes at Avignon, and England, the popes in Rome.

In 1404, the Roman pope Boniface IX died. The Roman cardinals reached out to the rival papal court at Avignon and said they would not elect a new pope if the Avignon pope, Benedict XIII, resigned. But Benedict refused, and the Roman cardinals went ahead and elected a new pope, Innocent VII. Thus, the Great Western Schism continued.

Many saints and holy people in the Church knew how terrible this situation was. It was very damaging to the faith of Christians and confusing for the governance of the Church. The schism could divide cities as well. When the rulers of the French city of Bruges pledged allegiance to Avignon in 1382, a great number of the city's merchants loyal to Rome chose to leave the city and practice their business elsewhere. It was a terribly divisive time for the Church.

Making the Church One Again
Many efforts were made through compromise and diplomacy to end the schism. Even the French monarchy tried to get the Avignon pope to resign for the good of the Church, but he refused. When the Church realized the popes themselves would not solve the problem, the cardinals called the Council of Pisa in 1409 to fix the schism without the cooperation of the popes. The Council of Pisa

declared both the Roman and Avignon popes deposed; *deposed* means removed from their position. With both other popes gone, the Council of Pisa elected a new pope. But there was no precedent in Church history or theology to support the idea that cardinals could get rid of a sitting pope. Thus, the two other popes did not recognize the Council of Pisa and refused to step down. This meant there were now *three* men claiming to be pope! The third pope set up his court at Pisa, making the situation even worse.

We probably cannot appreciate how confusing this was to the faithful. We take for granted that we have only one pope. Let's pause for a moment to see how this situation could affect even the most casual of encounters between Christians at this time:

———

It was a hot summer day in the country outside Turin. A dry wind blew over the hillside cut apart by a dusty road. Stephen, an English pilgrim returning from Rome, wandered up the lane, pausing near the hill's peak to rest. Behind him, in the Po Valley, sat the white buildings of Turin, glistening in the noonday sun. Before him loomed the shadows of the Italian Alps, which he would have to pass through on his way home.

Stephen wiped the sweat from his brow and sat down in the grass, taking a swig of water from his flask. He squinted in the sun, looking at a roadside shrine dedicated to St. Florian, the patron of soap makers and those who fight fires. The crudely carved, brightly-painted wooden statue depicted St. Florian dumping a bucket of water on a fire. Statues of Florian were very common in northern Italy.

The shrine stood at a crossing where the dusty road

met with another. The other road ran south along the coast, towards Genoa and Pisa. As Stephen looked at the statue and drank his water, he saw someone lumbering up the southern road. As he drew closer, it became clear he was a cleric of some kind. Stephen waved to him.

"God save you," said the cleric as he approached the crossroads. "A pilgrim, I see! Would you mind sparing some of your water for a thirsty servant of the Lord?"

"Certainly, Father," replied Stephen, rising and handing the priest his flask.

"Ah, an Englishman by the accent!" said the cleric, taking a swig of the water. "I am Father Giovanni, a priest of Pisa. I am coming to visit Turin to see my uncle, but I think I will rest here by the crossroads before I press on to the city; that is, if you don't mind the company?"

"Please, be my guest," offered Stephen. The two men flopped back down in the grass.

"So, you have gone to pray at the tombs of the apostles?" asked Fr. Giovanni.

"Indeed, and I had hoped to see the Holy Father, Pope Gregory XII. I was fortunate enough to attend one of his Masses in Santa Maria Maggiore and receive a papal blessing."

Fr. Giovanni flashed a warm but condescending smile. "That's right, you are English," he chuckled.

"What does that have to do with it?"

"Well . . . it is a touchy subject these days, but we Pisans know the real pope is Alexander V, whose court is at Pisa."

Stephen snorted. "Your council had no authority to appoint a new pope with two claimants already living. All you Pisans did was muddy the waters."

Fr. Giovanni was indignant. "Well, at least we are trying to help the situation. The claim of Gregory XII is illegitimate. The Roman line has been illegitimate for decades. Everybody knows that."

"How can the successor of Peter live anywhere but where St. Peter lived and died?" questioned Stephen.

"Yes," the priest continued, getting agitated, "but when the papacy moved to Avignon . . ."

"Did somebody say Avignon?" came a third voice.

The men looked up. Another traveler approached the crossroads from the road stretching out of the Alps. From his dress—an embroidered tunic and feathered hat—the man appeared to be a merchant of some sort. He made the sign of the cross in front of the statue of St. Florian and, smiling, said, "I heard you discussing the Holy Father at Avignon?"

"Sir, by your French accent and your words, may I assume you believe the true pope to be neither in Rome nor Pisa but in Avignon?" asked Fr. Giovanni.

"Of course," said the man, taking off his hat and wiping his brow. "But forgive me! I am Renauld of Nîmes, a merchant and banker. I am coming to Turin to check on my accounts here."

Renauld sat down in the grass beside the two men. He produced a large wine skin and a small wheel of cheese, which he broke in three. "A little midday repast, shall we?"

The priest and pilgrim thanked the merchant. The three men munched on the dry cheese and shared Renauld's flask of wine.

"But this question of the popes," continued Renauld, wiping the cheese crumbs from his beard, "'tis easily solved. The papacy was moved from Rome to Avignon well over a century ago. Everyone recognized the Avignon popes as legitimate. Benedict XIII has been on the throne at Avignon much longer than Gregory or

Alexander. Soon this will all be settled and we will all be toasting the pope in Avignon!"

"But the council has appointed Alexander!" replied Fr. Giovanni.

"That council is invalid and everybody knows it!" barked Stephen.

"That's the first time I've heard anything sensible out of an Englishman's mouth!" laughed Renauld.

Stephen did not take well to the Frenchman's condescension. "I've only just gone to confession; don't make me have to go again!" he said, raising his fist.

"I'd gladly take a blow from an English peasant in defense of the true pope!" shouted Renauld. He took his hat off and slapped Stephen with it.

"Oh dear," said Fr. Giovanni.

Stephen threw down his cheese and tackled Renauld. The two men began tussling about in the grass. Fr. Giovanni picked up a nearby stick and began whacking the two men on the back while they fought.

"Stop! Stop it!" he shouted. The men ignored the priest and continued with their brawl.

Exasperated, Fr. Giovanni looked around for help. He saw the image of St. Florian dumping a bucket of water on the fire. "Aha!" he said. He picked up the large wine skin the men had been sharing and dumped it all over their heads.

"Arghhh!" they growled, now drenched in water. The two men rolled onto their backs, panting. A moment later, they were laughing.

"You're both mad!" shouted Fr. Giovanni. "May St. Florian put out the fire of anger in your hearts!" Then, with a wry smile, he added, "And may you acknowledge Alexander V of Pisa as the true pope!"

———

In 1414, John XXIII, from the line of the Pisa popes, summoned another council at a place called Constance to solve the schism. The Roman pope Gregory XII agreed to participate as well. At Constance, two of the popes agreed to quit. But the Avignon pope, Benedict XIII, refused. The council excommunicated Benedict and he rapidly lost support. With all three popes out of the way, the Council of Constance could now elect a new successor of Peter, Pope Martin V. With the election of Martin V in 1417, the crisis was over. Martin V was universally acknowledged to be the true pope.

The period of the Great Western Schism was very damaging to the Church. Christ wills the Church to be one, as he is one with the Father (Jn 17:21). The Church could not be united when people were not sure who was in charge. And when the Church issued a decree in the name of the pope, people questioned whether it was binding or not. If the pope was not actually the real pope, did he need to be obeyed? The schism weakened the authority of the pope in the minds of many Christians.

This brings us to an interesting question: who was the real pope during all this chaos? Most historians and theologians teach that the popes at Rome were always the real popes. All the other claimants are considered antipopes, though the Church has never made an authoritative pronouncement on the question.

The Great Western Schism was a very complicated matter involving tricky legal questions. In our next chapter, we are going to turn from questions of law to matters of the spirit as we examine late medieval spirituality and mysticism.

CHAPTER 21

Late Medieval Mysticism

A Time of Interior Devotion

Have you ever heard the words *mystic* or *mystical*? What does it mean when we say a saint was a great mystic? Or that he or she had mystical experiences?

Let's start with mysticism. *Mysticism* refers to that aspect of the Christian faith which focuses on conditioning the soul to be transformed by the grace of God. It is the part of Catholic spirituality that dwells on the inner life of the soul and how God reveals himself to people interiorly. The Catholic faith has a rich tradition of mysticism.

A *mystic* is a person who devotes himself in a radical way to cultivating this interior life of grace. Some mystics are especially chosen by God to receive supernatural gifts and graces. Usually they lead lives of seclusion, praying and contemplating God's love. Sometimes they have visions or other experiences. They may write their visions down, as did St. Hildegard in Germany or St. Catherine of Siena in Italy.

In the late Middle Ages, Christians were very interested in mysticism—much more so than in previous ages. There were several reasons for this.

Europe was ravaged by the Black Death during the 1340s. This was a plague—a sickness or disease—that was highly contagious and killed millions. But by 1400, the plague had passed and life was improving. Cities were growing, living conditions were better, and people were getting paid more for their work. The average Christian was more educated and, in general, people were much more interested in working out their personal salvation. There was a great demand for devotional books, especially after the 1450s, when the invention of the printing press made it cheaper to produce books.

One of the most popular devotional books of the Middle Ages—indeed, of all time—was *The Imitation of Christ*, written by the English monk and mystic Thomas à Kempis, who died around 1471. Kempis's book is an imaginary discussion between Christ and the soul in which Jesus gives advice to the Christian on how to overcome temptations and persevere in holiness. *The Imitation of Christ* begins with advice about turning away from sin and leads the reader on into more profound subjects as the soul grows in grace. *The Imitation of Christ* was extremely well-known during the Middle Ages and is one of the best-selling books of all time. If you come from a devout Catholic family, you probably have a copy of *The Imitation of Christ* somewhere in your home.

Another well-known mystic of the Middle Ages was the German Dominican Johannes Tauler. Beginning in the 1330s, Tauler preached throughout the Rhineland in Germany. He encouraged lay people to devote great attention to their personal interior relationship with God. Tauler reminded people that holiness was not just for monks and nuns, that God dwells in the heart of every Christian, and everyone can be transformed by his grace to become saintly.

These sorts of ideas inspired many lay people to start their own groups to grow in holiness. In the Netherlands, two groups called the Beguines and Beghards emerged. The Beguines (for women) and Beghards (for men) were like little monastic communities of lay people. They lived in common and did not marry, but they did not take any vows. They split their time between doing good works among the poor and sick in the community and devoting themselves to spiritual study and contemplation. The Beguines and Beghards were very popular in the 1300s, but as time went on, they unfortunately began preaching heresy. Most Beguine and Beghard communities were disbanded or absorbed by other groups by the 1400s, but they demonstrate how Christians in the late Middle Ages were increasingly interested in mysticism and taking their personal faith more seriously.

Julian of Norwich

One part of medieval piety we do not often hear about is the lives of anchorites and anchoresses. The anchorite or anchoress was a man or woman, respectively, who lived in perpetual enclosure—that is, in a cell or room from which they never departed. Food and other items would be exchanged through a small window, but the anchorite or anchoress themselves never left their cell. Rather, they stayed there perpetually devoting themselves to prayer.

Many convents, abbeys, and even regular parish churches had anchorite cells built into them. Anchorites were well-respected in the community. People often went to them for prayer requests. A man or woman who chose to become an anchorite or anchoress had to receive permission from the local bishop and there was a liturgical rite for enclosing them. There was even a kind of rule anchorites followed regarding how they used their time, how they prayed, and so on. For example, in England there was a very popular book called the *Ancrene Riwle* ("Guide for Anchoresses"). Written in the thirteenth century, the *Ancrene Riwle* served as a kind of guidebook teaching anchoresses how to live.

One of the most famous medieval anchoresses was Julian of Norwich. Julian was an English woman who lived from 1342 to around 1416. When she was young, she had visions of Jesus and many other mystical revelations, which she wrote down in a book called *Revelations of Divine Love*. Not much is known about her life, but at some point, she may have become a nun, and later she adopted the life of an anchoress in the English city of Norwich. Nobody knows exactly what her enclosure ceremony may have looked like, but let's try to imagine:

———————

Sister Julian knelt before the crucifix in the church of Norwich. Her hands were clutched to her bosom and her mind was rapt in prayer.

"What does the Lord require of you but to do justice, and to love kindness, and to walk humbly with your God?" she prayed, quoting the prophet Micah. "Help me, O Lord, to be a pleasing sacrifice unto thee."

Someone else entered the small candlelit church and approached Julian. It was another nun, Sister Agatha. "Sister Julian, they are ready for you."

Julian made the sign of the cross and rose. She was silent, but joy welled up in her heart.

Sister Agatha led her out of the church sanctuary by a side door. She and Julian entered a long stone hallway. Nuns lined either side of the hall, holding candles that cast shadows on the dark stone walls. At the end of the hall stood the bishop of Norwich and Father Hugh, the parish priest. When Julian emerged into the hallway, the bishop shattered the silence with a booming chant that reverberated in the narrow hall. "*Libera me, Domine, de morte æterna, in die illa tremenda,*" he said. This was a prayer from the Church's Office for the Dead. It meant, "Deliver me, O Lord, from death eternal on that fearful day." This was usually sung at funerals. By praying the Office of the Dead, the rite signified that in accepting the life of an anchoress, Julian was truly dying to the world.

Led by Sister Agatha, Julian began a solemn walk down the hallway. Head bowed and hands folded in prayer, her ears were filled with the chants of the bishop and the responses of the sisters. Her heart warmed as she prayed silently, "Oh my Jesus, I am coming to thee."

Eventually she approached the bishop, standing with Father Hugh before a massive oaken door. The sisters continued to sing while he put his hand on Julian's head and prayed for the grace to serve God faithfully in the state of an anchoress. Then he turned to Father Hugh and the sisters and said, "Our beloved Sister Julian has renounced the world to embrace the cross of Christ in the life of an anchoress. Let us vow to support her with our prayers and sacrifices."

"Amen," the sisters responded.

"And you, Julian, remember us in your prayers," said the bishop, making the sign of the cross over Julian.

"Thank you, your Excellency," she replied, kissing the bishop's ring.

Father Hugh handed Julian a small book. It was a copy

of the *Ancrene Riwle*. "A small gift from myself and the sisters here. I'm honored to have such a holy woman enclosed in my church."

"May God be gracious to you," Julian said to Father Hugh. "And thank you for your support."

Two nuns pulled on the large wooden door. It creaked heavily as it opened. It revealed a small cell, plainly furnished with a cot, writing table, and kneeler which sat before a little statue of Christ in a niche in the wall. The opposing wall had a small window to the outside through which a single bright beam of light flowed into the cell. It was big enough for food and other items to be passed through. This window would be Julian's sole means of contact with the outside world.

"Embrace thy cross, Sister Julian," said Bishop Hugh.

"I will go unto Zion, to the hill of my salvation," said Julian.

With soft footsteps and eyes welling with tears of happiness, she crossed the threshold and walked into the room from which she would never depart. She lay on the ground, prostrate before the statue of Christ. The door creaked behind her, shutting loudly with a *boom!* It had the feel of a coffin lid being closed. On the other side of the door, she heard the clanking of the bolt, locking her in. The chanting of the nuns gradually faded as those on the other side of the door processed out. Finally, Julian was left alone in the solitude of the cell. She stood up and looked about her. All was still.

She set the copy of the *Ancrene Riwle* down on the table and sat down on her cot. She had never felt so happy as she gazed up at the statue of Christ.

Finally, alone with my Lord, she thought.

———

Julian spent the rest of her life in the cell, praying and writing. Her insights into the spiritual life were profound. We know about them today because her writings were copied and studied by other holy men and women. Though Julian died sometime around 1416, she would go on to become one of the most popular and beloved English mystics. Her book, *Revelations of Divine Love*, was also the earliest book ever written in the English language by a woman—at least the first that has survived.

Other Spiritual Classics

Not all mystics were monks, nuns, or anchorites. A great example is Margery Kempe, an Englishwoman like Julian. She was married to a town official in Norfolk and had children. But she felt called to a deep intimacy with Jesus. As a young woman, she began experiencing visions and other mystical graces. She wrote these down in a book that has come to be known as *The Book of Margery Kempe*. Many read it and it continued to be popular after her death, around 1438. It is considered the first autobiography in the English language.

Though her book was well-respected, Margery herself wasn't. She often went about in public weeping for the sins of the world and praying loudly for people to do penance. Her neighbors considered her a nuisance. She was called a madwoman and was locked up on several occasions.

We do not have the space to delve into all the wonderful mystical literature of the late Middle Ages—of works like St. Catherine of Siena's *Dialogues*, the *Revelations* of St. Bridget of Sweden, the books of the Dominican Henry Suso, *The Spiritual Espousals* of the Flemish mystic Jan Ruysbroeck, and many, many more.

What we must take away from this chapter is that by 1500, Christians were more literate than ever before. There were more spiritual works being printed, in addition to new editions of the Bible. Regular lay people were taking their faith much more seriously. The printing press made it easier to spread the Gospel and communicate wonderful teachings like those found in Julian's *Revelations of Divine Love* or Thomas à Kempis's *The Imitation of Christ*. This, of course, was a wonderful thing. But it was also very dangerous, as we shall see in our next chapter.

CHAPTER 22

The Outbreak of Protestantism

Heresies Abound

We've spent a lot of time examining the doctrine and practice of the Church in the Middle Ages, and in the process, we have learned many edifying things. The spirituality and intellectual curiosity of the High Middle Ages was bearing glorious fruit. By the 1450s, Christendom was in the full flower of the Renaissance as artists and scholars transformed the cultural life of Europe. In many places, the Church was in the midst of a great reform. It was an exciting time to be alive!

But we have also seen our fair share of problems. Things were not well everywhere. Priests were often less educated than they should have been, and bishops, as always, could be too wrapped up in political affairs. Simony was also still a problem; recall that simony means the buying or selling of spiritual things. The Church of the Middle Ages tried to end simony, but by the 1500s, men were still sometimes being appointed bishops and abbots not because they were good men but because they paid the most money. And too often the pope would behave more like a worldly prince than the successor of St. Peter.

Does it shock you that bad things like this could happen in the Church? It's always sad when people representing the Church of Jesus Christ act wickedly. But we must remember that though the Church is a divine institution, it is still made up of fallen persons. Though Christ promised the Church would continue to the end of time and would never teach error, men and women will always be capable of sinning or making bad decisions. Even among the twelve apostles, one of them was a traitor, and nearly all of them abandoned Jesus during his passion. It is certainly a shame when corruption creeps into the Church, but it is also inevitable from time to time. We all need grace, regardless of whether we are peasants, popes, or priests.

People of the Middle Ages were upset about the tales of corruption they were hearing. Sometimes this manifested itself in the rise of destructive heresies. We learned about heresy back in chapter 5, but it's good to review. Heresy is a teaching that is contrary to the Catholic faith. A heretic is someone who adamantly denies a certain truth of the Catholic faith.

Various heresies troubled the Church during the Middle Ages. In the twelfth and thirteenth centuries, a French sect called the Albigensians preached that the flesh was evil—that the human body was created by an evil spirit and only the soul was from God. The person was like a pure spirit imprisoned in an evil body. They had many other bizarre teachings as well. Thankfully, many of these heretics were converted by the preaching of the

Dominicans; others were destroyed in violent civil wars that rocked France in the early 1200s.

England also dealt with its own heresies. In the 1300s and 1400s, a sect called the Lollards were followers of a preacher named John Wycliffe. Wycliffe and the Lollards rejected many of the Church's traditions and taught that the Bible alone was the sole rule of faith. They also taught that the Eucharist was not truly the body and blood of Christ. Lollardy was condemned as a heresy in 1382, but Lollards would continue to roam about England for another century spreading their teachings.

In eastern Europe, similar ideas were brewing in Bohemia under the leadership of a man named Jan Hus. Hus's followers were known as Hussites. The Hussites wanted Church property taken away to force the Church to live in poverty. They also wanted a national church independent of Rome, taught peculiar doctrines about the Eucharist, and held that the Bible alone was the sole rule of faith for a Christian. Jan Hus was condemned and burned at the stake at the Council of Constance in 1415 at the behest of the Holy Roman emperor, but this only led to a generation of civil war between the Hussites within Bohemia.

Martin Luther

All these heresies had one thing in common: they rejected the authority and traditions of the Church. In 1517, heresy would again trouble Christendom, this time from a German monk named Martin Luther. Luther was an Augustinian friar who had been troubled by simony and other scandals in his diocese relating to the sale of indulgences. As we learned in chapter 14, an *indulgence* is a cancellation of penance for sins already confessed. After we go to confession, we receive a penance, which is usually a prayer or a work of charity you are supposed to pray or do. Penance helps strengthen our souls in God's grace and undo the damage caused by sin.

In the Middle Ages, penances could be severe. A sinner might be asked to fast for forty days on bread and water, go on a pilgrimage to Rome, or wear a hair shirt for a time (an uncomfortable shirt made of a rough cloth that makes you itch, a lot). However, if a sinner was given an indulgence, it meant they were allowed to exchange their severe penance for a smaller one. For example, a person whose penance was fasting for forty days might be allowed instead to simply say some prayers in their local parish. Indulgences had been a part of Christian life from the earliest days of Christianity, and Catholics still use them today. However, in Luther's diocese, indulgences were being sold and the money was being used to pay off the bribes of a corrupt bishop.

This scandal prompted Luther to write a document known as the *95 Theses*, which he posted on the door of the cathedral at Wittenberg in October of 1517. The *95 Theses* were a series of statements that called into question the Church's teachings on indulgences, purgatory, and the authority of the pope.

People were enthralled with Luther's ideas. With the aid of the newly invented printing press, he was able to spread his teachings to a large audience very quickly. He became popular, and the more popular he got, the more radical he became. Luther denied the authority of the Church's councils and taught that the Bible alone was the only authority a Christian needed—he said Christians should just read the Bible and come up with their own interpretation of it as best they could. Martin Luther also believed that people did not need to do penance for their sins. He taught faith alone—without anything else—was all one needed to be saved.

Word of Luther's teachings soon came to the attention of Pope Leo X. When Luther refused to back down, Pope Leo X excommunicated him in 1520. The pope hoped this would be the end of it.

But many princes and knights in Germany supported Luther. They hoped to use his movement to break Germany away from the Catholic Church and as an excuse to seize the Church's lands. Aided by powerful nobles, city after city throughout Germany fell under Luther's heresy. In places where his teachings took hold, Church property was seized and handed over to the government authorities. All over Germany, preachers were installed who would preach Luther's teachings, which had become known as Lutheranism.

Being as this is a book about the history of the Catholic Church, we are not going to spend too much time exploring the particulars of Luther's heresy or the history of Lutheranism. For that matter, we also won't delve too deep into the other heresies already mentioned so far or those we will address in the coming pages and chapters. What we are mainly concerned about here is setting the stage to see how the Church would respond to these troubling times.

That response came from the Holy Roman emperor Charles V, who was a devoted Catholic. He fought back against the Lutheran rebels, leading to warfare for decades in Germany between the Lutheran nobles and the forces of Charles V. By 1555, it was clear that neither Charles nor the Lutherans could prevail, so the two sides called a truce with the Peace of Augsburg. This agreement decreed that each noble could determine the religion in his realm—Lutheran nobles could make their territories Lutheran, while Catholic nobles could keep theirs Catholic.

John Calvin

Unfortunately, Luther's heresy was not the only one brewing. In France, a lawyer named John Calvin wrote a book called *Institutes of the Christian Religion*. The *Institutes* proposed a whole new understanding of Christianity that was different both from Luther and the Catholic Church. It would become popular in France and Switzerland.

Calvin's ideas were many, but we can explain some here, including his most well-known teaching of *predestination*. Calvin taught that because of sin, mankind is totally and absolutely evil. He is so evil, in fact, that he cannot even turn to God. Predestination states that God decides from all eternity who will go to heaven and who will go to hell. He chooses some to be saved and some to be damned, and this choice is not based on anything anybody does. This teaching is very different from the Catholic view, which teaches that our actions have real consequences, and that we have free will to take or not take those actions.

Calvin also taught that Jesus Christ did not die for all men, but only for the righteous. For those who are predestined to go to heaven, they have no choice in the matter. Calvin believed it was impossible for a person to lose their salvation. By contrast, the Catholic doctrine of mortal sin teaches that a person who dies unrepentant in serious sin can be damned, even if they had previously been faithful. Similarly, while Calvin thought a person destined to hell could do nothing to escape it, the Catholic Church taught sinners could repent and go to heaven.

John Calvin also had his own ideas about how the Church should be governed, arguing there should be no bishops. He wanted the Church to have no real authority above the parish level. He thought parishes should be ruled by groups of elders—called presbyters—who would select a pastor. When a parish is governed by bodies of elders, it is called *Presbyterian*.

Calvin's book and his teachings became influential throughout France and many Frenchmen went over to him. Those Frenchmen who followed Calvin's teachings were known as Huguenots. For a time, there was peace, but when the French king Henri II died unexpectedly in 1559, he was succeeded by his young and inexperienced son, Francois II. With an inexperienced boy on the throne, factions began to form behind different nobles, all of them wanting to seize as much power for themselves as possible. The Catholics tended to support the Duke of Guise, while the Huguenots supported the Duke of Bourbon.

Supporters of Guise and Bourbon began fighting each other in 1562, sparking what came to be known as the French Wars of Religion. These were confusing wars, partly political, partly religious, partly about the ambition of various men to the throne. The fighting was very nasty on both sides. Sometimes things were done that were not befitting of Christian people. That's why war is always such a dangerous thing; it is so easy to give in to anger and revenge.

For the next thirty-six years, Huguenots and Catholics would fight for control of the French throne. Queen Catherine struggled, too, with her three sons dying prematurely. For the whole duration of the war, France did not have a king that was scarcely more than a boy. Without a powerful king, the Guise and Bourbon families turned France into a battlefield for their ambitions.

King Henry VIII

England, too, was torn by the new heresies. King Henry VIII, who ruled from 1509 to 1547, was at first an opponent of Martin Luther and the other reformers who opposed the Catholic Church. He had even been granted the title "Defender of the Faith" by the pope. But by 1527, Henry's wife, Catherine of Aragon, had been unable to produce a son and heir for the king. Henry began to lose interest in Catherine and became enamored with Anne Boleyn, a noblewoman of the court.

He asked Pope Clement VII to grant him an annulment from Catherine—an *annulment* is a decree invalidating a marriage, thus allowing one to remarry. Henry was hoping to marry Anne and have a son with her. But Pope Clement VII disagreed with Henry and refused to grant him the annulment. This made Henry so angry he began to threaten the pope. Henry asked theologians all over the continent to give their opinions on the case. Some supported Henry, while others, like Bishop John Fisher, supported Queen Catherine.

Anne Boleyn was sympathetic to Martin Luther. As Henry moved closer to Anne—and as he got angrier with the Church—he considered the advantages that might come from breaking with Rome. Eventually, Henry decided that he wanted to be in control of the Church in England. He passed a law forcing every cleric and royal official to swear an oath that he was the Supreme Head of the Church in England. Once he did this, he sent Catherine away and married Anne instead. All Englishmen had to accept Anne as their queen.

This put Catholics in a dilemma. Only the pope was the head of the Church on earth. It was to St. Peter and his successors that Christ had entrusted the keys of the kingdom. Some would not swear the king's oath, including

Bishop John Fisher. He defended Queen Catherine and as a result, brought on Henry's wrath. Bishop Fisher was arrested and eventually beheaded for his opposition to the king.

Sir Thomas More was also in a tough spot. He did not want to swear the king's oath either, arguing that it went against the Catholic faith. He resigned from his office as Chancellor so he wouldn't have to swear, but King Henry had him arrested. Sir Thomas refused to say anything about his opinions. Even so, he was condemned by a lying witness and sentenced to death. Thomas More was beheaded in 1535.

As for King Henry, he was declared head of the Church of England, surrounding himself with people who supported his ideas. He replaced Catholic bishops with men loyal to him and had the Catholic Mass thrown out and replaced with a service that was much more in line with what Luther had envisioned. This new Church Henry created is called the Anglican Church. It still exists today and is still governed by the monarch of England.

With opponents like Fisher and More out of the way and no longer beholden to the pope, King Henry seized the wealth of the Church. He ordered all the monasteries and convents in the kingdom closed. Monks and nuns were turned out of their abbeys; those who refused to go were hanged, or worse. This scandalized some people, but Henry told them if he had the Church's wealth, he would never need to tax them again. Henry became fabulously rich as he took all the lands and wealth of the monasteries. Much of this money he wasted on useless wars and by giving it to his supporters. Within a few years, he was broke again.

What was it like for those monks who had to endure the closure of their monasteries? Let's visit the monks of a priory in Nottinghamshire to see:

———

The Carthusian monks of Beauvale Priory were standing about in confusion in the dew-soaked grass outside the abbey. It was barely dawn, but they had been turned out of their morning prayers by royal officials bearing a proclamation from King Henry that Beauvale was to be dissolved.

Workers had already entered the abbey and began carting out the valuables.

Brother Richard, one of the monks, approached the royal official. "Sir, has there not been some mistake? Our prior, Father Robert, has gone to London to speak with his Majesty's officials to keep the monastery open."

"Your Father Robert's been locked up for treason," grunted the official. "And I have my orders."

The sound of hammers and chisels ringing out from within the abbey broke the quiet morning silence. An old monk peered in the doorway. "Heaven help us!" he cried. "They are prying the silver right off the altar and pillaging the sacristy!"

"You must stop this at once!" Brother Richard called out. The agitated monk ran forward and grabbed the shirt of a workman carrying a gold chalice out of the abbey. The royal official took note and kicked Brother Richard from behind. The monk fell upon the dirty path.

"Lay another hand on my workmen and it'll be worse than that!" the royal official growled.

There was another smash. "Now they've smashed open the reliquaries!" cried the elderly monk by the door. "Mary help us, the bones of St. Aldhelm and the relics of St. Zita are getting scattered on the floor!"

"Shut that old man up or I will shut him up!" barked the official.

"Come, Brother William," said Brother Richard, leading the trembling old monk away. "It is best not to watch."

The monks, realizing the situation was out of their hands, wandered sadly away from Beauvale Priory towards town where they would take up lodging at the local inn and contemplate their next steps.

Meanwhile, the crew carted everything of value out of Beauvale. All the liturgical vessels, every piece of gold or silver or bronze, every reliquary—even the copper on the roof was pried off—and the furniture was dragged out to be sold. By nightfall, the abbey that had only twelve hours earlier been hosting divine services was an empty hull.

———

By 1540, King Henry had destroyed the thousand-year-old Catholic faith in England and replaced it with something entirely new. There were still Catholics in England, but they were a minority. They largely kept to themselves and celebrated their faith in private, for to deny the king was the Supreme Head of the Church would get one in serious trouble.

The irony is that Queen Anne never gave Henry the son he wanted, only a single daughter. Henry would eventually weary of Anne and have her head chopped off too. He would go through four more wives before dying in 1547.

By the second decade of the 1500s, Luther, Calvin, and those who opposed the Catholic Church had become known as *Protestants*, from the word *protest*. Though the Protestant movements were varied, they had several things in common: rejection of the authority of the pope, denial of the traditions of the Church, a belief that the Bible alone was the sole authority for a Christian, and the seizure of Church property by the state.

By 1540, Christendom was in a state of disarray. The spread of Protestantism had filled the continent of Europe with discord and violence. How did the Catholic Church respond? We shall find out in our next chapter.

CHAPTER 23

Trent and the Counter-Reformation

A Fractured Christianity

Believe it or not, the Protestants did not believe they were destroying the unity of the Church. Instead, they believed they were *reforming* it. For this reason, they are sometimes called "reformers" and the period of conflict with the Protestants is known as the "Reformation," or the Protestant Reformation.

But the Catholic Church took a profoundly different view. There is a difference between reforming something and destroying it. The plundering of Church property, the violence, and the rejection of Catholic tradition and authority did not look anything like a reform in the eyes of Catholics. Instead, it looked like revolution. And indeed, it was. The Protestant revolt marked a turning point from which Christendom would never recover. It fractured the unity of the medieval Church and created the situation we have today, where Christianity is fragmented into thousands of different sects.

In many places, the Catholic Church was caught off guard by the events of the Protestant Reformation. Few expected Henry VIII, who had once been called "Defender of the Faith" by the pope, to suddenly break with Rome, create his own Church, and dissolve the monasteries. Emperor Charles V had been unprepared for the chaos that swept over his empire because of Luther. And the French kings did not anticipate civil war to erupt in their country between Catholics and Huguenots.

The Council of Trent

But the popes knew that the challenge of Protestantism had to be answered. Throughout the first half of the sixteenth century, many popes wanted to summon an ecumenical council to address the heresies of the Protestants. We learned about ecumenical councils back in chapter 7. An ecumenical council is when bishops from the universal Church, in union with and under the pope, gather in a meeting to discuss matters of doctrine and discipline. An ecumenical council is often summoned in times when destructive heresies are confusing the Christian people.

Pope Paul III was pope from 1534 to 1549. He believed the Church needed to have an ecumenical council, so he summoned the Council of Trent in 1545. The Council of Trent had two purposes: first, to clarify Church teaching on things the Protestants attacked, such as the sacraments, how a person is saved, the relationship between the Bible and the Church's tradition, and much more; second, to reform the life and morals of the clergy so that priests, bishops, and religious could be holier and set better examples for their people.

The Council of Trent was held over many years.

Sometimes it was interrupted by wars or other problems, such as the death of a pope. But by 1563, the council was complete.

What sorts of things did the council teach? Well, it taught that Catholics get their faith from the Bible but also from the Sacred Tradition of the Church, unlike the Protestants, who said the Bible alone was a Christian's only rule of faith. The Protestants, starting with Luther, had also taught that a Christian is saved by faith alone. Trent reaffirmed the ancient Christian belief that faith, hope, and charity were necessary to go to heaven.

And there were other teachings from Trent. Luther and the other Protestants had said that indulgences, the veneration of saints, and the use of images in worship were all bad. The Council of Trent said that these things were all pious practices and encouraged their use. Trent also taught that the Body and Blood of Jesus Christ are truly present in the Eucharist, something all other Protestants denied.

Answering the second intended purpose of the council, it also reformed the life of the clergy. It commanded bishops to live in their dioceses and encouraged the reform of religious orders. It called for an end to the buying and selling of Church offices, and to make sure priests were well educated, it ordered bishops to establish schools for training priests. These schools were called *seminaries*.

As a result of the Council of Trent, the Catholic Church was indeed reformed. All over Europe, priests, monks, nuns, and lay people dedicated themselves to God with renewed piety. Artists created many works of religious art to promote the teachings of the council. This movement of spirituality and art that followed the Council of Trent is often called the *Counter-Reformation*, because through the Council of Trent, the Catholic Church attempted to counter the effects of the Protestant Reformation. Generally, the Counter-Reformation is said to have lasted from around 1534 (the beginning of the Council of Trent) to 1648, when the last of Europe's religious wars ended.

Saints and Martyrs of the Counter-Reformation

One of the things Trent called for was the founding of seminaries. The pope asked Cardinal Charles Borromeo, archbishop of Milan, to establish a model seminary in his city. He knew Charles was a saintly man and that other bishops would follow his example. Charles established the first real seminary in Milan to train and educate priests. He would also reform the religious orders of his diocese, promote beautiful music for the liturgy, and see to the religious education of children. In fact, have you ever been to Sunday school? The first Sunday school for children was established by Charles Borromeo in Milan.

All throughout his diocese, the saintly archbishop made sure his people and clergy were following the teachings of the Council of Trent. St. Charles Borromeo was eventually canonized and is the patron saint of bishops and catechists.

The Church also had many martyrs during this time in history, including the Englishmen Thomas More and Bishop Fisher, who we spoke about in the last chapter. There are too many martyrs to enumerate here, but just by way of example, we could consider the life and death of St. Fidelis of Sigmaringen. St. Fidelis was a Capuchin friar and theologian who was sent to preach among the Calvinists of Switzerland in order to return them to the Faith. St. Fidelis won many Calvinists of the region back to the Faith and administered sacraments to the Catholics he found living among the Swiss. He journeyed to many towns in eastern Switzerland, preaching and confounding the Calvinists.

The Calvinists eventually tired of him, however, and on April 24, 1622, they confronted St. Fidelis while he was returning home from preaching in a nearby village. Let's pause and take witness to St. Fidelis's last moments:

———

Fr. Fidelis stood calmly in the middle of the road. Around him in a broad circle stood twenty Calvinist soldiers from the nearby town of Grüsch, headed by their minister. The men were all armed with muskets, swords, and spears. St. Fidelis prayed silently to calm his nerves. He did not want the Calvinists to see his trembling.

"Well, if it isn't Fidelis!" said the Calvinist minister.

"The false prophet himself!" mocked one of the soldiers.

"He's the one who's been stirring up trouble and drawing people away from our church!" barked another one of the Calvinists, waving a sword angrily in the air.

"I have come to preach the Gospel of Christ and the truths of the Catholic faith," replied St. Fidelis calmly. "This should be good news for you. I mean none of you any harm."

"The Catholic Church teaches damnable error and blasphemy!" shouted the minister. "Its ministers deserve destruction." But then, stroking his beard and in a calmer demeanor, he added, "However, we'd be willing to overlook all that if you repudiate the pope and come over to our side."

"That's the only way you're walking outta here!" laughed a scruffy-haired soldier.

Something about this threat agitated Fidelis. His trembling stopped. He felt a swell of holy piety and zeal for Christ rise up in his heart. His fear was replaced by boldness. He clenched his fists.

"I've come here to confute, not embrace, your heresy," he said with a force that surprised the Calvinists and even Fidelis himself. "The Catholic religion is the faith of all ages. I fear not death."

The scruffy-headed soldier growled a furious, demonic howl. He raised his sword and whacked Fidelis across the head with the broad side of the blade. Fidelis stumbled at the blow as blood trickled from his head. He smiled and stood back up. Making a cross with his hands as if warding off an evil force, Fidelis said, "Pardon my enemies, O Lord. Blinded by passion, they know not what they do. Lord Jesus, have pity on me. Mary, mother of Jesus, assist me."

The invocation of the Blessed Virgin Mother enraged the Calvinists. The scruffy-headed soldier raised his sword and struck Fidelis again, this time with the sharp edge of the blade. The sword cleaved into the skull of the priest, knocking him to the ground. The soldiers swarmed about him like ants, piercing him all over with their swords.

"Hack off that troublesome leg," ordered the minister, "to punish him for all the many miles he walked through our countryside stealing members of our congregations for Rome."

The soldiers obliged, chopping off his left leg.

When they had had enough butchery, the crowd left, leaving the priest's mangled body lying in a bloody heap upon the road. For a moment there was no sound, save for the birds chirping playfully upon the trees and a small, gentle breeze.

The stillness was broken by a rustling sound. A woman

emerged from the bushes. Seeing the body of the priest, she made the sign of the cross. This Catholic peasant woman had been on the road when the Calvinist soldiers approached and had hidden herself in the underbrush. From there she had witnessed the entire bloody spectacle from beginning to end.

"Mother Mary!" she exclaimed, clutching the crucifix about her neck and covering her mouth with her other hand. "What barbarity!"

She knelt down to attend to Fr. Fidelis's wounds, rolling him over on his back. To her great surprise, his eyes were wide open. In his last wisp of breath, he whispered, "Christ . . . receive my spirit."

Artists of the Counter-Reformation

Besides the educational and disciplinary reforms of the Council of Trent, the council also ushered in an era of beautiful Catholic art and music. Catholic artists were inspired by the teachings of the council and wanted to infuse their creations with a spirit of piety and devotion. The Italian sculptor Gian Lorenzo Bernini, one of the greatest sculptors of all time, created the gigantic and ornate *baldachin*—the large canopy—that covers the altar of St. Peter's basilica in Rome. He also created many other marvelous sculptures, like his famous piece depicting St. Teresa of Àvila in ecstasy or David throwing his sling. His passionate sculptures are full of movement, intensity, and emotion.

Another one of the masterful Catholic artists of the Counter-Reformation was Caravaggio. Caravaggio was an Italian painter active in Naples, Sicily, and Rome. He was a master of light and shadow, which he used to produce very dramatic scenes. In his famous 1601 painting *Supper at Emmaus*, Caravaggio depicts the moment

Christ reveals himself to his followers at the dinner in Emmaus. The disciples are shocked, their arms and faces depicting exaggerated emotion. The dark shadows on the wall create a sense of theatrical drama. It is a powerful painting. Caravaggio uses theatrical lighting, exaggerated gestures, and powerful emotion in all of his works, such as the *Calling of St. Matthew*, *Judith Beheading Holofernes*, and the *Conversion of St. Paul*.

Indeed, this dramatic, emotional style was common throughout all the art of the Counter-Reformation. The 1500s and 1600s were turbulent times for Christians, full of strife, passion, and renewal. It was only natural that Catholics should translate that passion into the art they created.

Speaking of renewal, in our next chapter, we will learn about a new religious order that renewed the Church's system of education and evangelization during the Counter-Reformation.

CHAPTER 24

The Jesuits

Ignatius of Loyola

In the long history of the Catholic faith, great periods of renewal have always been accompanied by the founding of new religious orders. Brimming with zeal and a desire to save souls, these orders live out Jesus's counsels of poverty, chastity, and obedience in order to bear witness to God's saving power in each age. In this chapter, we will study the foundation and early history of one of the most important orders of the Counter-Reformation era, the Society of Jesus, better known as the Jesuits.

The story of the Jesuits begins with a Spanish soldier named Ignatius of Loyola. Born of the nobility in 1491, Ignatius dreamed of knighthood, fair ladies, and the glory of battle. He was a swaggering youth, arrogant, quick to pick a fight, and fond of fine clothes, women, and wine. At age seventeen, he entered military service as a *page*—a servant to a knight in training for knighthood—and

participated in many battles. He was praised for his brav-
ery and seemed destined to become an important military
commander for Spain.

But God had other plans for Ignatius. In 1521, when
Ignatius was thirty years old, he was defending the city
of Pamplona against a French attack. During the siege, a
stray cannonball struck Ignatius and shattered the bone
in his right leg, gravely injuring him.

Even today, shattering a leg bone is a serious injury,
but in those days, before modern medicine, a broken
bone could lead to fever, infection, and death. The doctors attempted to set the broken bone but failed to do it
correctly—at one point, a piece of bone had to be sawed

off (without any pain medication). Ignatius endured all this agony as best he could, but despite his resolution, the injury and the mangling of the doctors left him permanently crippled, with his right leg shorter than his left. Ignatius walked with a limp for the rest of his life.

But what does any of this have to do with the founding of the Jesuits? As it turns out, the wounding of Ignatius was providential. Ignatius was devastated that his injury had ruined a promising military career. During his long recovery, he was forced to come to terms with his handicap and rethink what he would do with his life. Let's stop in and visit the hospital where St. Ignatius spent much of 1521 recovering from his injury to see what happened to the once-proud warrior:

The still silence of the hospital's convalescence room was stifling. Ignatius looked absentmindedly at the ceiling, his hands folded calmly on his chest. There was no sound save for the buzzing of a fly near the window, until Ignatius's nurse, Sister Rosita, came in to check on him.

"How are you this morning, Master Ignatius?"

"Seven hundred and ninety-eight," Ignatius replied dryly.

"Excuse me, Sir?"

"Seven hundred and ninety-eight," he repeated. "The ceiling in this room has seven hundred and ninety-eight tiles on it."

"Oh goodness, you counted?" Sister Rosita asked, dabbing Ignatius's sweaty brow with a cloth.

"I did—twice—just to make sure."

"You should occupy your time more profitably, Master Ignatius."

"Believe me, I would like to. But that's difficult when

I can't get out of bed. Say . . . do you have anything I can read?"

"Certainly. I will have to see what we have available in the convent library. I will bring you some books when I come back this afternoon."

Sister Rosita glided away, leaving Ignatius alone to putter away the time with the fly and the ceiling tiles.

When she returned after None—the mid-afternoon prayers observed by all religious—she had two books for Ignatius.

"Here you are, Sir. I hope this will be more fruitful for you than counting tiles."

She set the books on the small wooden table beside his bed.

Ignatius leaned up and sorted through the books. "*De Vita Christi* by Ludolph of Saxony. *The Golden Legend* by Jacopo de Voragine. What is this stuff?" he asked. "Don't you have *Amadis of Gaul*, *Orlando Furioso*, or even something about King Arthur? Where's all the knightly romances?"

Sister Rosita rolled her eyes. "That chivalric nonsense you read is trash. If you want stories about fighting and battles, the lives of Christ and the saints are what you want. Their battles against the world, the flesh, and the devil were more epic than anything you'll read in your knight stories. And at any rate, this hospital is run by nuns, so all we have is religious reading," she added, thumping him playfully on the head with one of the books.

"Hey! Watch it!"

"Read," she snapped, thrusting the book into his hands.

"Fine, fine," he muttered, rubbing his head. "Let's see . . ." He picked up a book from the top of the pile as Sr. Rosita walked out. "So, *De Vita Christi* by Ludolph of Saxony. Well, let's see what you have to say."

Ignatius opened the cover, flipped to the first page, and began to read aloud.

"Lord Jesus Christ, son of the living God, grant that I, a poor and weak sinner, may keep the eyes of my heart fixed on your life and deeds, and imitate you to the best of my ability."

He closed the book and rubbed his eyes. "This is going to be some heavy reading." But, as it was either that or counting the ceiling tiles again, he opened the book up and continued to read.

As he read throughout that day and the following days, he became deeply impressed with the teachings of Jesus and the lives of prayer and penance lived by the saints. Gradually, a thought began to form in his head: "These saints truly were warriors, but warriors of charity and prayer. What if, instead of trying to rival worldly knights in deeds of valor, I set my mind to rivaling the greatest saints in prayer and penance? What if instead of doing battle for some earthly king, I resolve to do battle against my own sinful inclinations under the banner of Jesus Christ?"

———————

The pious thoughts these books placed in Ignatius's mind would bear fruit. After his release, he spent time living alone in a cave, took a pilgrimage to Jerusalem, and studied at the universities of Barcelona and Alcala. During this long period of prayer and study, Ignatius developed a unique approach to the spiritual life that focused intensively on examining one's own thoughts and deeds throughout the day, as well as a form of meditation that consisted in mentally imagining oneself in the scenes from the Gospels. These principles would be organized in a book Ignatius called *The Spiritual Exercises*. His book helped guide a person through a process of spiritual reflection. Its purpose was to help them identify their weaknesses, overcome them, and discern God's will for their lives.

Ignatius gathered a group of men around him who were devoted to the spiritual life and found value in *The Spiritual Exercises*. They decided to band themselves together into a company and live a common life dedicated to holiness, education, discernment, and missionary work. They called themselves the Society of Jesus, but they quickly earned the nickname of the Jesuits. Ignatius and his companions took their first vows in 1534.

Unlike most religious orders, the Jesuits did not have a rule. Rather, they placed a very high value on obedience to the commands of one's superiors. Instead of being governed by a rule, the order was governed by a kind of military structure based on the principle of obedience to those in command. This was exemplified by the special vow of obedience to the pope taken by every Jesuit. Pope Paul III approved Ignatius's plan for the Society of Jesus in 1540.

Jesuits Around the World

The Jesuits grew rapidly. Ignatius sent his new brethren to work on a variety of tasks for the building up of the Church. Some, like Francis Xavier, traveled abroad to spread the Gospel in foreign lands (we will read more about Francis Xavier in our next chapter).

Still, many Jesuits remained in Europe and became devoted to Catholic education. One of the most notable Jesuits was Peter Canisius. He traveled around Europe founding schools and lecturing at universities. He also founded printing presses to publish books defending the Catholic faith and answering the objections of the Protestants.

Some, like Peter Faber—the first priest ordained from among the Jesuits—worked tirelessly preaching the reform of the clergy. Fr. Faber traveled extensively throughout Portugal, Spain, and Germany. He was shocked by the chaos brought about by the Protestant revolution and encouraged the Catholic hierarchy to focus on bettering the life and morals of the clergy.

Other Jesuits trained to minister to Catholics who were stuck living in Protestant countries. England posed the most serious problem. After the deaths of King Henry VIII in 1547 and his sickly son Edward VI in 1553, England underwent a brief Catholic restoration under Queen Mary Tudor. Mary, the daughter of Henry VIII and Catherine of Aragon, was a devoted Catholic who restored England's union with Rome and abolished the Anglican Church created by Henry. Mary, however, was often ill and was unable to bear children. When she died in 1558, the throne passed to Elizabeth Tudor, Mary's half-sister and the daughter of Henry VIII and Anne Boleyn.

Queen Elizabeth, a zealous Protestant, had a long reign from 1558 to 1603. She revived all the old laws from the time of Henry VIII and proclaimed herself Supreme Head of the Church of England. She again broke England away from the Church of Rome, outlawed the Mass, and compelled all her subjects to worship in the Protestant Anglican Church.

The pope at the time, St. Pius V, was unhappy with how things were going in England. In the year 1570, St. Pius V excommunicated Elizabeth. He told English Catholics she was a false queen and that they did not need to obey her.

How do you think that made Elizabeth feel? If you thought it would make her more hostile to Catholics, you are right! She created all sorts of laws aimed at making it difficult to practice Catholicism in her realms. These were called the *Penal Laws*. The word *penal* means to penalize or punish. The Penal Laws punished Catholics for remaining loyal to the Church.

How did the Penal Laws affect Catholics? For one, they made it a crime to convert to Catholicism. All English subjects had to attend Anglican services or pay a fine. It was considered treason to print or share the decrees of the pope. The Penal Laws also made it a capital crime to even be a priest within the kingdom. This meant that any priest caught in England could be executed just for being a priest. All these laws were enforced in Ireland as well.

Even so, there were many Catholics who continued to practice their faith in England despite the Penal Laws. And there were many brave priests who came to England to minister to English Catholics in secret. Most of them were Englishmen themselves: Catholics who had fled England, entered the priesthood, and returned to their home country to hear confessions and say Mass secretly. As we mentioned, many of these priests were Jesuits.

These heroic priests did this at great danger to their own lives. Those who were captured—and there were many—could be executed by being hanged, drawn, and quartered. This meant they would be hanged from the neck until they were almost dead. Then, they would be taken down and have their bodies cut open and their organs removed and burned before their eyes. Finally, they would have their head chopped off and their body cut into pieces.

Obviously, this was horrific! And many priests suffered in this manner. Many of them, like St. Edmund Campion—a Jesuit priest who was put to death in England in

1581—have been declared saints. There were many other brave Jesuits who risked their lives to minister to Catholics living under Queen Elizabeth's tyranny. But for regular Catholics, practicing their faith was mostly a matter of keeping to themselves, while also evading the army of spies Queen Elizabeth had throughout the kingdom.

Ignatius himself would move to Rome in order to work on the founding of two colleges there. He labored ceaselessly to build up his schools while governing the order by a flurry of letters to Jesuit superiors all over Europe. In the summer of 1556, Ignatius fell ill with a fever and died suddenly.

St. Ignatius of Loyola was canonized in 1622. Peter Faber, Peter Canisius, Francis Xavier, and Edmund Campion have also been canonized or beatified, along with many more companions of the Society of Jesus.

We mentioned earlier that the Jesuits engaged in missionary efforts around the world. Indeed, with the discovery of the New World by Columbus in 1492 and all the new lands being opened up to European exploration, Christianity was beginning to expand beyond Europe and Asia into the newly discovered continents of North and South America, as well as the Far East. In our next chapter, we will learn about some of the missionary labors of the Catholic Church in these regions.

CHAPTER 25

Missions Abroad

The Spanish

In our last chapter, we talked about the life of St. Ignatius of Loyola and the founding of the Society of Jesus. In this lesson, we will learn about how Jesuit missionaries—as well as Franciscans and others—spread out across the globe, bringing the Gospel of Jesus Christ to the thousands who had never heard of Christianity. In this way, they answered Christ's call to "make disciples of all nations" (Mt 28:19).

The first missionaries in the New World were the Franciscan and Dominican friars who came over with the Spanish during the 1490s and in the early 1500s. The Spanish sent friars to teach the Catholic faith to the natives of Mexico, South America, and the Caribbean. They had mixed success. Some natives were eager to learn about the Catholic faith and many were baptized. The friars went about setting up missions for them. *Missions*

were communities for the natives centered around the church. Natives who lived there would learn the Catholic faith, as well as other valuable skills like woodworking or weaving.

Churches and monasteries began to spring up all over Mexico. However, some natives continued to adhere to the religious practices of their forefathers, and many remained hostile to the Spanish. This wasn't entirely without cause, as the Spanish did not exactly treat the natives gently. The Spaniards could be harsh masters who used the natives for their labor while keeping them impoverished. They also offered them no role in governing the lands that once belonged to them.

Many in the Church protested this treatment. The popes wrote multiple letters urging the colonial governments in the New World to be just and moderate in the treatment of natives, as well as commanding them to cease the practice of African slavery, which was just beginning.

There was a Dominican named Bartolomé de las Casas who saw the way the Spaniards mistreated the natives and protested against it. He urged the Spanish crown to adopt a more humane way of treating the natives and successfully got new laws passed to make life more bearable for those under Spanish rule. Later in life, Bartolomé also opposed the expansion of the African slave trade and all forms of slavery.

Other Catholic missionaries—such as St. Peter Claver—worked among the slaves themselves. St. Peter would minister to African slaves as they arrived in Spanish ports. He spent several months a year traveling from plantation to plantation to teach and baptize slaves, as well as fighting to see their conditions improved.

In South America, Jesuit missionaries traveled deep into the jungles of Brazil, Paraguay, and Uruguay to found missions among the Indians they found there. The Spanish and Portuguese authorities did not always approve of the presence of these missions. The Jesuits were ardent defenders of the Indians and often opposed colonial incursions into their territories. In future years, the Portuguese would forcibly eject the Jesuit missionaries from their territory altogether.

Religious life also flourished in the New World, especially in the Spanish colonies of Peru where the Dominicans had several religious houses. St. Martin de Porres, a Third Order Dominican of African descent, labored among the poor and sick of Lima, the colonial capital of Peru. He also ministered to slaves and was renowned as a miracle worker. When he died in 1639, the body of this humble Dominican was carried to his grave by the most high-ranking nobles and clerics of the city. St. Martin was canonized in 1962.

Another famous saint of the New World was St. Rose of Lima. Like St. Martin, she was a Third Order Dominican in the city of Lima, Peru. Though she did not live long, dying at age thirty-one, she desired nothing more than holiness and was exemplary in her life of prayer and penance. The entire city revered her as a living saint. When she died in 1617, thousands mourned her death. She was canonized in 1671, the first person born in the Americas to be canonized.

God even blessed Mexico and South America with supernatural apparitions. An *apparition* is a miraculous appearance of Jesus, the Blessed Virgin Mary, or a saint or angel. In 1531, the Blessed Virgin Mary appeared to a native man named Juan Diego at Tepeyac Hill in Mexico. This would be the famous apparition of Our Lady of Guadalupe. The fame of Our Lady of Guadalupe spread throughout Mexico and led to the conversion of thousands of natives.

A generation later, beginning in 1594, a Conceptionist nun named Mother Mariana de Jesús Torres in Quito, Ecuador, began receiving apparitions of the Blessed Mother that went on over several decades. The local bishop approved the apparitions in 1610, and ever since, Mary has been venerated in Ecuador under the title "Our Lady of Good Success."

Life in the missions of Mexico and South America was not easy for the early missionaries. In fact, it could be downright dangerous. In 1556, the Portuguese bishop Pedro Fernandes Sardinha was shipwrecked off the coast of Brazil and eaten by the natives who found him. (Yes, that's right, eaten!) Still, thousands of Catholics came to these new lands to bring the Gospel to the Indians and build up the Church in the New World. The Catholic heritage of Latin America that we still see and celebrate today owes its creation to the efforts of these heroic men and women.

The French

The French first arrived in North America in the 1520s and '30s with the voyages of Verrazzano and Cartier, around the same time St. Ignatius was forming the Jesuits. Jesuit missionaries soon arrived in the French settlements along the St. Lawrence River in what was then known as New France. Some of them, like Fr. Jacques Marquette and Fr. Claude Allouez, were also famous explorers. They not only spread the Gospel to the natives but brought back valuable information about the geography of North America and helped establish the French fur trade.

While French explorers were trying to establish new trade routes, French Jesuits were busy winning souls for Christ. Unfortunately, the Iroquois who lived along the St. Lawrence had become enemies with the French. In those days, the Iroquois were making fierce war on the French and their native allies in order to control the fur trade. They did not want to listen to the French Jesuits or learn about their God.

The Jesuits had better luck among the Hurons, another tribe living along the St. Lawrence and along the shores of the Great Lakes. Many missions were founded among the Huron and many of them converted to the Catholic faith. The Jesuit missionaries were called *Blackrobes* by the natives because of their black clerical garb.

Even so, the war with the Iroquois made it dangerous for the French to work among the Huron. Iroquois warriors were brutal enemies who frequently attacked the Huron. If they captured a Huron, they would take him back to their villages and torture him to death; Frenchman working among the Huron could face a similar fate, as the story of the Jesuit priest Fr. Jean de Brebeuf shows.

Fr. Brebeuf was a well-known missionary who had

worked for years among the Huron. He had done more than any other missionary to learn the Huron language, which was essential in teaching them about the Faith. He'd even published a Huron language catechism and written a Christmas hymn in Huron; you can still listen to it today—it is called *The Huron Carol*.

In 1649, Fr. Brebeuf was captured by the Iroquois. They put him through horrible tortures, dumping boiling water on his head, slashing him with knives, and pressing a red-hot iron into his flesh. As he lay dying, tied to a stake, they cut his heart out and ate it, then drank his blood. This was the sort of fate missionary priests risked in coming to Canada.

Another time, a group of French Jesuits under Fr. Isaac Jogues were traveling with the Huron and were attacked by the Mohawk along the St. Lawrence. The Mohawk were one of the Iroquois tribes and were fearsome, cruel warriors. Fr. Jogues and his companions were taken deep into Iroquois territory in present day New York to the Mohawk village of Ossernenon where they were tortured. The Mohawk did many horrible things to Fr. Jogues, even biting his finger off!

After they were done tormenting Fr. Jogues and his companions, the Mohawk made them slaves in their village. They killed another one of Fr. Jogues's companions, an aspiring Jesuit novice named Rene Goupil, who was killed with a single blow from a tomahawk for teaching an Iroquois boy to make the sign of the cross. The Mohawk tossed Goupil's body in the woods, but Fr. Jogues would later go out and recover it secretly, burying it lovingly in a ravine outside Ossernenon. Since Goupil was killed for teaching a boy the sign of the cross, Jogues regarded him as a martyr.

The Martyrdom of Fr. Isaac Jogues

Though Fr. Jogues would escape Ossernenon and re-turn to France, he later returned to the Mohawk lands where he was recaptured and again enslaved. This time, Fr. Jogues would follow Goupil in martyrdom. Let's take witness to his holy courage as we chronicle how his last hours unfolded:

———

Fr. Isaac huddled around a fire in the longhouse of the Mohawk family to whom he was given as a slave. These longhouses did not have proper ventilation, leaving the air smoky and smelly. Isaac shivered from the cold October air and from a fever that had taken hold of him.

An old Mohawk woman shuffled over to him. This woman, who referred to herself as his "aunt," draped a fur around his shoulders. "Take this, Ondessonk," calling him by his Indian name. "You look ill."

Fr. Isaac smiled at the woman, but his smile could not hide the sense of anxiety he felt. He looked down at the nub on his left hand where his pointer finger used to be. *It's been four years*, he thought. *Four years since my finger was bitten off when I was last captured.* The first time Fr. Isaac had been captured, he had been tormented but ul-timately managed to escape. He wasn't so sure this time. Something told him to prepare for martyrdom—that this time, there would be no leaving Ossernenon. Indeed, this time the Mohawk told him that if he left the longhouse he was assigned to, he would be killed immediately.

His Mohawk "aunt" could see the worry on his face. "Do not worry, Ondessonk. There are some warriors in this village who want you dead, but you have friends too. All we have to do is keep you inside the longhouse for a few weeks. Then the elders' raging anger will calm and you will be released."

"I hope it is as you say," replied Fr. Isaac.

The sound of footsteps could suddenly be heard approaching the longhouse. The old Mohawk woman shuffled to the entrance and pulled back the ratty old blanket that served as a door. A Mohawk warrior stood there, shrouded in a cloak.

"I'm here for Ondessonk," he said gravely.

"Ondessonk cannot come out," said the woman. "The elders have decreed that if he ventures outside, any man may kill him at will. We are protecting him."

"One of our men is sick," said the warrior. "He is dying. He is asking for the baptism of water that Ondessonk says will make him live forever in the next world."

Fr. Isaac rose to his feet. "I must go to him then."

His Mohawk "aunt" turned to him with a scowl. "Surely you know this is a trick, Ondessonk! It is a trap to lure you out in the open so they can murder you!"

"Perhaps it is," agreed Fr. Isaac. "But my enemies know me. They know that a Catholic priest may not resist the summons of a dying man."

"The only dead man will be *you* if you go out!"

"Aunt, please," pleaded Fr. Isaac. "It's my vows. I swore to God. I know not whether this be a trap or not. All I know is that I hear a dying man has asked for baptism, and I cannot do otherwise than go. It is my obligation as a Catholic priest."

Tears welled up in the old woman's eyes. "You stupid fool!" She pounded his chest with her fists before skulking away to a dark corner of the longhouse.

"Thank you for your kindness, aunt," said Fr. Isaac. Then, turning to the warrior, he said, "Take me to your friend."

The warrior led Fr. Isaac out into the open. It was the first time Fr. Isaac had been out of the longhouse in a long time. "This way," grunted the cloaked warrior. The village was silent, save for the crunching of the men's feet on the dried leaves that the fall winds had strewn about. Fr. Isaac prayed silently and with great intensity. *Lord Jesus, give me strength.*

"In there," said the warrior, pointing to a longhouse where Fr. Isaac knew many of his enemies lived.

"The dying man is inside there?" asked Fr. Isaac.

"Mhmm," grunted the warrior. He pointed to the blanket hanging across the door of the dark longhouse. "You go first," he said solemnly.

"Of course," stammered Fr. Isaac. The priest made the sign of the cross quickly before moving the blanket aside. The interior of the longhouse was dark but he could see the faint smolder of orange coals and dark figures huddled around it. Smoke stung his eyes. He timidly ducked under the blanket and began to walk into the structure.

As Fr. Isaac stepped into the longhouse, a Mohawk warrior hidden just beside the entranceway smashed a tomahawk down on his skull. The blow was swift, devastating, and brutal. Fr. Isaac collapsed immediately upon the dirty floor of the lodge, his skull smashed.

The Mohawk warrior spit upon the body of the priest. A round of fearsome hoots and war-whoops went up from the killer and the Mohawk gathered in the longhouse.

A few lodges away, Fr. Isaac's Mohawk "aunt" heard the whooping. She knew immediately what had happened and began to wail into the darkness.

"Ondessonk!" she cried. "Oh, my Ondessonk!"

———————

Today, St. Isaac Jogues, St. René Goupil, St. Jean de

Brebeuf, and many other French missionaries who gave their lives are venerated as the North American Martyrs. Their feast day is celebrated on October 19. As an interesting aside, the Mohawk warrior who killed St. Isaac Jogues later converted to Catholicism and was himself captured and put to death by a rival tribe—a fate he believed was given to him by God in retribution for his role in the death of St. Isaac.

St. Francis Xavier

Not all Jesuit missionaries came to North America. One of the greatest Jesuit missionaries was St. Francis Xavier, a friend of St. Ignatius and one of the first members of the Society of Jesus. While many Jesuits were traveling west to New France, St. Francis Xavier went east to the mission fields of Asia.

The Portuguese king John III had asked the pope to send Catholic missionaries to his territories in Asia to teach the people there about Christ. St. Ignatius sent St. Francis Xavier. In 1542, Xavier arrived in Goa, a city on the west coast of India and the capital of Portugal's Indian territories. Many of the Portuguese living there were hardened sailors—some of them were even criminals. St. Francis worked to restore Christian life among the Portuguese, as well as offer instruction to the people of southern India and Ceylon.

A few years later, he went further east to the islands of Malacca in Malaysia and spent two years preaching among the natives he met there. It was there, in 1547, where St. Francis Xavier met an exiled Japanese samurai named Anjiro who told him about the people and customs of Japan. Anjiro became the first Japanese convert to Christianity, taking the name Paul. Anjiro brought St. Francis back to Japan where he spent two years telling the

Japanese about Christianity. He had a very difficult time with the Japanese language, but managed to make a few converts. Future Jesuit missionaries would expand upon the little community begun by St. Francis.

During one of his voyages, St. Francis met a man from China who told him the Chinese were holding some Portuguese prisoners. St. Francis sailed to China to ask the Chinese emperor to release these men, but he fell ill and died from a fever while waiting to cross over to the Chinese mainland in 1552. St. Francis would be canonized in 1622 at the same time as St. Ignatius Loyola.

After St. Francis died, it became evident that his body was incorrupt; in Catholic history, a saint is said to be *incorrupt* when his or her body does not decompose after death, or decomposes at a much slower rate than normal.

His incorrupt body was eventually returned to Goa, India and buried there. The body of St. Francis is still intact to this day, retaining its hair, beard, nails, and form, despite the fact that it should have turned to bones long ago. The Christians of Goa take out St. Francis's incorrupt body every ten years and process about Goa for the veneration of the faithful.

During the 1500s and 1600s, Catholic missionaries traveled to the ends of the earth to bring the Gospel to people who had never heard of Christ or his Church. Whether we think of the Franciscan friars patiently instructing the natives of Mexico in the Faith, or the Dominicans of Lima sanctifying the New World with their prayers and penances, or the Jesuits working in far-off Japan or in the deep forests of Canada, the Faith was slowly becoming global, truly universal—more Catholic.

CHAPTER 26

Jansenism and Gallicanism

Tearing France Apart

During the Protestant Reformation, the Kingdom of France had been rent by civil war between Calvinist Huguenots and Catholics. The Huguenots were loyal to the Protestant house of Bourbon, and the Catholics to the Catholic house of Guise. After many years of fighting, it looked as if the Protestant Bourbons and their leader, Henry of Navarre, would win. But the Catholic people of Paris would never tolerate a Huguenot king. So, in 1594, Henry of Navarre converted to Catholicism, though not for the right reasons. He allegedly said, "Paris is well worth a Mass," meaning, he might as well convert if it gave him the power he sought. He was reconciled with the Church and accepted as king of France, becoming King Henry IV.

Thus, peace was restored and France was again united under a Catholic monarch—not at war but not truly united. The Huguenots maintained many fortified cities under their control, which Henry was willing to overlook. To make matters worse, a new heresy was rearing its head among the Catholic clergy. This heresy was known as Jansenism, after its founder, Cornelius Jansen.

Though Jansenism would split the French Church, Jansen himself was not French, but Dutch. He had studied theology in the Netherlands and applied to join the Jesuits but was rejected. Instead, he became a theology professor at the University of Louvain and began writing and lecturing on theology.

Though Catholic, it appears Jansen was influenced by the Calvinist theology that surrounded him in France and in the Netherlands. He wrote a massive book called the *Augustinus* which the pope at the time, Urban VIII, found scandalous and heretical. The pope accused Jansen of teaching that it was impossible for people to keep God's commandments, that Jesus did not really die for all men, and certain other things relating to God's grace that sounded very Protestant.

Jansen and his followers denied that his book *Augustinus* contained these teachings. They argued that the pope had every right to condemn errors, but he had no authority to prove that these errors were contained in a particular book.

"What good is it to say the pope can condemn heresy if I am unable to say where the heresy is found?" asked an exasperated Pope Urban. Meanwhile, the heresy of Jansenism was spreading, mostly due to a large convent of nuns in Port Royal, France whose abbot had introduced them to the heresy and began teaching it. Jansenist schools began popping up across France, and theologians and even several bishops began adopting the heresy. This alarmed Pope Urban, as well as the French king, Louis XIV.

Jansen died in 1638 but the Jansenist movement continued. It appealed to sophisticated intellectuals who thought Jansenism provided a superior form of Catholicism to the popular piety enjoyed by the commoners. It sometimes led to bizarre expressions of piety, such as the Convulsionary movement of Paris. Centered on the cemetery of St. Medard, the movement began when people started reporting strange occurrences at the site of a Jansenist deacon's grave. But these were not miracles in any sense which Catholics understood them. In fact, they were . . . well . . . let's visit Paris during the time of the Convulsionaries to get a sense of what was going on:

———

It was a busy evening on the streets of Paris. Down on one of the city's many winding side streets walked Monsieur Moreau, a visitor from Bayonne in the city on business. He was reading the city newspaper, the *Gazette*, while he walked when he heard a familiar voice call his name.

"Joseph Moreau! Is that really you, my friend?" called a well-dressed, mustachioed man standing outside a shop.

"Goodness, if it isn't my old companion, Gustave-Pierre Richambeau!" exclaimed Moreau, tucking the newspaper under his arm and waving to his friend.

"In the flesh!" replied Richambeau, bowing. "What brings you to Paris?"

"Oh, business," said Moreau, walking up to Richambeau. "I see your law practice is doing well?"

"It certainly is," responded Richambeau. His eyes fell on the paper tucked under Moreau's arm. "Ah, I see you are reading the Paris *Gazette*. It is probably full of wild stories about what's been going on here."

"Indeed, now that you mention it, I was just reading about a strange Jansenist sect called the Convulsionaries. It was a most . . . eh, *interesting* read."

"And what does the *Gazette* have to say about them?" asked Richambeau.

"That they congregate at the cemetery of St. Medard over the tomb of some heretic deacon. And there they do bizarre things like swallow stones, eat pieces of metal, and roll around on the ground shouting and babbling. Is this all true?"

"Oh, that and more, Moreau. It's a kind of madness that has overtaken the weak-minded. I myself went to St. Medard last Saturday to see one of their spectacles and it was much worse than what was written in the newspaper."

"You have my curiosity," admittted Moreau. "Please, go on."

"It was horrific! There were two women, Rachel and Felicité, who were nailed to crosses."

"Nailed to crosses! *Mon dieu!* Whatever on earth for?"

"The convulsionaries say they can undergo the most extreme torments and feel no pain. This Rachel and Felicité, these wretched creatures, had nails driven through their hands and feet and stayed fastened to the crosses for three hours!"

"How did they endure it? Did they feel pain?"

Richambeau shrugged. "Sometimes they pretended to sleep or be in a trance; other times they just jabbered nonsense, like infants in a nursery. At any rate, the nails were eventually removed and a great quantity of blood flowed from their wounds. The women then sat down to take some food. Their followers asserted that they felt no pain, but to everyone who saw them, it was easy to see that they were in the utmost agony."

"What other sort of crazy things did you see?" asked Moreau.

"What sort of crazy things *didn't* I see? Women laid on the ground and were beat in the head with clubs and stepped on—and I was told this was supposed to give them comfort! Some were poked with swords in the sides and tried to pretend it felt delightful."

"Lord, have mercy! This heresy is a mental disorder," exclaimed Moreau. "I also heard something about a fire?"

"Ah yes," Richambeau said gravely. "The spectacle concluded with a woman named Francoise who had announced that God commanded her to burn the gown off her back and that she should not be harmed."

Moreau scratched his head. "God himself commanded her to burn the clothes she was wearing? Why? And doesn't God have better things to do?"

"I don't know, Moreau. These people have lost their minds. So as I was saying, this Francoise actually set her clothes on fire, but instead of experiencing any peace or delight, she screamed out in terror and ran about the place wildly. Her attendants poured several buckets of water on her and carried her off, half-roasted and half-drowned and utterly ashamed of her exhibition."

"How long has this sort of thing been going on?"

"Almost twenty years. A few unworthy priests connected with the Jansenists are at the heart of it. It's pure insanity."

Down the street, the bells of a nearby church began to ring. "Well, I am going to try to make it to the Vespers service," said Moreau. "I shall say a prayer for you and the people of your city."

"Many thanks," replied Richambeau, shaking his hand warmly. "We need prayer. It seems like everyone is going mad."

––––––––

As you can imagine, the archbishop of Paris condemned this nonsense and instructed Catholics to stay away from the movement and the cemetery of St. Medard. Meanwhile, the pope compelled all Jansenist clergy to sign a profession of faith and to refrain from promoting their heresy. King Louis XIV closed Jansenist schools and removed Jansenists from positions of authority. The crisis seemed to be averted, but Jansenist sympathies took a long time to die out. As late as 1713, Pope Clement XI was still dealing with the Jansenist problem. That year he published a papal bull called *Unigenitus* condemning the heresy again.

Gallican Liberties

But Jansenism was not the only problem coming from France. Before the Protestant Reformation, during the long period of the Avignon papacy, the French Church had gotten used to its bishops having a lot of independence and getting away with whatever they wanted. And why not? For almost seventy years, the popes were all French, the papacy was beholden to the French king, and the Church in France prospered as a result.

This continued during the Protestant Reformation. The Church was so torn with controversy and chaos that the French bishops continued to do pretty much what they wished without the popes paying much attention. Thus, by the 1600s, French bishops had for several centuries possessed certain privileges and liberties that the bishops of other countries did not enjoy. The French bishops referred to these as their "Gallican liberties"—from *Gaul*, the old Roman word for France.

Even as Pope Urban VIII and his successors were combating Jansenism, certain French bishops objected to the pope intervening in the French Church at all. Citing their so-called Gallican liberties, they said that it was the job of the French king, not the pope, to see to the affairs of the Church in France. Among other things, they also argued that the pope could not take certain actions without the consent of the bishops and that his teachings were not infallible.

In 1682, a group of French bishops published a declaration on the so-called "Liberties of the Gallican Church." This document called for the pope's authority to be drastically reduced. The Gallican bishops repeated their earlier claims that the king, not the pope, would manage the Church's affairs in France. It also said that the pope had no right to summon French bishops to Rome without the king's approval, that the pope could not send legates into France without the king's approval, and that his papal bulls and decrees could not be published without royal approval.

Needless to say, this was a very radical document. King

Louis XIV condemned it and wrote a personal letter to the pope protesting the spread of Gallicanism within his territories. Indeed, the ideas of the Gallicanists were spreading to other countries, such as the Netherlands and Italy. Bishops jealous of the pope's power tried to assert their own version of the Gallican liberties in their own countries.

The popes and the French bishops went back and forth on the problem of Gallicanism for the better part of the 1700s, but by then, there were much bigger things afoot in Europe that drew the attention of the Church, as we shall see in our next chapter.

CHAPTER 27

The Age of Revolution

Anti-Clericalism

Gallicanism was only one manifestation of the new spirit of the age creeping over Europe in the 1700s—another was anti-clericalism. *Anti-clericalism* means opposition to religious authority or to the hierarchy of the Church. Gallicanism was a form of anti-clericalism because the Gallicans wanted the king of France rather than the pope to lead the Church in France.

Anti-clericalism or Gallicanism in various forms was adopted by some monarchs, even ones who claimed to be Catholic. Take the case of Holy Roman Emperor Joseph II. Joseph's mother, Empress Maria Theresa, had been a devout Catholic and very loyal to the Church. Joseph, however, was very much influenced by the anti-clericalism of his day. When Joseph became ruler of the Holy Roman Empire in 1780, he used his new power to weaken the Church in his dominions. He did this by putting seminaries under government supervision, depriving the Church of its tithes, making bishops swear an oath of loyalty to the crown, abolishing ecclesiastical courts, and closing over seven hundred monasteries and convents. Emperor Joseph had a special dislike of contemplative religious orders, which he viewed as useless. When he closed monasteries, he specifically targeted those orders whose members spent their days in prayer and contemplation. Orders who did some sort of "useful" work in the world—such as teaching or ministering to the sick—were allowed to remain.

In only valuing "useful" orders, Joseph demonstrated that he did not believe in the supernatural mission of the Church. All good Catholics know that prayer is one of the most useful things we can do. But Emperor Joseph—and many like him—was being influenced by a movement throughout Europe known as the Enlightenment. The *Enlightenment* was a time of scientific discovery, when many of the principles of modern science were worked out in physics, medicine, astronomy, and other areas. We discuss the Enlightenment in great detail in the eighteenth chapter of *The Story of Civilization: Volume III*, so we will not review it all here, but it is enough to know that all of the scientific discoveries of the period gave people an exaggerated confidence in the ability of science to solve mankind's problems. Increasingly, the Church of Jesus Christ and her teachings came to look outdated, old fashioned, and as an enemy to progress.

This anti-Catholic spirit was very evident in the suppression of the Jesuits. Kings and intellectuals who were anti-clerical especially hated the Jesuits for two reasons: first, the Jesuits were the ones running many of the best Catholic schools throughout Europe, so whoever wanted to control the education of Christendom needed to do away with the Jesuit schools; second, the Jesuits took a special vow of loyalty to the pope, which obviously bothered the Gallicans and anti-clericalists.

Many European rulers began forbidding the Jesuits within their dominions. The Jesuit order was outlawed in Portugal and all its dominions—including Brazil—in 1759. France followed in 1764, and in 1767, they were outlawed in the Kingdom of the Two Sicilies, Malta, Parma, and the Spanish Empire. Austria and Hungary followed suit, banning them in 1782.

Seeing the Jesuits thwarted everywhere and facing increasing pressure from the rulers of Europe prompted the pope at the time—Clement XIV—to issue a decree dissolving the Jesuit order throughout Christendom. The Society of Jesus founded by St. Ignatius Loyola was no more—for the time being.

Indeed, what was going on throughout Europe was nothing less than a growing spirit of revolution against the authority of the Catholic Church and the Christian culture she gave rise to.

The French Revolution

This revolution became political in 1789 with the outbreak of the French Revolution. We discuss the details of the French Revolution in chapter 20 of *The Story of Civilization: Volume III*, so we will not be delving into all the politics here, but we can offer a summary.

After being plagued by financial troubles for many years, King Louis XVI of France summoned a meeting in 1789 called the Estates-General. This was a gathering of all the notables of the French kingdom for the purpose of approving financial reform. However, a dispute broke out over the role of the commoners in the proceedings, and when King Louis tried to evict the commoners from the Estates-General, they formed a National Assembly and called for a constitution that would limit the king's authority and grant a much greater role to the common people in governing France.

King Louis tried to go along with the demands of the National Assembly, but things got out of hand. The National Assembly was taken over by radicals called the Jacobins who abolished the monarchy and imprisoned the king and his family. They passed laws restricting the activities of the Church and compelled all clergy to take an oath to the new government of France. Clergy who would not swear the oath were ordered to leave France. As for the king, Louis XVI was charged with treason against the French people and beheaded in January of 1793. But the killing would not stop there.

The Jacobins established something called the Committee of Public Safety, ruled by a man named Maximilien Robespierre. Its job was to protect the French republic from rebellions. In practice, this meant killing anyone suspected of supporting the French monarchy—or the Catholic Church.

From 1792 to 1794, France endured something called the Reign of Terror. During this time, Robespierre's Committee on Public Safety executed around forty thousand French people. Most were killed by the *guillotine*, a device made of a wooden frame with a sharp blade that dropped onto the victim's neck, chopping their head off.

Robespierre's victims were sometimes nobles or people who had worked for the king. Most victims were simply commoners who did not like the new republic. But Robespierre had a special hatred for the Catholic Church. In a place called the Vendee, royalist Catholics who had banded together to resist the Committee of Public Safety were ruthlessly slaughtered by troops of the republic. In other places, even priests and religious were victims of the guillotine. Nobody was safe, no matter how peaceful.

There were many martyrs during the Reign of Terror. Priests and religious who would not swear obedience to the French state could be killed. Sometimes angry mobs simply slaughtered any clerics or religious who fell into their hands. One such story involves the martyrdom of St. Salomone Leclercq:

———

Brother Salomone Leclercq was ejected from the cart along with dozens of other priests, seminarians, and religious who had been rounded up by the revolutionaries.

"Move, priest scum!" growled a guard, waving a musket in Salomone's face.

"I'm not a priest," he replied calmly. "I am a religious of the Lasallian Brothers."

"I don't care! Move!" the guard shouted, grabbing Brother Salomone by the cowl and dragging him

towards the entrance of the Hôtel des Carmes Carmelite monastery.

"Why are they taking us to a monastery?" asked a young seminarian walking next to Salomone.

"I doubt they're interested in joining," Salomone answered.

Brother Salomone and the others were hurried through the arched stone corridor that led into the monastery. Guards shouted at them, shoved them, or prodded them with the tips of swords or muskets. They eventually passed out of the corridor and into the sunny garden of the monastery. The bushes were well trimmed and the lawn was immaculately manicured.

As Salomone and the crowd moved into the garden, the Carmelite brothers came flocking out of the monastery, as well as some other clerics who had taken refuge there.

"Are they coming out to greet and receive us?" asked the seminarian hopefully.

"No," replied Brother Salomone. "They, too, are being driven. Look! They are flanked by guards even as we are."

Indeed, it was so. As the Carmelite brothers came streaming out of the monastery, revolutionary guards could be seen behind them, prodding them on with swords and guns.

"They must've arrived just before we did. They're cleaning the place out."

The brothers and other clergymen were massed together in the center of the garden, both those from the monastery and those who had arrived with Brother Salomone—about two hundred men in all. The revolutionary guards formed a circle around them.

Brother Salomone made the sign of the cross. "I commend my soul to you, O Christ," he prayed. Other men made similar acts of faith, hope, and charity, entrusting their souls to God.

For a moment, there was a tense silence. Salomone watched a butterfly flit upon a bush, oblivious to the chaos going on around it.

The silence was broken by a single musket shot from the commander of the revolutionary guards. "*Tuer!*" he shouted, which means, "Slay!"

A hail of musket fire tore into the priests and brothers. Several bodies dropped as the garden became clouded with dense gray smoke. The guards armed with swords and knives leapt forward and plunged into the crowd of defenseless men, stabbing and slashing in indiscriminate fury. The air was rent with the groans of the dying.

A guard wielding a long saber approached Brother Salomone, who was withering on the ground in pain but was not yet deceased. "Do . . . what you've come . . . to do," Salomone managed to stammer as he threw wide his arms in the form of a cross.

The guard thrust him through the gut with a single strike. Salomone cried out, clutching his belly. The guard gave him another quick thrust through the throat, silencing Brother Salomone's final cries.

————

The Reign of Terror was filled with many sad stories such as this. But soon people got sick of Robespierre and all the killing. He was arrested and sent to the guillotine, a fitting twist of fate. The Committee of Public Safety was replaced by a new government as things began to calm down and the killings slowed. Catholics were safer now that the Reign of Terror was over.

Napoleon

By this time, others had had enough of the Revolution altogether. In Paris, a mob of royalists banded together and demanded the return of the French monarchy. A young general named Napoleon Bonaparte was sent by the revolutionary government to stop the mob. Napoleon loaded his cannons full of small balls of metal and fired them into the crowd. Thousands of the little balls struck the crowd like little bullets. Many were killed and the royalists fled. Napoleon was a hero of the Revolution.

But the fight was not over. Other kingdoms were so horrified at what was going on in France that they mobilized their armies against the French republic. France found itself at war with Britain, Spain, Austria, and Holland.

Luckily, France had a promising young general in Napoleon Bonaparte. The French government sent Napoleon to lead its armies in Italy against the Austrians. Napoleon had many stunning victories and forced the Austrians to make peace with France. Napoleon was spectacularly successful in all his campaigns, but we will meet up with him again in our next chapter.

In the bloody persecutions of the French Revolution, we see how barbaric society becomes when people turn their backs on God. The hatred of the revolutionaries for the Faith—the way they killed priests and religious, desecrated churches, and tried to wipe out all traces of Christianity—was demonic in its intensity.

In our next chapter, we will learn about how the Church reacted to the changes in France and all of Europe brought about by the chaos and ideals of the French Revolution.

CHAPTER 28

After the Revolution

Napoleon and the Church

In the last chapter, we learned how the outbreak of the French Revolution unleashed a wave of anti-Christian violence that terrorized France for years. In 1799, the military successes of Napoleon Bonaparte enabled him to seize power in France and subsequently rule as a dictator for the next fifteen years.

Unlike the French revolutionaries, Napoleon wanted to make peace with the Church. He thought having the Catholic Church on his side would help solidify his reign, so he made a concordat with the Church. (Remember, a concordat is an agreement the Church enters into with the government of a nation.) The concordat between Napoleon and the Church acknowledged Catholicism as the French people's majority religion and allowed the bishops a large degree of independence in exchange for an oath of

loyalty to the state. Pope Pius VII even participated in the coronation of Napoleon as emperor in 1804.

But things eventually went sour between Pius VII and Napoleon. Though Napoleon had made peace with the Church, his ambition knew no bounds. He wanted to be a great conqueror and he cast his greedy eyes upon the Italian lands governed by the pope. In 1808, his armies invaded central Italy and seized the Papal States. Pope Pius VII was taken prisoner and held captive in the northern Italian town of Savona.

There is a lovely story about Pius VII's time in Savona and some neighborhood boys who wanted to help the Holy Father feel better in his captivity. Let's pause for a moment and see how this story unfolded:

———

Gaetano and Luigi crept behind a large bush outside the

episcopal palace of Savona. "Be careful!" Gaetano scolded his friend. "Don't crush the package."

Luigi nursed the small brown-paper package carefully. "It's fine," he said. "I won't let anything happen to it."

"This is where the French keep the Holy Father," said Gaetano.

"How are we going to get this to him?" Luigi asked. "The guards won't let us in."

Gaetano smiled. "I'm glad you asked. I've got a plan. Follow me."

The two boys scampered behind the bushes towards the rear of the palace. This was near the corner spot where the splendid Baroque era cathedral joined to the episcopal apartments, where the pope and his entourage were actually living. It was a quiet corner, shaded and obscured by some trees and tall grass.

"What are we doing back here, Gaetano? We're going to get in trouble."

Gaetano rummaged around in the weeds by the foot of the trees and produced a tall ladder. "I left this here last night," he said, propping the ladder up against wall of the episcopal apartments. "Come on!"

The two boys scrambled up the ladder and, in a moment, were dashing nimbly across the ridged tile roof of the building. Yet they had not reached the upper floor; they still had to clamber up another short wall to get to the highest point on the roof—the point from which they could see down into the gardens of the palace.

The two boys lay flat upon the roof tiles to remain hidden. Gaetano squinted, peering down into the well-manicured garden. "This is the spot," he whispered. "Papa Pio takes a walk here every morning before lunch."

"It's already half-past eleven," said Luigi. "He should be out any minute."

"Just don't crush the package! That's all you have to worry about."

The boys lay there on the roof baking in the Italian sun for fifteen minutes before they heard the commotion of the pope's entourage entering the gardens through the portico connecting the gardens to the living quarters. Pius VII himself walked out onto the gravel garden walkway first—the boys recognized him by his blazing white cassock and matching white *zucchetto*, the small white skullcap worn by the Roman pontiffs. Pius was followed by a small group of cardinals and some other clergy. They appeared to be talking casually.

"Okay, Luigi, get the package ready!" Gaetano slapped his friend on the arm.

"They are almost under us!"

"Gaetano, ah . . . how am I supposed to get this to the pope?"

Gaetano shrugged. "I guess you're going to have to throw it."

"You want me to throw this at the pope? I can't do that!"

Gaetano rolled his eyes. "You always have such a dreary way of seeing things. Oh! Here he comes! Papa Pio!" Gaetano shouted. The pope and his entourage turned toward the roof. "Now! Throw it!" hissed Gaetano.

Without a second thought, Luigi flung the bag from the rooftop. It thudded on the gravel a few feet in front of Pope Pius.

Luigi made the sign of the cross. "Thank God it did not hit him."

The pope bent down and picked up the package. With a furled brow and a curious grin, he carefully unwrapped the brown paper. A few curious cardinals peered over his shoulder as well.

When the package was finally opened, a huge smile beamed across his face. He looked up at the boys, and instead of a solemn papal blessing, he waved and blew them a kiss. The boys waved back and scampered away.

"Holy father, what are those?" asked one his cardinals.

Pius held up what looked like a massive, dark-brown brick and sniffed it with delight.

"Well, my dear cardinal, looks to me like a month's supply of chocolate."

———

While this story may not be as grand or influential as some of the others we have read, it shows that the people cared for their pope and were saddened that he was exiled from Rome. It was yet another troubling episode for the Church following the French Revolution, as Pius would be held as a prisoner until 1814, when Napoleon finally fell from power

In *The Story of Civilization: Volume III*, we spent a great deal of time discussing the French Revolution and the rise and fall of Napoleon Bonaparte, so we will not revisit all of that here. All you need to know is that Napoleon became a very ambitious man and began to invade too many foreign lands. You could say his pride got the best of him and he essentially wanted to rule the world. His army suffered losses and he once abandoned them, which caused him to lose their respect. His army and his people eventually turned on him and sent him off to live in exile.

A Liberal Movement

By 1815, with Napoleon living in exile, the Bourbon dynasty returned to the French throne. The monarchy was restored and the generation of chaos that followed the

French Revolution was finally over. It seemed that normalcy had returned to Europe.

Yet despite the passing of the French Revolution, its ideals lived on. Throughout Europe, many people sympathized with the ideas of the French Revolution, even if they were not French. The ideas of the Enlightenment were causing people to slowly lose faith in the Christian message. More people left the Church, wrongly seeing it as an enemy to progress.

The revolutions in France (and the American Revolution as well) led many people to desire democratic governments. A *democratic* government means a government where people elect others to make laws. Some began to demand their kings and queens give them written constitutions, like the American Constitution, or the one proposed by the French revolutionaries. People who wanted these things were known as *liberals*, from the word *liberty*, which was the slogan of the French and American revolutions. The half-century following the fall of Napoleon consisted of a struggle between the forces of liberalism and those of *reaction*, meaning those who disagreed with the ideals of the French Revolution and reacted to them by working to enforce the powers of traditional monarchies and the Catholic Church.

Throughout Europe, the popes of this age worked tirelessly to promote traditional Catholic morality and political theory against the rising tide of liberalism. We will learn more about this in our next chapter, but one way they hoped to accomplish this was by the restoration of the Jesuits. We learned in our previous chapter that Pope Clement XIV disbanded the Society of Jesus due to pressure from various European monarchs. But after the fall of Napoleon, the political situation had changed in Europe. Those monarchs were no longer around, and

Pope Pius VII thought the Jesuits were sorely needed if the Faith was to be rebuilt in Europe. Pius VII called for their restoration in 1814, and within a few years, the Jesuits were again active, teaching and preaching in all the countries from which they had been expelled.

Another development of the age was the restoration of the Catholic hierarchy in Britain. The Catholic hierarchy was abolished and outlawed in England at the time of the Protestant Reformation. Anglicans assumed governance of all the old churches that had formerly been Catholic, and from the time of Queen Elizabeth onward, simply being a Catholic priest within England could get one executed. In Ireland, Catholics were subject to the most monstrous persecutions, being deprived of land, title, and often life itself. But these anti-Catholic sentiments and laws were beginning to fade.

Though Catholicism for so long had been an outlawed faith and so practiced in secret, the situation for Catholics in England became more tolerable under the Stuart dynasty of the seventeenth century; there was even a brief reign of a Catholic king, James II. By the 1800s, the mood of the British government had changed. For one thing, the ruling Hanoverian dynasty was more sympathetic to Catholicism than previous monarchs had been. Furthermore, English cities were being swarmed with thousands of Irish Catholic immigrants fleeing to England to escape the famines in Ireland. And with the advent of liberalism, people didn't think religion was worth bickering about anymore. The days when Protestants and Catholics fought wars against each other seemed like ancient history. Religious persecution had no place in the modern, enlightened Kingdom of Great Britain.

In 1829, the British Parliament passed the Catholic Relief Act. This law repealed almost all of the old laws against Catholics and restored their political rights. With the passage of this law, thousands of British citizens began converting to Catholicism. In 1845, England was shocked when one of the most eminent Anglican scholars, John Henry Newman, converted to Catholicism. As an Anglican, Newman had long argued that the Church of England ought to return to many of the Catholic Church's practices. Newman converted because he became convinced that the Catholic Church was the true Church of Christ. He would go on to become a renowned Catholic writer, be elected a cardinal, and be canonized by Pope Francis I in 2019.

Seeing conditions in England becoming much more favorable for Catholics, Pope Pius IX officially reestablished the Catholic hierarchy in England in 1850 with the bull *Universalis Ecclesiae*, appointing Cardinal Nicholas Wiseman as archbishop of Canterbury. It had been almost three centuries since English Catholics had a regular episcopacy. This was a very good time to be a Catholic in England, and the restoration of the hierarchy there only brought about more conversions.

The Church abroad was thriving as well. In 1808, Pope Pius VI created the first diocese in the United States (Baltimore) and named John Carroll its archbishop. Carroll came from an eminent family of American Catholics (his cousin Charles had been a signatory of the Declaration of Independence). Though Catholicism would remain a small religion in the United States for a long time, the establishment of the Diocese of Baltimore would be followed by many others, and as the American frontier spread west, Catholic missionary priests came as well, preaching to Native American tribes and ministering to the remote Catholic homesteads that dotted the American wilderness.

Revolution was not only a European ideal; the spirit of revolution came to Latin America as well. Between 1800 and 1820, the vast Portuguese and Spanish empires that had been built up in Mexico and South America since the 1500s broke away from Spain and Portugal in a series of revolutions. The Catholic Church found itself divided in many of these conflicts. In some places, like Mexico, the lower clergy sided with the revolutionaries while the higher clergy sided with Spain. Many new liberal regimes also adopted anti-clerical policies towards the Church.

During the first half of the 1800s, the Catholic Church attempted to recover from the chaos of the French Revolution. Things seemed to be going well in Europe and throughout the world. The Church had been restored in France, and in England the Catholic hierarchy had re-emerged. The United States established its first diocese, and Catholicism continued to spread throughout the New World and into mission territories abroad. Some of this success could be traced back to the return of the Jesuits, as we already mentioned.

Meanwhile, holy popes like Pius VII, Gregory XVI, and Pius IX worked tirelessly to promote Catholic morality. This last pope, Blessed Pius IX, would become one of the most important popes in the history of the Church. We will dedicate our next chapter to the events of his pontificate.

CHAPTER 29

The Age of Pius IX

The Growing Threat of Liberalism

By the middle of the nineteenth century, it was evident that the French Revolution marked a turning point in European history. People were enamored with the liberal ideas introduced by the Revolution. Every traditional authority—whether monarchs or the Catholic Church herself—had to decide how to respond to this new change in thinking.

This uncertainty made things tense in Europe. Cardinals debated whether the Church should take a hard line against the rising tide of liberalism or be more sympathetic to it. In the papal conclave of 1846, the cardinals elected Giovanni Maria Mastai Ferretti, the bishop of Imola, who took the name Pius IX. As bishop of Imola, Ferretti was known as a friend to the liberal reforms sweeping across Europe. The cardinals who elected him thought perhaps as pope he would help reconcile the Church to the new mood of the age.

But that would soon change. In 1848, liberal revolutions broke out across Europe, including within the Papal States themselves. Pius was briefly forced to flee Rome before it was safe to return. He was shocked at the violence and anti-clericalism of the liberal uprisings and grew skeptical towards the liberal movements. He began to see liberalism and the Church as enemies, between whom no truce was possible.

Pius soon became a target of Italian liberals. During the 1850s and 1860s, a movement within the Italian peninsula sought to unify all of Italy under the House of Savoy. In order to do this, the Italian liberals needed to wrestle control of the Papal States away from Pius IX. They needed to steal the land that had been under the rule of the popes for over a thousand years.

Pius IX was not going to allow this to happen without a fight. He formed an international force of Catholic volunteers called the Zouaves to defend the Papal States. The Zouaves came from all over the Catholic world to fight for Pius IX. The papal army was passionate, but they were still small. This forced Pius to turn to Napoleon—not Napoleon Bonaparte, who was long dead, but his nephew, Napoleon Bonaparte III, who had become first president and then emperor of the French in 1852. We will not go into the story of Emperor Napoleon III's reign here, but you can read about it in *The Story of Civilization Volume III*. At any rate, Napoleon kept French troops stationed in the Papal States to help Pius IX and the Zouaves fight off the Italian army.

The Battle of Mentana

The French and Zouaves fought many battles against the Italians. One of their most notable victories was at the 1867 Battle of Mentana, a conflict at the central Italian village of Mentana which was being held by the Italian army. Let's dive into a scene from this battle to see what it was like:

———————

The Zouaves' scouts took cover among the rocks and hills outside the slopes leading to Mentana. The dirt road led straight into the heart of the medieval city, but the Italian forces of Giuseppe Garibaldi were lined up in the trees on either side guarding the way. A hail of gunfire from the Italians had forced the Zouaves to find cover from the stinging bullets.

"Blimey, we're pressed down something fierce!" yelled Seamus Reilly as bullets flew past his head. Seamus was an Irishman who had seen more than a few battles with the Zouaves.

"Saints alive, keep your head down you crazy Irishman!" cried Heinrich Zimmer, a German Bavarian who had only recently arrived in the Papal States to fight for Pius IX. Heinrich ducked behind a rock as bullets continued to strike all around them.

A third man came running up—Joe Parker—an American cowboy who'd lived a life of adventures in the Wild West before coming to Europe to fight as a mercenary. He fired a few rounds from his pistol at Garibaldi's men in the trees before diving into the grass beside Heinrich and Seamus.

"Hang tight, boys," he said. "Ol' Captain Gonny is bringing up the company now. We're gonna give these fellas a run for their money!"

"Captain Gonny" was the French Captain le Gonidec, commanding officer of one of the four companies of Zouaves approaching Mentana. Indeed, as Joe Parker had promised, Captain le Gonidec led several hundred Zouaves barreling into the skirmish, eager to drive the Garibaldian forces from the woods.

"Attack!" Captain le Gonidec cried. "Clear the trees and open the way to the town!"

The company of Zouaves shouted *"Pro Petri Sede!"*— "For the Chair of Peter!"—and darted up the embankment before the woods in a jagged line, firing in rapid bursts towards the Italians. The Italian line began to waver at the assault as several men were struck and many began running off towards the town.

"It's still not enough," lamented Seamus. "We need a little more force."

"There's yer force!" yelled Joe Parker, pointing.

The scouts looked back. Another company of Zouaves was approaching, several hundred men strong.

"They're led by Colonel de Charette himself!" Joe

exclaimed. Colonel de Charette was one of the commanders of the entire campaign, a fearless warrior devoted to the pope's cause.

"Men, fix bayonets!" he called.

The Zouaves quickly affixed the long, pointed knives to the ends of their rifles, designed to inspire terror in the enemy. The Italians began to waver. They could see that the Zouaves were preparing to storm the tree line.

"Charge!" yelled Colonel de Charette, waving his sword.

Hundreds of Zouaves charged the hillside, bayonets gleaming. Heinrich, Seamus, and Joe also leapt from their hiding places and charged with their fellow soldiers.

The Italians were in no mood to fight off two hundred sharp blades coming at them. The men who remained broke ranks and fled, running for the safety of the city. Colonel de Charette's bayonet charge opened the way for the Zouaves to march straight up to Mentana and take the city.

Prisoners of the Vatican

The French and the Papal Zouaves stopped the Kingdom of Italy's advance, at least temporarily. In 1870, France got into a war with Prussia, and Napoleon III called the French troops home. With Rome unprotected and Pius left defenseless, Italy's army attacked, allowing the Italian king, Victor Emmanuel II, to take control of the Papal States.

When the Italian troops attacked Rome in 1870, Pope Pius IX ordered the commander of the papal forces defending the city to fire a few shots at the Italians before ultimately surrendering. Pius knew he could not win a battle against Emmanuel's forces, making the shots were more symbolic in nature. He didn't want the people to think he was inviting the Italian forces in; he wanted it known that he did not agree with the occupation of Rome. The shots were signals of his opposition.

It might seem strange that the Kingdom of Italy would attack the Papal States, but Italy was very anti-Catholic at this time. King Victor Emmanuel's government shut down monasteries and convents and the Jesuits were expelled from the kingdom. Many Church lands were confiscated, laws were passed making it difficult to send children to religious schools, and Victor Emmanuel pressured Pius to renounce his claims to the Papal States.

Pope Pius IX thought the Kingdom of Italy was behaving wickedly and refused this demand. In fact, he refused to even leave Vatican City and set foot in the Italian kingdom. He feared that if he entered the kingdom, people would see that as a measure of his support for the policies of King Victor Emmanuel. Pius did not want to give any reason for people to suspect this. He didn't leave the Vatican for the rest of his life, and future popes did the same. For almost sixty years, no pope left the Vatican. The popes of this time were known as "prisoners of the Vatican" because of their refusal to set foot on Italian soil. Thus, the tiny Vatican City, an area of only 109 acres, became all that was left of the thousand-year-old kingdom once known as the Papal States.

The Legacy of Pius
The Church was also under attack elsewhere. In the new German Empire, the powerful German chancellor Otto von Bismarck also attempted to weaken the influence of the Catholic Church. The German government tried to decide who could and could not become a priest, and many other anti-Catholic laws were passed. Pope Pius IX

and the German bishops heroically resisted these laws, and eventually Bismarck backed down.

France, meanwhile, had lost its war with Prussia and Napoleon III was forced out of power. The French proclaimed another republic, which passed more anti-Catholic laws. Everywhere liberalism progressed, the Church found herself under attack.

One way Pope Pius IX sought to defend the Church was by summoning the First Vatican Council in 1870. At the First Vatican Council, the Church taught that the pope is infallible when he teaches officially on matters of faith and morals. *Infallible* means not capable of being wrong. This teaching is known as the doctrine of papal infallibility. It is based on Christ's promise to St. Peter in the Gospel of Matthew where Jesus says, "You are Peter, and upon this rock I will build my Church. And the gates of hell shall not prevail against it" (Mt 16:18). It means that when the pope officially teaches something about the faith or about the morals of the Church, his teaching is certainly true. The Catholic Church had always believed this. But with all the attacks on the Church's authority, Pius IX thought it was the right time to declare this to the world.

Another marvelous thing Pope Pius IX accomplished was the definition of the dogma of the Immaculate Conception. This refers to the Catholic belief that the Blessed Virgin Mary was conceived without any stain of original sin. Catholics had believed this for a very long time. In fact, way back in the first centuries of the Church, it was common to refer to Mary as *Panagia*, the "All Holy," or the "Sinless Virgin Mary," or many other such names. In 1854, Pius published a papal bull declaring as a truth of the Faith that Mary was in fact conceived without any

original sin—by a special grace of God—and that this should be believed by all Catholics.

Pope Pius IX died in 1878 as one of the longest reigning popes in history. He was later beatified and today is known as Blessed Pius IX. This holy man fought a long fight against forces that he believed were working to destroy the Catholic Church and erode the Catholic faith. In our next chapter, we will learn more about the tumultuous battles the Church and the popes fought against the evils of the modern world.

CHAPTER 30

A New Century With New Challenges

The Rise of Communism

During the long pontificate of Pius IX, the popes and the Church abroad had fought tirelessly against a rising anti-Catholic sentiment throughout Europe. With the loss of the Papal States, the passing of anti-Catholic laws in France, Germany, and elsewhere, and the threat posed by the popularity of anti-clerical and liberal ideas, the Church was under attack everywhere. In this chapter, we will see how these troubles only intensified moving into the twentieth century. But we will also see how valiant Catholic men and women rose to the occasion to defend the Church and proclaim Christ's Gospel in a new age.

Blessed Pius IX was succeeded by Pope Leo XIII, also a good and holy man. Leo cared very much about the plight of the working poor in the cities. As the world became more modern, less people were farming and more were working in city factories. Leo grew concerned about these people, as conditions in the factories and the cities could be very poor. In many places, common people no longer owned land or property. They were crammed together in crowded slums working dangerous and dreary jobs in factories or mines, and for very little pay. Poverty was rampant, as was drunkenness and all the other vices that come with poverty.

These conditions were prompting the growth of a movement called *Communism*. The Communists were radicals who believed the rich and poor would always be locked in an endless struggle. The solution to poverty, according to them, was for the poor workers of the world to unite and overthrow the rich. All private property, whether of individuals or of the Church, should be taken away. Instead of working for themselves, people would work for each other and the goods of the wealthy would be taken away and given to the poor. There would be no more rich or poor. Mankind would be one single community, which is why it was called Communism. The word *communism* means owning things in common.

While striving to help the lower class is a noble goal, many of the tenets of Communism were misguided or even corrupt. Forcibly taking money from one group of people (who may have earned their money through hard work and sacrifice) and giving it to another is essentially stealing. Furthermore, the Communists wanted to build their society through violent revolution. They were not opposed to killing their opponents to get their way. The Communists were thus enemies of nobles, kings, and queens—and especially of the Church and of religion in general. In fact, Communists were atheists. An *atheist* is someone who does not believe God exists. Communists believed God was an invention to scare people into obedience. They thought religion was like a drug that made people forget their current troubles by focusing on eternal life. In their future society, they imagined there would be no more religion.

All throughout Europe and even in the United States, people were embracing Communism. There were not many at first, but the Communists were well organized. They met in homes and taverns and plotted the destruction of the Church and society.

Communists wanted to solve the problem of poverty, but it is one of those ideas where the solution is worse than the problem. Communism is a very anti-Christian idea. God wants us to be charitable to the poor, but he also does not want us to steal things from others. God also wants us to come together as one human family—but one human family centered on Jesus Christ, not on the empty possession of worldly goods. The popes at the time immediately condemned Communism, and the Church still today speaks out against it.

But Pope Leo XIII also realized that Communism was attractive to people because it claimed to offer a solution to the problem of poverty. If Christians would step up and address the inequality in the world, poverty could be alleviated and people would not be lured away by the lies of Communism.

In 1891, Pope Leo published an encyclical called *Rerum Novarum*; its English title was *On the Condition of the Working Classes*. *Rerum Novarum* was a groundbreaking document. It was the first time a pope had asked the Church to consider social problems like poverty, ownership of property, and workers' rights in such detail. In this encyclical, Pope Leo encouraged employers to treat their employees with justice. He also encouraged workers to turn to Christ and the Church for their inspiration and to avoid the evils of Communism. And he said that workers should band together into workers unions to protect themselves from being taken advantage of by greedy bosses.

Across the world, Catholics enthusiastically responded to Pope Leo's message. Catholic worker organizations were formed in many cities and articles were published in newspapers to address social problems. Socially-minded Catholics everywhere attempted to put Pope Leo's vision into practice.

Modernism

In our last chapter, we talked about certain liberal political leaders—such as Garibaldi or Bismarck—who wanted to attack the Church in hopes of changing the way society was structured. It was bad enough that political leaders were attacking the Church, but what's worse was that many even *within* the Church herself became obsessed with the idea of change. There were priests and theologians who began applying the idea of change to Catholicism.

"Everything changes," they said. "This is true of the Church's teaching as well. Even God can develop! The Church needs to become more modern!"

These people began to teach all sorts of wild things. They said Christians should stop believing in miracles and that Jesus never rose from the dead. They also said the Bible was not true and many other damaging things. But at the heart of their teaching was the idea that God himself can change. They believed that what was true in ages past was no longer true today. Modern man had developed, and so must God. These ideas were being taught in Catholic seminaries and published by certain Catholic authors, especially in France and in Germany.

The next pope, St. Pius X, who was pope from 1903 to 1914, called these people "Modernists" and said they were teaching heresy. Pope St. Pius X published an encyclical called *Pascendi* in which he identified the main problems with Modernism. The heart of Modernism, according to Pius X, was the idea that religion is ultimately a feeling. It is not based on any objective truth about God but rather how a person *feels* about the idea of God. For the Modernist, religious practice—such as worship, prayer, festivals, and so on—are just ways that cultures express their religious feelings.

But because society changes over time, how people express themselves will change as well. This is why the Modernists thought religion could always be changing, always be evolving into something different—because it was not ultimately about what was true or good but rather about what people feel, which can always change.

This was a very destructive teaching. The Catholic faith was founded upon the fact of the resurrection of Jesus Christ. The things Catholics profess in the Creed every Sunday are not feelings but things we believe to be absolutely true. If Modernism were accepted, it would mean that no truth of Christianity could be certain anymore. This is why Pope Pius called it the "synthesis of all heresies"—this meant that Modernism contained every heresy in some way because it called into question every teaching.

Pope St. Pius X took strong action against the Modernists. He forbid them from teaching in seminaries and religious schools, he discouraged Catholic publishers from publishing their writings, he refused to promote them to important Church offices, and he made all new priests swear an oath against Modernism.

Signs of Hope

It might sound like this was only a troubling time for the Church, but there were signs of hope too. In Britain, since 1850 the Church had been undergoing a kind of Renaissance. Converts were flowing into the Church and there was a vibrant literary Catholic movement within Great Britain dedicated to expounding and defending the Catholic faith. Two of the most famous Catholic literary figures of this movement were G. K. Chesterton and Hilaire Belloc. Belloc was born Catholic, while Chesterton was a convert to the Faith. The two men became friends and wrote many excellent books and articles arguing that a return to Catholicism was the only way to remedy the evils of the modern world. They also vigorously supported the teaching of Pope Leo XIII and founded newspapers and organizations dedicated to promoting the Church's social teaching. Many of these and other works by Chesterton and Belloc are still read today.

Pope Pius X also published an important decree calling for a restoration of sacred music. He reminded Catholics that music used in worship should be especially suited for the Catholic Mass, meaning it should be reverent and use traditional chants. This led to many wonderful and sacred songs being composed or arranged during the time of St. Pius X.

St. Pius X also lowered the age for First Communion. Prior to his pontificate, it was common for children to not receive First Communion until they were eleven or twelve. But Pope St. Pius knew how important Holy Communion is for growing in grace and believed children needed all the graces they could get. In 1910, he published a decree allowing children to receive First Communion as young as seven years old. If you made your First Communion when you were seven, you can thank the saintly Pope St. Pius X.

In the United States, too, the Church was thriving. Throughout the latter part of the nineteenth century, the growing Church in the United States gathered together in several synods in Baltimore, Maryland to address issues facing American Catholics. The most important of these was the Third Council of Baltimore, held in 1884. This was the largest synod ever held in the United States up to that time. The council made reforms concerning the education of youth, clerical discipline, and many other subjects. But it is probably most remembered for publishing a little catechism that young American Catholics still use today. Have you ever seen *The Baltimore Catechism*? This nifty little book on the essentials of the Catholic faith was the product of the Third Council of Baltimore. It has been a foundation of religious education among American youth for well over one hundred years.

The Little Flower
We should also mention one of the greatest Catholic saints who lived during this age. Many of you may have heard of St. Thérèse of Lisieux, known as "the Little Flower." St. Thérèse was a French Carmelite who entered the convent at a young age. She came from a very holy family: her parents have both been canonized, several sisters were nuns, and one of them—Leonie—is being considered for sainthood.

St. Thérèse wanted to enter the convent at the age of fifteen. Normally, girls this young were forbidden from taking vows, but St. Thérèse wanted so ardently to become a Carmelite that her family took her to Rome during the Jubilee year of 1887, when Pope Leo was celebrating the fiftieth anniversary of his ordination to the priesthood. They hoped that perhaps she could have the opportunity of getting the pope's permission to enter the convent early. The story of her meeting with the pope is very touching and reveals the depth of her love for God and her Carmelite vocation:

————————

Young Thérèse was excited but nervous about her audience with Pope Leo XIII. Thérèse and her sister Celine stood expectantly outside the pope's chambers, waiting for their summons to enter. A French priest named Fr. Reverony who had accompanied them turned to Thérèse and said sternly, "Now listen, girl, you mustn't speak in the pope's presence!"

"But Father, we are here to ask permission for me to enter Carmel. How can we present my petition if I cannot speak?"

"No talking! We don't want to annoy the Holy Father and prolong the audience unnecessarily. Forget asking him about your petition. Let the superiors at Carmel decide that for you. You just hush up. Do you understand?"

Thérèse looked up at her father with tears welling in her eyes. "Papa?" she whimpered.

"We understand," said her father, a note of disappointment in his voice. "Thérèse, listen to Fr. Reverony! Keep silence!"

Thérèse nodded.

A moment later, an attendant opened the door. "The Holy Father will see you now."

Thérèse and her family, along with Fr. Reverony, entered the papal audience chamber. Leo XIII was seated on an ornate wooden chair on an elevated dais. He was a thin man with a worn but kind face, and two tufts of

fluffy white hair protruding from the sides of his head. He was clothed in a white cassock and the white biretta.

Celine nudged her sister. "Speak," she whispered, with a sly grin on her face. "It's your only chance."

Thérèse lifted her head and looked directly into Leo's dark, thoughtful eyes. At the sight of the pope, Thérèse burst into tears. She flung herself at the Holy Father's feet and grasped the hem of his cassock.

"Most Holy Father, I have a great favor to ask of you!" she blurted between sobs. "Holy Father, in honor of your jubilee, permit me to enter Carmel at age fifteen!"

She looked up at the pope's kindly face, tears still streaming down her cheeks.

Fr. Reverony glared at her. "I . . . apologize for this outburst Holy Father. This girl wants to enter Carmel at age fifteen. The Carmelite superiors are already aware of her request and are considering it."

"Well, my child," said Pope Leo, "you must do what the superiors tell you then."

Thérèse leaned forward and grasped the old pope by the knees. Fr. Reverony gasped. Her father put his face in his hands. "Oh, Holy Father!" she cried, "If you say yes, everybody will agree!"

Pope Leo smiled. He took Thérèse's hands in his own, and gazing at her with fatherly love, said slowly, "Go. Go. You will enter—if God wills it!"

Thérèse cried and buried her head in the pope's lap. He touched her head gently, blessing her.

"Thank you, Holy Father," Fr. Reverony said awkwardly, motioning for the group to withdraw.

Thérèse's father and sister kissed the pope's ring and tried to lift Thérèse, but she continued to cry at his feet. Leo nodded to his Swiss Guards. Two of them walked up, and each taking hold of Thérèse under the armpit, lifted her and carried her to the door. While being carried through the air, she continued to keep her arms folded in supplication and cry out to the pope.

After the party was ushered out of the door, Pope Leo's attendant scoffed. "A girl with such uncontrollable emotions will never make a good Carmelite."

Pope Leo turned to the attendant. "And how did St. Mary Magdalene behave when she wept at the feet of the Lord? No different than this girl. And what did our Lord say to her? 'Her sins are forgiven, because she loved much.' Clearly this young girl loves much. Indeed, she may one day be a great saint. Who are we to say otherwise?"

The attendant's head dropped. "I'm sorry, Holy Father."

"I forgive you, you knucklehead," Leo said playfully. "Now go show in the next group of pilgrims."

The attendant bowed and hastened to do as the pope requested. Leo was left momentarily alone. He thought of Thérèse's tearful face and smiled. "God grant her the desires of her heart," he whispered, crossing himself.

———

St. Thérèse did indeed enter the convent soon after this story occurred. However, her life there would not be very long. St. Thérèse suffered from a disease called tuberculosis that slowly killed her. Because she was restricted in what she could do, she developed a path to holiness that has become known as the "Little Way." Here is how St. Thérèse explained the Little Way: "Love proves itself by deeds, so how am I to show my love? Great deeds are forbidden me. The only way I can prove my love is by scattering flowers and these flowers are every little sacrifice, every glance and word, and the doing of the least actions for love."

In other words, instead of doing extraordinary things for God, St. Thérèse would do ordinary things with extraordinary love. Simple things like washing the dishes, putting up with the annoying habits of others, or sweeping the hallway could be done with intense love and devotion and become paths to holiness.

St. Thérèse died from her illness in 1897 at the young age of twenty-four. But her writings were preserved and published, and many Catholics benefited from her Little Way. The Little Way offered a plan for ordinary Catholics to strive for holiness. Those who went through their daily routine of laundry and chores, or went off every day to boring jobs, or lived an otherwise "normal" life could all use the Little Way to find meaning and holiness in their everyday activities. This was very valuable indeed.

In many respects, the Little Way was not new; it was simply a restatement of what Jesus Christ had taught about being sincere in our actions, doing things for love of God, and referring all things to Christ. But in the modern world—with all its conveniences and new technologies and things to distract us—St. Thérèse thought the Little Way was especially suited to the time she lived in. And the Church agreed with her. She was canonized in 1925 and proclaimed a Doctor of the Church in 1997. Today she is one of the most popular saints in the Catholic Church and millions practice her Little Way.

It may seem like these last two chapters have focused excessively on things said and done by the popes. This may be true, but then again, the deeds of the popes of this age were very relevant to what was going on in the Catholic Church as a whole. Holy popes like Blessed Pius IX, Leo XIII, and St. Pius X knew the Church was being threatened by enemies without and heresies within. They fought back against the spirit of the times valiantly, standing up for the oppressed, defending the rights of the Church, and calling all men to turn to Christ. Unfortunately, the world would increasingly ignore the teaching of the popes, as we shall soon see.

CHAPTER 31

Under Fascism and Communism

The Great War

In the summer of 1914, while Pope Pius X lay dying, the countries of Europe were preparing to slaughter each other in the bloodbath that would be known as the Great War. The causes of the Great War—later known as World War I—are complex and way beyond the subject matter of this book. We recommend *The Story of Civilization: Volume III* (chapter 27) to learn more about the history of this horrific war. Essentially, the war pitted the German Empire, Austro-Hungarian Empire, and Ottoman Empire against France, Britain, Italy, Russia, and the United States.

The Great War raged from 1914 to 1918. When it was all done, Germany and her allies lay defeated and about sixteen million people had been killed. It was the most destructive war in human history up to that time. When Pope Pius X heard about the war, he was horrified.

Already sick, he fell into deep anxiety and died the very day the German armies marched into Belgium.

And yet, in the midst of all the chaos and death of the Great War, God showed his care for the Church and the suffering people of Europe. He did this by sending the Blessed Virgin Mary with a message.

Our Lady of Fatima

On a spring day in 1917, the Virgin Mary came and visited three humble shepherd children in the quiet foothills of Portugal, in a small village called Fatima. Their names were Lucia, who was the oldest, and her cousins, Francisco and Jacinta, who were brother and sister. Over a period of six months, Mary came to the children in the pastures where they tended their sheep and told them how upset God was over mankind's sins. She asked them to pray constantly, especially the Rosary, and said they should make reparations for sinners. She asked that they spread a message of prayer and penance.

Over the course of her visits, Mary warned the children that if humanity did not stop offending God with

all their sins, an even worse war would rip the globe apart and Russia would spread errors throughout the world. She also warned that the Church would be persecuted and the pope would have much to suffer. To prevent these things, she said God wanted the world to be consecrated to her Immaculate Heart. To *consecrate* something means to make it sacred by setting it apart for a specific religious cause; in this case, the world would be entrusted to Mary's heart so that she could lead it back to her Son's heart.

Many in the village and the surrounding areas did not believe the children. But Mary had promised a miracle to make sure everyone knew Lucia and her two cousins were telling the truth. On October 13, 1917, with almost 100,000 people packed into the pasture, something truly remarkable took place:

———————

Ten-year-old Maria and her eight-year-old brother João were milling about the Cova da Iria, the broad pasture where thousands awaited the miracle promised by the children. But nothing felt miraculous at the present moment. The sky was full of dark storm clouds and torrents of rain poured upon the crowd, turning the pasture into a muddy mess. Many were hiding under umbrellas.

Maria and João were from a poor shepherd family in Fatima. They had only ragged coats and had not brought umbrellas.

"Let's go home," João said with purple, trembling lips. "Mom told us not to stay out too long. Nothing's going to happen anyway."

Maria wiped strands of soaked hair from her face. Her old, worn shoes were not keeping out the muddy puddle forming at their feet. She actually *did* want to go, but something made her feel like they should stay.

"I know, João, but . . . let's just stay a few more minutes."

The three children—Lucia, Francisco, and Jacinta—were praying near the trees at the edge of the forest. The rain continued to beat down, and by noon the pasture was flooded.

"We're standing in three inches of water!" João complained.

"Maybe it will clear up," said Maria. "Look, now the clouds are parting a bit. The sun is starting to come out."

Indeed, the muddy pasture was suddenly illumined by rays of the sun beaming down through a break in the clouds. But then something seemed . . . strange—the sun did not appear to be stationary. Instead, it seemed to roll back and forth, rocking in place.

Maria blinked. She knew staring at the sun could cause one's eyes to play tricks on them, but when she heard all the others in the crowd gasping and pointing, she knew she was not seeing things.

"Maria! The sun is moving!" cried João.

Moving was not all. It was changing colors: first blue, then yellow, then many colors all at once. And it did not hurt to look at it—in fact, it was easy. The staring crowds gasped and cried out. Many fell to the ground or knelt in prayer. The vibrant colors of the sun shone all upon the Cova da Iria, rich blues and yellows and greens lit up the earth. It reminded Maria of being inside a church and seeing the colored light passing through the stained-glass windows.

As if the moment could get any more astonishing, the sun then appeared to fold in on itself, as if turning itself inside out. It began to plummet towards the earth, growing larger as it dropped towards the Cova da Iria! The crowds screamed. People flung themselves on the ground and confessed their sins.

"This is it!" cried an old woman, clutching Maria's jacket. "It is the end of the world!"

"Jesus, have mercy!" Maria called out.

She and João laid face down upon the earth. The children could feel the heat of the sun as it approached. Their backs were warm, then even hot. João peeked his eyes up. The sun seemed to consume the entire sky; its rays seemed to be dancing on his very shoulder.

Then, suddenly, it was over. The children looked up. All was calm. The sun was back in its place. People were still lying on the ground; hundreds more were kneeling in prayer. Maria and João stood up, shaking. The sky was a rich, deep blue, with not a cloud in sight. A strong wind blew, and the trees rustled near where the children were standing. Lucia was calling out: "Pray! Pray the Rosary every day for sinners!"

Maria looked at the ground. The dirt beneath her feet was dry and crumbly, with no sign of dampness. She realized her feet were dry. "My hair!" she cried, running her hand through it. "It's dry!"

"I'm completely dry too!" João exclaimed.

And it was not just them. Thousands of others were completely dry as well. There was no sign there had been a rain storm.

————

This astounding event is known as the Miracle of the Sun. It was witnessed by almost 100,000 people, including many atheists who would go on to write about what they saw in papers that spread all throughout the world.

Though it took many years, the Church would eventually approve the apparitions at Fatima. This meant they were worthy of belief, something Holy Mother Church does not declare about all apparitions. Still, the story of

Fatima is an example of *private revelation*. While public revelation is the Word of God found in Scripture and must be believed by all Christians, private revelation is defined as divine messages delivered privately to an individual or group of individuals. If the Church deems them worthy of belief, Catholics are permitted to believe in them and practice the messages and spirituality associated with them, but they are not *required* to. In other words, you can refuse to believe that Our Lady of Fatima visited the three shepherd children and still be Catholic, but you can't be Catholic if you don't believe Jesus is the Son of God (an example of public revelation).

Today, nearly all Catholics believe in the story of Fatima and millions of people incorporate the message and spirituality into their daily life. It is arguably the most impactful Marian apparition in the history of the Church, though Our Lady of Guadalupe may have something to say about that!

Fascism, Communism, and the Church

One of the many things Mary said at Fatima was that if people did not learn from the destruction of World War I and repent of their sins, an even worse destruction would come upon the world. Sadly, people did not heed the warnings of Fatima, as we shall see.

After the end of the war, Italy was in turmoil. Communists were trying to take power, but another movement, called the Fascist movement, rose to combat the Communists. The Fascists wanted a very strong national government. They were opposed to Communism but also to democracy. The Fascists wanted a strong leader who would suppress opposition and free speech.

The leader of the Italian Fascists was a newspaper publisher named Benito Mussolini. Mussolini was a

powerful speaker who held huge rallies attended by thousands of Fascists. The Fascists would hold marches and public demonstrations; sometimes they would battle the Communists in the streets. Facing an impending war between Communists and Fascists, King Victor Emmanuel III invited Mussolini and the Fascists to take power in Italy. Mussolini became dictator of Italy in 1922.

Mussolini was not a devout man and thought little of the Church, but he recognized the Catholic Church was important to Italian identity and a valuable ally against Communism. Since the time of Pius IX, the popes had not recognized the Italian state. The popes had not even left Vatican City, referring to themselves as "prisoners of the Vatican." In 1929, the government of Mussolini and the Church—now led by Pope Pius XI—came to an agreement called the Lateran Treaty. According to the

Lateran Treaty, the Vatican would be recognized as an independent state and Catholicism would be recognized as the official religion of Italy. Mussolini's government agreed to pay the pope millions of dollars to compensate the Church for the theft of the Papal States in 1870.

Thus, the long struggle between the Church and the Italian state was settled. That's not to say Mussolini and the Fascists were allies of the Church; Mussolini was a brutal dictator, and within a few years, Pope Pius XI would accuse Mussolini of violating the Lateran Treaty in various ways.

But the rule of the Fascists was preferable to a Communist takeover. When Communists took over Russia in 1917, all public exercise of religion was outlawed and children were raised to be atheists. Priests and bishops were silenced or faced death or exile in labor camps in far-off Siberia if they dared oppose the Communist authorities.

Wherever Communists came to power, they did everything they could to exterminate the Church and the influence of religion. In Spain, a civil war between Communists and Fascists under the General Francisco Franco raged from 1936 to 1939. Around 6,800 members of the clergy were killed and many lay persons as well. As of the writing of this book, 1,915 of these victims of the Communists have been beatified as martyrs; 11 have even been canonized.

In Mexico, too, the socialist government of President Plutarco Calles unleashed a rabid persecution of the Church that lasted from 1926 to 1929. Priests were forbidden from ministering without the government's permission; the government also restricted the number of priests allowed in certain areas, leaving many parts of Mexico without access to any priest whatsoever. Priests found ministering to people in spite of these laws faced execution. One famous priest who suffered under the Calles government was Blessed Miguel Pro, a Jesuit priest who was ministering in secret during the persecution.

Fr. Pro was eventually arrested and shot. President Calles was so spiteful he had the execution photographed as a warning to other priests. Yet this deterrent had the opposite effect, inspiring other Catholics to resist. The people of the Church banded together, calling themselves the Cristeros, which, loosely translated, meant "the Catholic militant." The Cristeros fought back against President Calles, adopting the battle cry motto of *Viva Cristo Rey!* This meant "Long live Christ the King!" They organized themselves into a militia and fought a bitter guerrilla war against Mexican government forces that lasted until 1929, when the anti-Catholic laws were lightened—partially due to the influence of the United States.

Pius XI published an encyclical called *Divini Redemptoris* in 1937. This encyclical explained the dangers of atheistic Communism and called for Catholics to vigilantly oppose the errors of the Communists. Pius XI taught that the essential error of Communism was in trying to replace the supernatural salvation won by Christ for a promise of an earthly salvation that was merely political.

Despite these awful things going on in the world, there were bright spots in the 1920s and '30s. In England, the Catholic renaissance we spoke of in chapter 30 continued as converts flooded into the Church. Pius XI published a beautiful encyclical on Christian marriage called *Casti Connubii*. This document reminded Catholics of the traditional idea of marriage as a life-long union of a man and a woman who come together in faith to establish a family. *Casti Connubii* was also the first modern encyclical to speak out against artificial contraception (but it would not be the last).

The Church faced many troubles during this period, but if it did, it was only because the world itself was extremely troubled. In places like Spain and Italy, the violent strife between Communists and Fascists tore at the very fabric of society. In countries like Mexico and Russia where socialists or Communists took over, the Church faced horrific persecution. But we have not even begun to talk about what was going in Germany, which was perhaps worst of all. This dark story will have to wait until the next chapter.

CHAPTER 32

The Church in the Second World War

The Nazis

In this chapter we will be talking about the era of 1933 to 1945, during which the Church and the world had to deal with the rise of the Nazis in Germany and the Second World War. These subjects are extremely broad, impossible to summarize in one chapter. In *Story of Civilization Volume III*, we have three entire chapters dedicated to teaching about the World War II era. It's too bad we don't have the space to go into a lot of the politics and military history here, because it's really fascinating stuff (even if sad and scary). But in this chapter, we will have to restrict ourselves to discussing how these events affected the Church. Readers who want to learn more about the World War II era should definitely read *Story of Civilization Volume III*.

After World War I, many European countries were

torn by conflicts with Communist or Fascist movements. The Communists took power in Russia and formed the Soviet Union, while in other places, like Italy and Spain, Fascists took power. In Germany, too, there was a strong Fascist movement led by Adolf Hitler and the National Socialist German Workers Party, known as the Nazi Party for short. Hitler and the Nazis took power in Germany in 1933. Like other Fascist leaders, the Nazis were willing to tolerate the existence of the Church if it could be pressured to support the government.

Nazi ideology was extremely wicked. Hitler and the Nazis considered the Germans a master race, meaning they were superior to other peoples in intellect, creativity, and culture. Hitler believed Germany lost World War I because it had been betrayed by Communists and Jews. Hitler especially disliked Jewish people. He believed they were like a parasite on German civilization that made Germans weak and corrupted their culture. He argued that Germany should be only for Germans. Hitler wanted Germany to be free of Jews and other races he deemed to be less perfect than Germans. The Nazis passed laws that persecuted Jewish people and took away their civil rights. Later, they would be arrested and sent to concentration camps to be killed.

Pope Pius XI was still reigning when Hitler came to power. In 1933, the Church and Germany signed a concordat, similar to the one signed with Mussolini. The concordat was meant to ensure that the rights of Catholics were respected in Germany. But Hitler had no intention of keeping his word with the Church.

As the Nazi persecution of Jews grew more intense, Pius XI wrote an encyclical called *Mit Brennender Sorge*, which means *With Burning Concern* in German. This document condemned the racist theories of the Nazis. It also accused the Nazis of breaking the concordat by trying to force Catholic schools to indoctrinate children with Nazi teachings, among other things.

The Nazis were less than thrilled about the encyclical. Let's visit a Catholic parish in the southern German town of Bamberg to see how local authorities responded to *Mit Brennender Sorge*:

————

It was early Sunday morning. The first rays of sunlight were only beginning to peer in through the windows of St. Jakobskirche, one of several Catholic churches in Bamberg. The church was empty save for an old man sitting in one of the front pews: Fr. Klaus, St. Jakobskirche's pastor.

Fr. Klaus would normally be spending this time praying or preparing a homily, but not today. Today, he was thumbing through a little booklet, squinting through his reading spectacles to read the pope's new encyclical.

"Oh dear," he said quietly to himself as he perused the pages of the document. "The Nazis will not like this. Not one bit."

The Vatican had shipped 100,000 copies of the encyclical into Germany in hopes that German priests would read portions of it from the pulpit and distribute copies amongst their congregations. St. Jakobskirche had received their delivery of thirty copies the day before.

Fr. Klaus put down the encyclical and looked up at the dull, red light glowing in the tabernacle. "What should I do, O Lord? If I don't read this encyclical to my people, I will be disobeying the wishes of the Holy Father, but worse, I will be guilty of keeping the light of the Gospel's truth hidden. But if I stand up today and read this, well, who knows what those Nazi thugs will do? They will probably be waiting at the door to take me away to a camp right after Mass. They might close the parish, and then my parishioners will be without the sacraments, without guidance." He leaned forward and thumped his head on the pew. "O Lord, help me figure out what to do."

Just then, a loud thud *boomed* on the door of the church. Fr. Klaus rose, startled. Three men in long, dark coats were standing in the narthex with blank, expressionless faces. Fr. Klaus gulped. It was the Gestapo—the secret police of the Nazi regime.

"Can I help you gentlemen?" Fr. Klaus said, his voice wavering.

"Perhaps," said the leader of the men. "We have heard that Pope Pius has sent shipments of a certain document to every parish in Germany. Have you received any shipments from Rome?"

"Why . . . yes," stammered Fr. Klaus, holding up his copy of *Mit Brennender Sorge*. "Just yesterday. I am reading it now."

One man stepped forward briskly and snatched the booklet from the priest's old hands. "Thank you," he snapped. "Are there more copies?"

"Um . . . yes, there is a box in the sacristy, but—"

Two of the Gestapo men strode back into the little room beside the sanctuary where the priest vested for Mass. A ruckus ensued. Fr. Klaus could hear the noise of rummaging and of drawers being slammed. He winced when he heard a loud crash. The Gestapo captain took out a cigarette. "Mind if I smoke?"

"This . . . this is a Church. We don't smoke in here."

The Gestapo captain smiled. He raised the cigarette to his lips, struck a match and lit it. He took a big puff and threw the match on the floor as the sound of breaking glass shattered in the sacristy.

A moment later, the Gestapo agents returned carrying a box with the extra copies of the encyclical.

"Ah!" said the captain. "We have found what we needed. We will be relieving you of these, Father. We wouldn't want your possession of them to put you in a difficult situation." Then turning to his men: "Alright, let's go. We've still got more churches to visit this morning."

The captain threw his barely-smoked cigarette on the floor before walking out. The heavy wooden doors slammed shut, leaving Fr. Klaus alone.

Shaking his head, Fr. Klaus trudged back to the sacristy. Genuflecting before the tabernacle, he passed by the altar and through the door into the vesting room to see what kind of damage the Gestapo had done. He gasped when he saw the room. The closet where he kept his vestments was ransacked and all his liturgical garments where thrown about on the floor. The dresser where he stored his liturgical books was also rummaged through, the drawers pulled out, books tossed everywhere, and some of the wooden cabinets smashed in—one of these broken cabinets had been in St. Jakobskirche since the seventeenth century. The old mirror against the wall where Fr. Klaus used to give himself a look after he had vested was smashed. Broken glass was everywhere.

Tears welled in his eyes. "Why did they do this? The box was sitting out in the open. They could have just asked me to go get it."

He fell to his knees sobbing amidst the broken glass and wreckage of his sacristy.

––––––––––

This sort of thing was common after the publication of *Mit Brennender Sorge*. And that wasn't all. In response to the encyclical, Hitler cracked down on the Church in

Germany. The Nazis closed a dozen Catholic printing presses, arrested hundreds of prominent Catholics, and issued a wave of anti-clerical statements. Catholics within Germany were faced with the difficult prospect of being suspected of treason to the German state for maintaining their loyalty to the Church. The German bishops hoped that the Church and Hitler would work out their problems. But the doctrines of the Nazis were so repugnant to Christianity that this was not possible—and Hitler made it clear that he was not the sort of man to bow to the Church's demands.

Pius XI died in 1939 and was succeeded by the Vatican secretary of state, Eugenio Pacelli. Pacelli took the name Pope Pius XII. Pius XII was a courageous and deeply thoughtful man. The Church and the world would need his leadership; only a few months after he became pope, the Germans invaded Poland. The Second World War had begun.

St. Maximilian Kolbe

World War II lasted from 1939 to 1945. Once the war broke out, things got much worse for Jews living under German occupied areas. They were rounded up and sent to concentration camps where they were killed. Millions of Jews perished.

But Jews were not the only victims of the Nazis. Anyone who opposed the Nazi regime could be arrested and sent away. The Nazis especially targeted Catholic priests. A famous Catholic priest of this time was the Polish Franciscan Fr. Maximilian Kolbe. When the Nazis invaded Poland, Fr. Kolbe helped Jews escape. He also used his monastery to print anti-Nazi publications. He was eventually arrested and sent to the notorious concentration camp at Auschwitz in 1941.

While imprisoned there, the Nazis had plans to execute a certain man. When the man protested that he had a wife and children, Fr. Kolbe volunteered to die in his place. The Nazi guards were astonished. Why should this man want to die for a stranger?

"I am a Catholic priest," was Fr. Kolbe's reply. He knew this simple answer was the truth, that he was a shepherd who would sacrifice himself for his flock, even if the Nazi guards couldn't fathom such an act.

Fr. Kolbe was put to death in Auschwitz in August of 1941. The man whose life Fr. Kolbe saved survived the war and lived a good long life—long enough to attend the canonization ceremony of Fr. Kolbe in 1982. Today, St. Maximilian Kolbe is one of the most beloved saints of the twentieth century.

Of course, there were other Catholic heroes during the war, including the pope. Italy and Germany were allies, but even in Italy the Jews were threatened, first by anti-Jewish laws passed by Mussolini's government and later by the Nazis themselves when they came into Italy to help the Italian Fascists during the war. Pope Pius XII took it upon himself to hide thousands of Jews throughout the Vatican so that the Nazis would not find them. Pius hid so many Jews that after the war was over, he was honored by Jews worldwide for his work. The chief rabbi of Rome even converted to Catholicism and took the name Eugenio, after Pius XII.

Catholic Sufferings

The years of the Second World War were hard on Catholics. Catholic priests in particular were often targets. In some places, the chaos of the war caused a disruption of sacramental life. Catholics in certain areas did not have regular Masses, marriages, baptisms, or confessions. In Poland, around six million Catholics died as a result of the war.

But what was particularly painful was that Catholics could be found on all sides. There were a great many Catholics among the Americans and French who were fighting to save Europe from the Nazis, but there were also Catholics within Germany and Italy. No matter who won, Catholics suffered. Catholics died when the Allies bombed the German city of Dresden, or when the Allies bombed the old monastery of Monte Cassino in Italy (founded by St. Benedict) because they mistakenly thought it was being used to hide German soldiers. In reality, it was full of monks and villagers who had fled to the monastery to escape the war. Catholics died when the Americans dropped an atom bomb on the Japanese city of Nagasaki in 1945, which for centuries had been the center of Japanese Catholicism. And any religious person living under the Soviet Union in Russia suffered as well. It was a time of sadness and loss for everybody.

Fortunately, by April of 1945, the German front was collapsing all over Europe. Seeing no hope for a German victory, the German dictator Adolf Hitler committed suicide. In Italy, Mussolini also perished, captured and shot by Communists. The Japanese, too, surrendered in August after the United States dropped its terrifying nuclear weapons on them. By the fall of 1945, the horrors of World War II were over.

But its effects continued to be felt for years to come. An entire generation of Catholics came of age during the war, including thousands of priests, religious, and theologians. The war experience had a profound impact on how they viewed the world and the Church's role within it. We will learn more about this in our next chapter.

CHAPTER 33

The Second Vatican Council

Catholicism Around the World

The world had been through a flurry of changes in the past hundred years: the coming of new industry that changed the way people lived and worked, the rise of nation states hostile to the Church and its mission, the coming of Communism, the carnage of two world wars, and changing morality that increasingly rejected Christian revelation.

The Catholic Church had boldly met these challenges. Pope Leo XIII had strongly argued for the rights of workers in the new industrial society. Pope St. Pius X worked tirelessly for peace even as Europe was about to explode in the fires of World War I. Pius XI had urged the German people to reject Nazi racism. And Pius XII opened his own palace and basilica up to hide Jews from the Nazis during World War II.

Despite the heroic witness of the Church and her saints,

many modern people had begun to give up on Christianity. This was seen in many ways but chiefly through Mass attendance, which was low throughout much of Europe. Additionally, after World War II, much of Eastern Europe fell under the control of Communism. Countries behind the "Iron Curtain," where atheistic Communism reigned, left millions of Europeans being raised with no faith whatsoever.

Things were not so dire in other parts of the world. In places outside of Europe, people were converting to the Catholic Church by the thousands. Part of this growth of Catholicism around the world was simply due to modern means of communication, such as the television and radio, which made it easier to bring the message of Jesus to the far-flung corners of the earth. Another important reason for the Church's growth was the work of missionary orders. The recently formed Missionary Society of St. Columban (known as the Columban Fathers) labored in China for fifty years until they were expelled by Chinese Communists in the 1950s. The Columban Fathers continued their missionary work elsewhere in Asia, notably in the Philippines, Japan, Burma, and Korea, bringing thousands into the Church.

Africa, too, was home to many missionary orders. For example, the Holy Ghost Fathers had a lively missionary presence throughout Africa. Scores of Holy Ghost Fathers gave up their lives for the Gospel in Africa. In 1961, twenty Holy Ghost Fathers were massacred in the Congo by government troops who wrongly believed the missionaries were stirring up a rebellion. But these martyrdoms were not in vain; throughout the twentieth century, the Church grew faster in Africa than anywhere else.

Thus, even while Catholicism was weakening in Europe, it was growing around the world.

The Summoning of a Council

Pope Pius XII died in 1958. His successor, Pope John XXIII, believed that the Church needed to update its message for the new age. He wanted to summon an ecumenical council to do this. Some bishops and theologians were confused. "The Church's teaching never changes. It does not need to be 'updated' for the modern world," they said.

But Pope John did not want to change the Church's teaching, only the way it was explained. "The substance of the ancient doctrine of the deposit of faith is one thing, and the way in which it is presented is another," he said.

For Pope John and others governing the Church in the early 1960s, the experience of World War II had profoundly affected them. During the war years, they had witnessed hateful, anti-Christian ideologies lead to the deaths of millions of innocent people. They had seen millions perish from the horrors that come with battle, such as disease, starvation, and the bombings of civilians. They had also witnessed the development of nuclear weapons, mighty bombs that harnessed the nuclear power of the atom to create devastating explosions capable of obliterating entire cities.

And these horrors did not take religion into account. In the Nazi concentration camps, Catholics perished alongside Protestants, Jews, and anyone else the Nazis deemed unfit. In Communist Russia, Catholics as well as Russian Orthodox suffered if they dared stand up for their religion. The nuclear bomb dropped on Nagasaki, Japan killed Japanese Catholics alongside Japanese Buddhists and anyone else caught in its blast.

Essentially, Pope John XXIII believed that the developments of the twentieth century had put mankind in a new position. The challenges facing the world in the

twentieth century were very serious problems that affected the entire human race, regardless of religion, race,
or nationality. People were facing a new and uncertain
future that required a fresh response from the Church.
As we noted before, Pope John did not want to change
the Church's teaching. "Jesus Christ is the same yesterday, today, and forever," the Bible tells us in the New Testament book of Hebrews (13:8). Still, Pope John believed
that the new situation in the world required Catholics to
rethink how the Faith was presented to the rest of humanity—as well as how the Church's message could ben-
efit the world as a whole by focusing on things that unite
people instead of what divides them. At least, this was

Pope John's goal. Whether he was successful is another question.

Pope John asked bishops from all over the world to submit ideas to discuss at a council. The bishops responded enthusiastically, recommending everything from stronger condemnations of Communism, to a reform of the liturgy, to a clarification on the Church's teaching on marriage. Pope John XXIII summoned what became known as the Second Vatican Council in the fall of 1962.

The Second Vatican Council took four years, from 1962 to 1965. Pope John died before the council ended, but his vision was carried on by the new pope, Paul VI.

The council gave the Church many important teachings. It taught that the Church is the people of God and reminded Catholics that holiness is for everybody, not just priests and religious. It encouraged Catholics to participate in the liturgy prayerfully and studiously, and suggested that in a world where so many people did not believe in God, it would be better for Catholics and Protestants to focus on what unites them rather than on what divides them. Much of this was not necessarily new but a new way of teaching to the modern man and woman.

The Novus Ordo

One thing the Second Vatican Council requested was a reform of the liturgical books the Church uses for Mass and various rites. After the council ended, Pope Paul VI formed a special commission to reform the sacred liturgy. The result was the *Novus Ordo Missae*, the "New Order of the Mass," which was drafted in 1969 and set to become the new Mass of the Church in 1970.

The creation of the Novus Ordo was very controversial and the transition to it was awkward. The traditional Mass in use before the Second Vatican Council was over a thousand years old. Catholics knew it intuitively. With the introduction of the *Novus Ordo Missae*, Catholics were uncertain what the Church was envisioning. Should the priest continue to offer Mass facing the tabernacle or should he face the people? Or for that matter, where should the tabernacle be located? The laity should actively be engaged during the Mass, but what does that mean? Does that mean the laity are to merely pay close attention and pray attentively, or does that mean they must be given active roles in the liturgy, such as singing or doing the readings? And if the laity can perform readings and other functions in the Mass, what is the role of the traditional Minor Orders, such as acolyte and lector? The council said that *vernacular languages*—that is, the language spoken locally in a given place—could be incorporated into the liturgy. But how much? Where? And what would become of Latin, which the council also said should be retained?

There were a great many confusing questions following the introduction of the new Mass. For the first time in centuries, the Catholic Mass might look very different depending on where it was celebrated. This was not only because the new liturgy offered so many options for a priest to choose from but also because priests often took considerable liberty with how they celebrated, sometimes doing things not permitted in the Missal.

It has been a long time since Pope Paul VI's Novus Ordo Mass became the ordinary Mass in the Latin Rite. People still argue about it. For example, the Second Vatican Council taught that Latin and Gregorian Chant should be preserved in the Novus Ordo. But in fact, Latin and Gregorian Chant have disappeared almost everywhere in the Catholic West. People continue to debate about what the Second Vatican Council actually envisioned.

Vatican II's Legacy

The years after the council were chaotic and confusing for Catholics. Some people took the council's teachings and used them to justify all sorts of wild things the council never envisioned. In some places, a person could go to Mass in the 1970s and the liturgy would look so foreign as to seem like a different religion from the Mass as it was said before the Novus Ordo. People assumed that because the council had changed a few things, now everything was subject to change. It was as if the spirit of revolution had entered the Church. Indeed, some people took the Second Vatican Council as a kind of French Revolution within the Church, in which everything old was overthrown and replaced by new ideas.

Rather than lead to a rich harvest of new conversions to the Church, people were dejected and confused. Fewer and fewer Catholics attended Mass than even before the council. In many places, bishops openly defied the pope and did whatever they wished. Additionally, vocations to the priesthood and religious life plummeted. Pope Paul was extremely sad and perplexed at how this all could have happened.

In the years after the council, both the world and the Church seemed like they did not know where they were going. Things seemed adrift. In our next chapter, we shall further examine some of the problems the Church faced in the post-conciliar era.

CHAPTER 34

Hopes and Fears

Striving for Unity

Popes John XXIII, Paul VI, and the fathers of the Second Vatican Council had hopes that the years after the council would bring about a great rebirth of the Christian faith in the West. Instead, it was a period of confusion and disappointment. In this chapter, we will learn about some of the issues facing the Church in the years after the Second Vatican Council and how the Church tried to correct things.

But let's start on a more positive note. The Second Vatican Council had stressed the need for all Christians to be unified. When Catholics work together with non-Catholic Christian groups, it is called *ecumenism*. The council fathers believed this was necessary in order to combat the rising tide of secularism, atheism, and Communism. As a result of ecumenism, new discussions with Protestant groups were opened up in an attempt to repair old wounds. But perhaps the most striking gesture of ecumenism came while the council was still in session, when in 1964, Pope Paul VI and Patriarch Athenagoras of Constantinople met and greeted each other in Jerusalem. The historic meeting happened on the Mount of Olives. The pope and patriarch prayed the Our Father together, exchanged gifts, and promised to work together for the good of all Christians.

This may not seem like a big deal, but it had been five hundred and twenty-five years since a Roman pontiff and patriarch of Constantinople had last spoken to each other. This quiet meeting opened up a new era of better relations between Catholicism and the Eastern Orthodox Church. Though the schism that began in 1054 still persists to this day, relations between Catholics and the Orthodox are better now than they have been for many centuries.

One thing that brought a sense of unity to these two faiths was suffering. Most members of the Eastern Orthodox Church lived in Eastern Europe and in the Middle East. During this period, the countries of Eastern Europe were universally under the control of Communist dictatorships. Catholics and Orthodox suffered alike under the brutal regimes of the Communists, who treated Christians like traitors to the state and believed Christianity was a plague that needed to be eliminated.

Tortured by the Communists
Before the council, the Church had condemned Communism repeatedly. But in light of the millions of Catholics now living under Communist rule, Paul VI believed a softer tone was required. Perhaps Communists could be shown that Catholics were not enemies of the state? Perhaps if the Church softened its tone against Communism,

the Communists would be more respectful of the rights of Catholics living in Communist countries.

This was a controversial strategy that some disagreed with. Had the Communists not shown over the years that they could not be trusted? Some Catholic leaders continued to vigorously oppose Communism. One notable example was Josef Cardinal Mindszenty of Hungary. Mindszenty had good reason to oppose the Communists. Let's see how they greeted the cardinal when they first took over Hungary back in 1948:

————

A club slammed down on the cardinal's head. He collapsed to the floor of his cell with a grunt, blood now streaming down his face.

"Confess!" shouted the Communist officer who had struck him.

"I told you," panted Cardinal Mindszenty, "I have nothing to confess. I have committed no crime."

A guard kicked him in the stomach. Mindszenty collapsed, wheezing.

"Sure you do," he said. "You must confess to being a traitor, a conspirator against the People's Republic of Hungary."

"People's Republic," the cardinal chuckled, even as he spit out blood. "This so-called republic has nothing to do with the people. This is a Communist tyranny, plain and simple. And I am guilty of nothing other than being a good Catholic who wants to defend the rights of the Church and her flock."

"You are a member of the clerical opposition seeking to overthrow the Communist Party!" The officer whacked him on the back. Cardinal Mindszenty collapsed on his stomach, sprawled out on the clammy concrete floor of his cell.

Cardinal Mindszenty mumbled something.

"What's that?" asked the officer. Then to the guard, "Stand him up!" The guard reached down and hauled the wounded cardinal to his feet. Mindszenty was still mumbling. The guard slapped him across the face.

"Speak clearly, swine, so the commandant can understand you!"

The cardinal looked at the guard, staring at him with his bloodshot eyes and blood trickling down his chin. A weak, crooked smile came across his face. His gums and teeth were red with blood.

"What I said was, praise be to Jesus Christ who has deigned that I should suffer for his sake."

With a trembling arm, the cardinal began to raise his hand to make the sign of the cross. The officer would have none of it. He screamed as he struck Mindszenty's hand with the club before he could bring it to his forehead. Mindszenty grunted as the bones in his hand shattered. He fell mumbling to the ground again.

The officer put his boot on the back of the cardinal's neck. "Let's get one thing clear, Your Eminence. The Party sent me down here to get a confession out of you, and I *will* get it, even if we have to stay here all day."

———

The Communists continued to torture Mindszenty until he could no longer think clearly and confessed to all manner of ridiculous crimes. He was eventually sentenced to life in prison.

This was in 1949, when Pius XII was still pope. Pius denounced the torture of Cardinal Mindszenty and excommunicated those involved in his trial. Mindszenty would spend seven years in prison. He was released in 1956 when the Communist government was briefly overthrown, but when the Communists returned, he fled to the United States embassy in Budapest, where he would remain for the next fifteen years—technically a free man, but unable to leave the grounds of the embassy without being arrested by Communists.

By the 1970s, the Church's attitude had changed somewhat. Pope Paul VI believed he could offer a compromise to get Mindszenty freed. He declared Mindszenty to be a "victim of history" and agreed to not publicly hold the Communists responsible for the cardinal's condition. He also lifted the excommunication on those whom Pius XII had condemned. The Communists liked this, and Mindszenty was released in 1971, after almost twenty-two years in constant confinement. He lived out the rest of his life in Vienna, Austria, dying in 1975. Cardinal Mindszenty was later considered for canonization; as of today, his cause is still in progress and he is known as Venerable Josef Mindszenty.

The Church in China

Eastern Europe was not the only place where the Church was suffering. In China, too, Catholics were in a very difficult state. After Communists took over the country in 1949, they set up a government-run church called the Chinese Catholic Patriotic Association (CCPA). The CCPA rejected the primacy of the pope and tried to blend Communist teaching with the Christian Gospel. The CCPA created its own priests and bishops and held services that resembled the Catholic Mass. Catholics who wanted to practice their faith were expected to attend the services of the Chinese Catholic Patriotic Association.

The problem was that the Catholic Church did not

recognize the CCPA as a legitimate Catholic organization. It was a fake church propped up by Communists
for the purpose of keeping the pope from exercising any
control over the Church within China. Chinese Catholics who wanted to remain faithful to the Catholic
Church needed to attend secret, so-called "underground"
churches—not literally underground, but hidden. Catholic priests had to say Mass in houses, the backrooms of
stores, abandoned warehouses, or other out-of-the-way
places.

As you probably could've guessed, Catholics were ex-
posed to persecution from the government for attending
the underground church, and priests and bishops faced
even stiffer penalties. Priests were often kidnapped by the
government and never seen again; even bishops and cardinals could suddenly go missing. Sometimes their dead
bodies would be found days later in an alley. One of the
most famous Chinese bishops to suffer under the Communists was Cardinal Ignatius Kung Pin-Mei, who at the
time the Communists took over was bishop of Shanghai.
He was arrested by the Communists in 1955 and spent
over thirty years in prison. Upon his release in 1988, he
learned that he had been made a cardinal in secret by
Pope John Paul II.

Confusion and Dissent
While the Church was trying to build bridges with other
Christians and soften its tone against Communism, Paul
VI struggled to maintain order within the Church. As we
discussed in our last chapter, there were some within the
Church doing things in the name of the Second Vatican
Council that the council never called for. The use of Latin
was scrapped from the liturgy, Gregorian chant virtually
disappeared, replaced by folk songs, contemporary music,

or Protestant hymns, and even though the Missal of the Novus Ordo did not call for it, priests began celebrating Mass facing the congregation and eventually distributing communion in the hand, something that had been very rare for most of Catholic history. There was a strong sense throughout the Church that the liturgy had become like the Wild West where anything was permissible.

Meanwhile, progressive theologians began openly challenging some of the Church's moral teachings. They clamored for the Church to change its teaching that married couples must be open to having children, among other things. This prompted Pope Paul VI to issue an encyclical in 1968 called *Humanae Vitae*, which means "On Human Life." *Humanae Vitae* reaffirmed the Church's traditional teaching that Catholic couples must be open to having children, and it condemned certain immoral practices that for centuries were seen as sinful but were now becoming commonplace.

While faithful Catholics rejoiced at this clear proclamation of the Church's truth, *Humanae Vitae* was rejected by others who wanted the Church to change its teaching.

This dissent was widespread—*dissent* in this context is when people disagree with the Church's Magisterium. For example, the bishops of Canada issued their own document challenging the prudence of Paul VI in issuing *Humanae Vitae*, warning that people could have a difficult time obeying the Church's teachings.

Much to the chagrin of Paul VI, there were other things people were questioning too. Fewer Catholics believed in the Real Presence of Jesus in the Eucharist; nuns and monks began to leave the religious life to take up more active vocations in the world; new vocations to the religious life and priesthood declined drastically. Others began to wonder why they should remain a Catholic, arguing that all religions were more or less the same and it didn't matter which one you subscribed to so long as you were a "good person."

By 1978, Paul VI was sick and near death. He was perplexed at how the council's promising, optimistic vision for the Church in the twentieth century could have gone so wrong. He died, sad and demoralized, in August of 1978.

The '60s and '70s were a time of trial for the Church. While Communists oppressed Catholics in China and Eastern Europe, Catholics in the free West struggled to understand what to make of the chaos following the council. Though there were some beacons of light—such as *Humanae Vitae*—we have certainly discussed a lot of negative things about this era: persecution, confusion, dissent, and disappointment. Fortunately, that's not the end of the story. The Church may suffer from persecutions without and turmoil within, but Jesus promised to not leave the Church helpless. In our next chapter, we'll see how a new pope tried to remedy this sad state of affairs.

CHAPTER 35

The Pontificate of Pope St. John Paul II

The Election of Karol Wojtyla

By now we have covered almost twenty centuries of Christianity. And one thing we have learned is that sometimes God can drastically change things by raising up one single man or woman to say yes to his plans. Think of how St. Benedict, retiring to find peace in the wilderness of Italy, ended up composing a monastic rule that would lead to the establishment of Western monasticism. Or how St. Francis brought thousands of people back to God through his simple love of poverty and simplicity. Or how the Blessed Virgin Mary brought the Son of God into the world by her faithfulness. Similarly, in this chapter we will learn about how one saintly pope attempted to stem the tide of chaos that followed the Second Vatican Council and did more to shape the modern Church than any other pontiff.

When Pope Paul VI died in 1978, the cardinals of the Church gathered in Rome to elect a new pope. The cardinals chose the patriarch of Venice, Albino Luciani, who took the unusual name John Paul, choosing it as a means of demonstrating his support for the vision of the previous two popes, John XXIII and Paul VI.

The Church was excited about Pope John Paul. He was a friendly man—known by Italians as "the Smiling Pope." He wanted to stay faithful to the reforms of Vatican II while restoring discipline to the Church. But Pope John Paul's time as successor of St. Peter was brief. After only thirty-three days on the throne, he was found dead in his bed. He apparently died of a heart attack late at night while reading *The Imitation of Christ*. The world was stunned. The cardinals, many of them just returned home, re-boarded their planes and returned to Rome for another papal conclave.

This time they elected the young archbishop of Cracow, Poland, Karol Wojtyla, to become pope. Karol Wojtyla took the name John Paul II in honor of his predecessor. Wojtyla's election was big news for two reasons. Karol Wojtyla was the first non-Italian to be elected pope since 1522, and at fifty-eight years of age, he was exceptionally young—for a pope, that is. This meant that he would probably sit on the Chair of Peter for a long time and have decades to guide the Church.

In his first words to the Catholic Church and the people of the world, Pope John Paul II came onto the balcony of St. Peter's Basilica and said, "Brothers and sisters, do not be afraid to welcome Christ and accept his power. Help the pope and all those who wish to serve Christ and with Christ's power to serve the human person and the whole of mankind. Do not be afraid. Open wide the doors for Christ."

Pope John Paul II was a new kind of pope, full of warmth and energy and ready to tackle the problems facing the Church and the world, which stemmed from the same issue: men had forgotten God. When people forget God, they no longer understand themselves. If people would return to God, they would not oppress each other or murder each other or turn to destructive systems like Nazism and Communism to solve their problems.

John Paul II and Communism

Pope John Paul II was popular for many reasons, but mainly because he gave people hope. In a world marred by destructive wars and threatened with nuclear weapons that could annihilate the human race, the pope tried to teach people to have faith in God and in each other.

Yet not everybody liked John Paul. This became painfully clear one spring day in 1981 when a Turkish assassin named Mehmet Ali Ağca shot him as he moved through St. Peter's Square. Pope John Paul survived after surgery and a long period of rest, but his health would suffer for many years because of his injuries. The assassination attempt happened on May 13, the feast of Our Lady of

Fatima. John Paul believed Our Lady of Fatima had helped him survive that day.

As for Ağca, nobody knows what his reasons were. He gave so many different stories to police and contradicted himself so many times, nobody could believe anything he said. Some people thought it was the Communists who put him up to it, others said he acted alone. Whatever the reason, John Paul II showed incredible mercy by visiting Ağca in prison and forgiving him. Ağca ultimately repented of his action. He kissed John Paul's ring as a sign of his sorrow for what he did. Mehmet Ali Ağca was sentenced to life in prison, but the authorities later let him go after John Paul asked for Ağca to be released.

You may have wondered why people thought the Communists might've put Ağca up to it. Well, the Communists didn't like John Paul very much. In fact, they were afraid of him. He often spoke out against the evils of Communism, and because he was so well respected and had such a big platform, the Communists thought he would stir people up against them.

John Paul's homeland of Poland was a Communist country. He took a famous trip there in 1979 and held a public Mass in Warsaw, in a place called Victory Square. Hundreds of thousands came to celebrate God in the Holy Eucharist. In the face of the Communists watching from the rooftops, the people chanted, "We want God!" The Communists had spent years trying to suppress the people's desire for God, often in hostile ways, so this made them nervous. It's why some think they tried to have him killed just a few years later.

As it turns out, the people behind the Iron Curtain did indeed reject Communism. Perhaps the teaching of John Paul II was partially the reason. But they were also tired of being oppressed by their Communist governments and wanted freedom. We discuss the collapse of Communism in detail in *The Story of Civilization Volume III*. Between 1989 and 1991, Communist governments all over Europe collapsed and were replaced by democracies—including in Russia, which had been the center of world Communism since 1917. Poland, the homeland of John Paul II, was also liberated.

Europe rejoiced. The United States rejoiced. The millions of Christians in Eastern Europe who could now practice their religion freely rejoiced. And Pope John Paul II smiled and rejoiced as well. Europe was free. His native Poland was free. A new day of freedom was rising across the lands of old Christendom.

The New Evangelization

We mentioned in chapter 33 that there was chaos in the Catholic Church after the Second Vatican Council. This was another issue Pope John Paul II tried to fix. He published a new *Catechism of the Catholic Church* to serve as a reference for people who wanted to learn about the Church. This was the first universal catechism that had been published since the Council of Trent. With the new catechism, it was much easier for average Catholics to read and understand the Church's teachings.

He also wrote important documents about the Eucharist, marriage, the liturgy, and many other important things. And he was always traveling; he traveled all over the world encouraging people to have faith in God—but he also taught that there was a valuable place for science and reason in the Catholic faith as well. "Faith and reason are like two wings on which the human spirit rises to the contemplation of truth," he taught. Because of John Paul's efforts, which he encouraged the lay faithful to join him in, the Church got better. He hoped people would join him in what he called "the new evangelization," which meant finding new and fresh ways to bring people into the Church (or keep them there). It was very slow work—sometimes agonizingly slow—but things did improve.

John Paul's Last Moments

Pope John Paul II became sick when he was old and suffered for a long time before he died. Many people were inspired by his suffering. He demonstrated that life still has value even if it is hard, because everything can be offered to God, even our pain. John Paul II died in the spring of 2005.

Have you ever wondered what happens when a pope dies? The rituals surrounding the death of a pope are very old and hearken back to a time of kings and royal courts. Let's visit the papal apartments of the Apostolic Palace in the Vatican on April 2, 2005, the day St. John Paul II passed into eternal life:

———

The pilgrims gathered around St. Peter's knew that John Paul II had passed into eternity. They knew not because any announcement had been made but because the bell of the *Arco delle Campani*—the fortress tower of the Swiss Guards—began ringing solemnly. Within moments, other bells around the Vatican and all of Rome began doling their mournful tones. Pilgrims wept and prayed. All throughout the city people paused in silence. For many days, John Paul II had been on the edge of death. The tolling of these bells announced that the moment had come.

Within the Vatican, everything came to a grinding halt. The See of Peter was vacant. An American bishop named James Harvey hurried through the corridors of the

Apostolic Palace. Bishop Harvey was the prefect of the papal household, the man who supervises the pope's private affairs. He was looking for another special individual, the papal camerlengo. The camerlengo is a cardinal who, among other things, is in charge of administering the transitional period between the death of one pope and the election of another. The papal camerlengo for John Paul II was the Spaniard Cardinal Eduardo Martinez Somalo.

Cardinal Somalo was pacing under the shaded porticoes of St. Peter's when he saw Bishop Harvey approaching with a grave look on his face.

"It's time, isn't it?" asked Cardinal Somalo.

Bishop Harvey nodded. "The papal household awaits your eminence to verify the death of the pontiff."

Cardinal Somalo and Bishop Harvey headed off together towards the papal apartments where the body of John Paul II rested. These private chambers had been closed off and were being watched by the Swiss Guards. In the old days, it was not uncommon for people to try to break in and loot the pope's apartment after his death. Though such things no longer occurred, the brightly uniformed Swiss Guards still kept a vigilant watch over the papal apartment.

Several other cardinals and members of the papal court met Harvey and Somalo outside the doors, those of the Apostolic Camera. These members of the Roman Curia were summoned to witness Cardinal Somalo verify the pope's death. Seeing the camerlengo approach, the guards opened the doors and admitted the men, who all filed in behind Cardinal Somalo.

The lifeless body of Pope John Paul II lay still in the large bed. His wrinkled face was peaceful; he looked like he was sleeping. Cardinal Somalo produced a small object from his pocket. It was a tiny, golden hammer. He sat down on the bed. Taking the hammer, he struck John Paul's body lightly on the forehead. "Karol?" he called, using the pope's birth name. When only silence called back, he tapped his forehead again with the hammer. "Karol?" Then, a third time. "Karol?"

Cardinal Somalo stood up and solemnly declared, "The sovereign pontiff, John Paul II, is dead." Everyone present made the sign of the cross.

A flurry of activity ensued in the hours following. Various cardinals went off to inform others, while Bishop Harvey told the dean of the college of cardinals, Josef Ratzinger, who in turn began contacting all the cardinals of the world. Cardinal Somalo sent off a messenger to the vicar of Rome, Cardinal Ruini, who in turn composed a message to the people of Rome.

Meanwhile, Cardinal Somalo slipped the ring of the fisherman off of the dead pope's hand. An attendant emerged from the pope's study holding the papal seal with which John Paul had stamped all official documents. The ring and seal were put on a small, movable marble column that had been brought in and placed beside Cardinal Somalo. The camerlengo struck each with the little golden hammer. The ring cracked and the seal shattered. The ritual signified that the authority of John Paul II had come to an end.

Eventually, everyone filtered out of the apartment and John Paul's body was taken away to be prepared for burial. He would be vested in the white simar, or robe, of the pope, the white alb, cincture, and amice, then clothed in a red and gold chasuble with a pectoral cross around his neck.

Cardinal Somalo was the last one to leave the papal apartment. With the apartment now vacant, he closed the large, solid doors and locked them with a massive iron padlock. The apartments would remain locked until the election of a new pope.

———

John Paul II had spent almost twenty-seven years on the throne of St. Peter, one of the longest reining popes in history. He was soon canonized and is now known as St. John Paul II. His feast day is on October 22.

John Paul worked hard to bring reform to the Church. Things were much better by 2005, but there still remained much to be done and many challenges to face across Christendom. And Christendom was no longer only a European reality; in the twenty-seven years John Paul was on the throne, the Church grew and spread more on other continents than ever before. Africa, Latin America, and Asia were all vital centers of Christian life.

By the late twentieth century, Western civilization was at a crossroads. With the collapse of Communism, it was uncertain where Europe would go. The twentieth century had seen the rise and fall of Fascism, Nazism, and Communism. What would be the driving idea or force that guided her peoples into the future? Would the people of old Christendom return to the teachings of Jesus Christ to understand themselves and their world, as John Paul II believed? Or would they turn to some other system or idea to take them into the unknown future? In our final chapter, we will attempt to answer these questions.

CHAPTER 36

The Church in the Twenty-First Century

Benedict XVI

John Paul II had made a tremendous impact on the development of the Church in the period after the Second Vatican Council. From the chaos of the post-conciliar period, John Paul II gave the Catholic Church the form it would take for the next several decades. His contributions were truly immense: a new Code of Canon Law issued in 1983, the *Catechism of the Catholic Church*, first published in 1992, not to mention fourteen encyclicals, visits to 129 countries, and 482 new saints canonized. John Paul II set the trajectory the Catholic Church would follow into the third millennium.

For all these reasons, he left some big shoes to fill. The papal conclave summoned after his death elected the German cardinal Joseph Ratzinger, who took the name Pope Benedict XVI. Ratzinger had served for years as the

prefect of the Congregation for the Doctrine of the Faith, the body within the Vatican responsible for clarifying and defending Catholic doctrine.

Whereas John Paul II had been a charismatic speaker and dramatic leader, Benedict XVI was a quiet, thoughtful, scholarly pope. He continued the work of John Paul II in restoring the Church. Benedict believed that in the aftermath of the Second Vatican Council, people had become too taken up with the idea of change for the sake of change—that too many Catholic customs had been lost, too many teachings had been obscured, and too many new things had been introduced into the Church. Catholics needed to return to the roots of their traditions to reclaim their identity and rediscover what it means to follow Jesus Christ.

To this end, in 2007, Benedict issued a decree promoting the celebration of the old Mass. If you recall from chapter 33, Pope Paul VI had replaced the traditional Mass with the Novus Ordo Mass in 1969. The Novus Ordo is the Mass most Catholics in the West are familiar with today. After 1969, celebration of the Church's traditional liturgy virtually disappeared; in many dioceses, bishops were outright hostile to it. Benedict's 2007 decree, *Summorum Pontificum*, said that this never should have happened. Furthermore, he said any priest is free to celebrate the traditional Mass if he wishes. Pope Benedict hoped that the riches of the old Mass would help today's Catholics recover the beauty of their traditions. Since 2007, celebration of the traditional Mass has blossomed around the world and more and more young Catholics are interested in learning about the Church's liturgical traditions. Benedict also gave the Church many beautiful teachings with encyclicals on love, hope, and the obligation of Christians to put their faith into practice by helping the poor and sick.

One other unique thing Benedict did was help the Catholics in China. Back in chapter 34, we discussed how the government of Communist China had put Chinese Catholics in a very difficult spot. They outlawed the Catholic Church, creating instead a fake, government run church called the Chinese Catholic Patriotic Association, or CCPA for short. The CCPA had its own parishes, priests, bishops, and congregations. It looked very much like the Catholic Church, but was in fact a tool of the Communist authorities. Meanwhile, Catholics who wanted to attend the real Church had to meet in secret and could be persecuted or killed.

Benedict wrote a letter to Chinese Catholics encouraging them to reconcile with the CCPA. If Catholics of the underground Church and the official church could both profess the same faith, they could celebrate the Eucharist together. He gave suggestions for how both the Chinese government and the Catholic Church in China could work to bring the Church out of the shadows to full participation in Chinese life.

A few years later, in 2018, Pope Francis I (Benedict's successor) and the Chinese government agreed to a concordat. According to this agreement, the Chinese government would recognize the pope as the head of Chinese Catholics. The pope would have the right to choose Chinese bishops, but only among candidates selected by the Chinese government. If the pope didn't like any of the government's choices, he has the right to veto them—that means reject them. The Communists would also stop persecuting the Church.

This agreement was a small step towards fixing the situation in China, but it remains to be seen whether the Communists will hold up their end of the agreement. Communists have historically not thought twice about breaking agreements with religious authorities. In fact, scarcely a month after the concordat was signed, the Chinese Communists destroyed two Marian shrines, indicating their persecution of Catholics was far from over.

The Years Following Benedict's Resignation
Though Benedict's papacy had a strong beginning, there were problems as things went on. Scandals and corruption in various places plagued the Church. In some places in the United States and elsewhere, priests, bishops, and religious were implicated in committing deeds of great wickedness and immorality. People were scandalized by

these evils. Pope Benedict, old and worn out from the weight of these problems, announced he was resigning the papacy in February of 2013. He was the first pope to resign the papacy since Pope St. Celestine V in 1294.

The cardinals of the Church gathered in Rome and elected an Argentinian cardinal named Jorge Bergoglio, who took the name Pope Francis I. At the time of this book's publication, Francis is still reigning today.

And what does the Church founded by Jesus look like today? In many respects, things are much better than they were a generation ago. The invention of the internet has made Catholic teachings more accessible to more people than at any time in history. The average Catholic who wishes to be educated about the Faith has a vastly greater opportunity to learn than at any time in history. The Catholic faith is more international that it has ever been, with the Church growing in places like Africa and Asia.

Additionally, a growing number of Catholics worldwide are interested in recovering the Church's traditions, especially among the young. New religious orders dedicated to preserving our Catholic heritage are thriving with vocations. While many dioceses suffer from shortages of candidates to the priesthood, the priests coming through the seminaries today are much better prepared for priesthood than those forty years ago.

Many new and wonderful saints have also been canonized—such as St. Kateri Tekakwitha, the Native American saint known as the Lily of the Mohawks. We even have a few more doctors of the Church: St. Gregory of Narek, St. Hildegard of Bingen, and St. John of Avila.

Mother Teresa

One of the most popular modern saints recently canonized was a nun named St. Teresa of Calcutta, who during her life was known as Mother Teresa. Mother Teresa lived from 1910 to 1997. She founded a religious order called the Missionaries of Charity and was known for her work as a missionary in India. Over the decades, Mother Teresa and her Missionaries of Charity worked among the poorest of the poor in Calcutta, ministering to the sick and dying. She achieved worldwide fame and her order grew into the thousands, spreading all over the globe. She would be canonized by Pope Francis in 2016.

Mother Teresa had a deep trust in God's provision. Though there were many people in the world with their own motivations, she believed God worked through all of it to show his love for people. One well-known story about Mother Teresa and a wealthy Indian business owner shows both her wisdom and her trust in God:

————

Mr. Hunjan adjusted his glasses while he looked at the charts spread out in front of him on the ornate wooden table. His senior managers were briefing him on how his business was doing that year.

"If you'll direct your attention to page seven of the quarterly budgetary report," said one of the managers dryly, "you'll see that profits in the third quarter have surpassed our year-to-date projections from the January review."

The other managers nodded.

"Mmm," Mr. Hunjan said blankly.

The figures on the graph seemed to blend together. His mind was elsewhere, for later this morning he was going to have a meeting with Mother Teresa of Calcutta. He had long wanted to meet the famous nun who had done so much good in the world. In fact, he was going to offer her one of his company's properties for her work in India. But he felt . . . odd. Maybe even nervous. It had been a long time since he had met someone who made him feel this way. Usually people were nervous to meet him! After all, he was the powerful billionaire. He couldn't understand why meeting this little nun intimidated him so much.

"Mr. Hunjan? Does that sound good?" his manager suddenly interrupted his reflection.

"Oh . . . um . . . huh?" Mr. Hunjan looked at the graphs.

"The actuarial summary? Are we hitting the numbers you'd hoped?"

"Oh yes . . . eh . . . fine, fine," Mr. Hunjan said absently.

The intercom in his office buzzed.

"Mr. Hunjan, she's here," said his secretary.

"Wonderful! Gentlemen, that will be all for now!"

The managers cleared out of his office. Mr. Hunjan paced about the room, straightening paintings on the wall and picking up little stray pieces of paper off the floor. He had a nervous, sinking feeling in the pit of his stomach. He was meeting Mother Teresa to offer her something, but he found himself desperately wanting something from her—her approval.

A moment later, there was a gentle knock at the door. "Come in," Mr. Hunjan said, his voice cracking.

His office door slowly opened and a tiny, bent woman entered. She was draped in the blue and white Indian *sari* which served as the habit of her order, now recognized worldwide. Mr. Hunjan rushed to the kindly old woman with the excitement of a child meeting his hero. He reached out his hand.

"It's so good to meet you, Mother!"

She clasped his hands between her own frail, wrinkled hands. "And you as well, Mr. Hunjan. May God bless you!"

Several other sisters entered with Mother Teresa, attendants who helped her in her travels. They all sat around Mr. Hunjan's conference table. The sisters asked Mr. Hunjan a bit about his business, and he answered cordially. Mother Teresa herself said nothing; she only sat with her hands folded, smiling.

She's so . . . small, Mr. Hunjan thought. *I had no idea how tiny she would be. And she's very old. No wonder she needs all these attendants. I wonder . . . can a simple nun of such advanced age really manage a property of the size I want to give her? Perhaps this whole thing is too much.*

"Mr. Hunjan," said Mother Teresa suddenly, "we are all friends here. Tell me plainly what's in your heart."

"Well, managing a property of this size is a big deal. I'm just wondering, what sort of financial experience do you have? How do you manage your budget?"

Mother Teresa gave Mr. Hunjan a smile that made him shrivel. He felt dumb as soon as he'd asked.

"Let me ask you a question," she said. "You wanted to see me. Why? Where did the idea come from?"

"I guess I just felt . . . an urge . . . inside me."

Mother Teresa smiled. "I see lots of people like you. And they all say the same. They felt an urge. Mr. Hunjan, it's clear that God sent you, just as he sends everyone who comes into my life in whatever way. And those people provide the material means we need for our work. The grace of God is what moved you. You are my budget, Mr. Hunjan. God sees to our needs, as Jesus promised. We do what we will—we come here, we go there, we do this, and we make our decisions based on our own best judgment. But behind it all is the hand of God working, always working, as he is now working through you."

Mr. Hunjan sat quietly for a time. A moment later, he signed the paper officially giving the property to Mother Teresa and her sisters.

The Greatest Treasure in the World

In a way, Mother Teresa's words to Mr. Hunjan are really the best way to understand the history of the Church as a whole, whether ancient or modern. People act freely, making their own choices for their own purposes, but God works his providence through them. Divine grace and man's free will are always acting together in this world, like an endless dance between God and mankind following the music of the Holy Spirit.

Similarly, the Church is human and divine. It was divinely founded on the promise of Jesus Christ and sanctified by his blood. It operates by his power and, under the guidance of the Holy Spirit, will always be a beacon of truth in the world, preserving the deposit of faith unstained until the end of time. But insofar as it is governed by human beings, there will always be sin, bad decisions, corruption, and occasional stupidity. We can pray that such things happen as rarely as possible. And even in the dark times we have studied, God never failed to raise up shining examples of saintly men and women to proclaim his truth.

The Church is the mystical Body of Christ, so said Pope Pius XII. Behind its exterior there is a mystical reality. It is like the stable of Bethlehem: on the outside, simple, solid, perhaps a little dirty, but on the inside, it holds *the greatest treasure in the world*. And though society continues to change and will continue to change, there will always be people responding to his call. Just as the ancient Church had to adapt to the fall of the Roman Empire, so will Christians in the future learn how to build up the kingdom of Christ in the world of tomorrow, whatever it may look like—until he comes again in glory.

INDEX

Margaret of Scotland, Saint, 154
Mark the apostle, Saint, 10, 14
Marquette, Jacques, 263
marriage, 325
Martelm Charles, 104
Martin de Porres, Saint, 261
Martin Luther, 227–30, 233
Martin V, 214
martyrs: apostles, 9–12; Bishop John Fisher, 233–34;
    Counter-Reformation, 242–46; Father Isaac
    Jogues, 264–68; Fr. Jean de Brebeuf, 263–64,
    268; Holy Ghost Fathers, 338; North American
    Martyrs, 268; Pope St. Fabian, 38; Reign of
    Terror, 283; Rene Goupil, 264; Sir Thomas More,
    234; St. Agatha of Sicily, 38; St. Agnes of Rome,
    65; St. Boniface, 111; St. Clement, 19; St. Justin
    Martyr, 28–32; St. Lawrence, 199; St. Polycarp,
    20–24; St. Rene Goupil, 264, 268; St. Salomone
    Leclercq, 283–85; St. Sebastian, 65; St. Tarcisius,
    26–27; Thomas Becket, 128–33; Thomas More,
    243; victims of Communists, 324–25
Mary, Mother of God, 245–46, 353; apparitions, 164,
    262, 318–22; brown scapular, 166–68; icons, 99;
    Immaculate Conception, 303–4; Our Lady of
    Fatima, 318–2, 355–6; Our Lady of Good Success,
    262; Our Lady of Guadalupe, 262; Pentecost, 3;
    St. Dominic, 164
Mary Magdalene, Saint, 314
Mary Tudor, 255
Mass, 31, 365; music, 350–51; Novus Ordo Missae
    (New Order of the Mass), 341–42; second century,
    24
Matthew (New Testament), 54, 184, 259, 303
Matthew the apostle, Saint, 10, 14